THE ALCHEMISTS

THE ALCHEMISTS

THE INEOS STORY

An industrial giant comes of age

Jim Ratcliffe
Ursula Heath

Biteback Publishing

First published in Great Britain in 2018 by
Biteback Publishing Ltd
Westminster Tower
3 Albert Embankment
London SE1 7SP

ISBN 978-1-78590-388-5

10 9 8 7 6 5 4 3 2 1

A CIP catalogue record for this book is available from the British Library.

Set in Minion Pro and Avenir

Printed and bound in Great Britain by
CPI Group (UK) Ltd, Croydon CR0 4YY

MIX
Paper from
responsible sources
FSC® C020471

CONTENTS

INTRODUCTION

Frankly, I was not sympathetically inclined, a year or so ago, to the proposal to write a book about INEOS's first twenty years. It had undertones of self-indulgence written all over it, it risked being a hostage to fortune, and, if one is at all superstitious, then telling the world publicly how wonderful we have been over two exciting decades has all the hallmarks of the kiss of death!

So, no, I wasn't enthusiastic. Nor were John and Andy, my two colleagues and lifetime friends.

So how come the U-turn? Did vanity ultimately win the day?

Here I struggle a little. We – John, Andy and myself – have enjoyed a most extraordinary twenty years, which has seen INEOS grow from a small obscure chemical company in Antwerp to, quite frankly, a colossal enterprise today. Now we have chemical plants the size of the City of London. We have over 100 chemical sites worldwide. We have annual sales of $60 billion, comparable to the GDP of a medium-sized country. We produce 50 million tonnes of chemicals and 50 million tonnes of oil and oil products. We own 1 billion barrels of oil still in the ground. We have eight tankers shuttling shale gas from America to Europe. We have a car company, a clothes company and a football club, not to mention my hotel business. It's difficult to keep up sometimes. Last year every single business in INEOS beat its budget. Our safety record is genuinely world-class. Profits hit $7 billion in 2017.

So, is the story worth telling? Who knows? But John, Andy and I were lobbied persistently and, ultimately, we weakly relented.

To accomplish what we have in such a short timeframe requires taking some risk. We have experienced some strong headwinds on our journey (some might say cyclonic is a better description!) and many moments are indelibly seared into memory. All of this will, hopefully, make interesting reading.

There has never been a dull moment. It has been an absorbing time and tremendous fun, in the main. We weathered the crisis in 2008, no thanks to Gordon Brown, but our ship was close to foundering. We stood our ground with the unions in Grangemouth four years ago and, ultimately, saved Grangemouth and many thousands of jobs. Today, Grangemouth is tremendously successful, but it teetered for weeks on the verge of closure. And we brought US shale to Europe, whose stubborn refusal to entertain such a cost-effective energy source threatened the whole European chemical industry when oil was over $100 per barrel. Exciting times. Although I admit it has been exciting in a 'manufacturing' sense. I was born in the heart of industrial revolution territory and I suppose it runs in my blood. I believe we benefit if we actually make some of the goods we buy rather than just sell services. And, just as importantly, much of the northern economy in Britain depends on manufacturing jobs which today are few and far between. Britain has its own rust belt, as America did before its shale revolution resolved a lot of that. I'm optimistic we could do the same here.

It's traditional to offer thanks in such a book as this, and INEOS has cause to be grateful to many people who helped it along the way, but we certainly wouldn't be where we are today without John Reece and Andy Currie. Both clever chaps from Cambridge, unlike like my humble red-brick, they share my northern values, hailing from Sunderland and Doncaster grammar schools respectively. We work closely together. We almost always reach a consensus when important decisions come our way and, likewise, they both enjoy good humour. Northern values include hard work, good manners, grit, rigour and an essential sense of humour, with wit as a bonus. Life is short!

My family, I am told, has endured the occasional bout of grumpiness from my direction – I am sure only on a microscopic level and exceedingly infrequently – but has given much support and helped keep my feet firmly planted on the ground. The family always come first, and we make this message clear throughout INEOS.

I am fortunate in that I can switch off, so family holidays offer a real rest. My father once said that there is little point worrying about things you can do nothing about. It was good advice.

So, for better or worse, here follows the tale of INEOS.

Jim Ratcliffe
April 2018

FOREWORD BY PROFESSOR SIR ANDREW LIKIERMAN

Professor Sir Andrew Likierman was dean of London Business School between 2009 and 2017. Educated at the University of Vienna and Balliol College, Oxford, Andrew's career has spanned the public and private sectors as well as many years in academic life. In the public sector he has been an official in the Cabinet Office and the Treasury, non-executive chairman of the National Audit Office, and a director of the Bank of England among other posts. Roles in the private sector include director of Barclays plc and non-executive director of Times Newspapers. Andrew taught Jim Ratcliffe during his MBA at London Business School in 1978.

There is something irresistible about the story of a plucky upstart making good. Even better, this story is real life. And in an entrepreneurial world dominated by services and high-tech, INEOS is a sighting of that rarest of birds, the highly successful UK manufacturing entrepreneur.

There's always a danger of companies writing their own stories, as Jim frankly acknowledges. This is also a story still very much in the making, with major developments in recent years including building a fleet of tankers in China to bring US shale gas to the UK, buying North Sea oil fields and pipelines, and – planning and public opinion permitting – fracking. More are on the way.

But even if it's mid-story, there are good reasons to tell it. INEOS is now a force in international petrochemical and energy supply, including the North Sea. Its operations in Scotland alone make it a significant national player. But as a private company it has to provide less information than those that are listed and this book gives a context for those who want the background to INEOS. The company is also proud of what it has achieved, and wants to share where it comes from and what it has done. Then there are some real insights for those wanting to learn from others, and understand what it takes in terms of risks and rewards, inspiration and perspiration, to turn dreams into reality.

The obvious question from a success story of this magnitude is: why INEOS, and why not so many of the hopefuls who started at the same time, full of enthusiasm, most of whom will have failed? While each start-up is different and each entrepreneur has his or her own strengths and weaknesses, there are certainly some lessons from INEOS for tomorrow's aspiring entrepreneurs to think about, including those a world away from manufacturing.

First, there is the combination of technical and managerial professionalism. The management team are a group who understand their fields and can apply their knowledge and experience. The combination of detailed technical knowledge with professional management has been crucial in overcoming challenges to build the business. All too often a great idea fails because there are not the management skills to turn it into a viable enterprise and it isn't an accident that, contrary to so many other cases, a high proportion of INEOS acquisitions have been successful. The logic of acquiring underperforming assets has been backed up by the skills and ability to make them perform. But while the basis of the company's fortunes has been turning the oil majors' unloved chemical plant into highly profitable operations, the lateral moves to other energy fields in recent years show that the professionalism is not confined to making the original concept work.

Another key factor is the advantage that has come from continued private ownership. This is most evident in two contradictory aspects of speed: the ability to take decisions quickly, combined with the opportunity to be patient without being pushed by the capital markets. It is also clear that these freedoms have come at the cost of increased risk that comes with reliance on debt in troubled times.

Then there is the management culture. Most important is a lack of complacency – the one characteristic I have found common to well-managed organisations throughout my own working life. At INEOS this is combined with openness, a lack of pomposity and a down-to-earth approach. In Lancashire parlance, spades are called bloody shovels. Management of risk has also been crucial. INEOS is a company which has taken huge risks in terms of the sheer scale of acquisitions, the moves to new spheres of operation and geographic spread. This is 'Boys Own' stuff, with bold moves followed by testing times. Anyone who wants to know how resilient you need to be in a crisis should read Chapter 5 on the rocky road through the financial crisis, and Chapter 8 on the Grangemouth showdown.

Finally, there is the leadership. The company has the character of the founders all over it – the managerial and technical professionalism, the lack of complacency and the management of risk are not accidents. 'The tone from the top' is often cited as a reason why companies fail. Here it is very much the basis of INEOS's success, with all the above qualities allied to a clear strategy and values, and with a deep commitment to the business. It also reflects the founders' northern grit and pragmatism, allied to experience on the ground in manufacturing and finance. Jim Ratcliffe has a combination of qualifications in chemical engineering, management accountancy and from business school, and it shows.

Leadership has also meant teamwork. While Jim is the leading shareholder, driving force and public face of the company, INEOS is not a one-man band. The founders remain the shareholders, and the fact that turnover among the senior team is so low is a sign of the strength of a group of colleagues working together to make things happen.

One factor not on the above list is luck. Every new enterprise needs some, and those who are lucky understandably want to take the credit for what follows. In the case of INEOS, it could be said that their ambitions coincided with the desire of the oil majors to divest their petrochemical operations, but without the skill to pull the operations round, the fortune of timing would have been irrelevant. They were definitely not lucky in the timing of the financial crisis so soon after acquiring such a huge slug of their assets. So overall, they can't be said to have relied on luck, other than in Pasteur's sense that 'fortune favours the prepared mind'.

What next? As ever, the only thing that can be said with certainty about the next twenty years is that they won't be like the last twenty. I've no doubt they will be full of excitement, but INEOS starts Year 21 as a world player in the publicly sensitive area of energy, not a hopeful start-up. There are positions to defend as well as new areas to conquer. New skills and qualities will be called on. The balance of interests of the founders may change, and in due course they will need to think about succession. There will be a lot more scrutiny. This is where the culture of the company is so crucial. The flexibility, open-mindedness and lack of complacency will be essential in maintaining the ability of the company to thrive.

The remarkable achievements of INEOS can be seen as an outstanding example of the excitement and gloom, the fun and the angst of entrepreneurship. This book has plenty of food for thought for those wanting to follow this company's example. Or those who just want a good story.

Professor Sir Andrew Likierman
April 2018

To my mother and father, Alan and Marie

JIM RATCLIFFE ON INEOS

Before writing this opener, I circulated a note around the top thirty senior execs in INEOS, asking them for their uninhibited and personal reflections on why INEOS has been so successful in such a relatively short time span. Consequently, the insight that follows is a blend of my own views and those of the movers and shakers in INEOS who have experienced this remarkable growth first hand. There are many occasions in this chapter when I am unable to match the clarity of thought of these executives, in which case I use their exact words rather than mine, and these can be identified by passages in italics.

Let's begin at the top, so to speak. I have known and respected and worked with John and Andy for twenty-five years. We are good friends. Twenty-five years is a long time never to have had an argument, but it's a fact. We have had our differences and debates over the years but never a sour word. We have never had a 2:1 vote. We have never had a vote!

We all grew up in modest surroundings in the north of England: John in Sunderland, Andy in Doncaster and me in Manchester and Hull. All three of us were educated at grammar schools when education was sensible and grounded in common sense, subjects were evenly split between sciences and arts, you got your ear clipped if you misbehaved, you stood up and showed respect when the teacher entered the classroom and joyously you could play oodles of sport! John and Andy went off to Cambridge and I had a choice of Birmingham, Leeds, Manchester and Imperial College (London) to read chemical engineering. Birmingham was good for sport!

So, we shared similar upbringings – which came with similar values. A work ethic was required to rise from these modest beginnings. An appreciation of the value of money was naturally acquired. None of us had any! A grounding in common sense was quite normal where we came from. A sense of humour, or, more accurately, a need for humour, is present in us all. Les Dawson always said that humour was related to adversity – the Geordies, the Liverpudlians, the Mancunians, we collectively enjoy a good laugh. Seldom does a board meeting start without some banter, generally football-related. I simply cannot cope with a dry board meeting. I lose the will to live. We (I think) are approachable. We don't have airs and graces. We are not particularly PC. In the USA, we would have been shut down years ago. We don't enjoy politics, or bureaucracy, or bullshit. We do like honesty, good manners, directness and normal people. That said, we can equally tolerate quirkiness. We are not impressed by a suit and tie and we don't expect people to stay late if there is no necessity, just to put on a show.

I believe that the three of us are highly complementary. John does the finance stuff with great professionalism. I have not met his equal. I fluff around at the top and think about strategy and deals, and some of my guiding principles of safety, rigour and ensuring the right people are in the right roles – that sort of thing! Last but not least, Andy is peerless in picking up the pieces (usually, in fact, almost always my pieces!) and making the organisation tick smoothly. Again, I have not met his equal.

So, there goes the John and Andy bit. We are good mates, we are all driven, and we stick by each other.

I like structure, so I'll use headings in attempting to describe the INEOS 'mojo' and why INEOS has achieved success.

SUCCESS

I asked the execs, 'What made INEOS so successful?' But firstly, let's ask whether it *has* been successful. I happen to think it has. In spades. That said, I could have a bias! Before we examine the question, it's worth saying that I can categorically state I had no vision at the beginning of INEOS's life in 1998 of what INEOS was to become, or what it might achieve. Not that, in reality, it would have much occupied my mind twenty years ago, as it would have constituted 'dreaming', and I don't indulge in that.

We have around 100 chemical sites, most with multiple chemical plants. Some are the size of the City of London, and they can be found in most corners of the world. We are fully international, from Korea and China to the UK, Germany and the USA, and many more in between. Our sales level at $60 billion is the same as a small- to medium-sized country such as Bulgaria, Costa Rica, Uzbekistan or Tanzania. On a sales basis, we would be 118th in the current Forbes list, on profits number 99. We are one of the top five chemical companies in the world. We are the size of Facebook plus McDonald's combined. We are the largest petrochemical company in Europe. We have one of the largest and most successful chemical plants in North America. We supply one in ten households in the UK with gas. By bringing shale gas from America, we rescued Grangemouth, the largest manufacturing facility in Scotland. We may yet rescue the likes of the Defender. It feels like we are the only organisation to recognise that shale might just revive manufacturing in the north of England. We made $7 billion of profit (EBITDA) last year. Not bad for twenty years' work, in my view. So, what characteristics helped us achieve these milestones?

ORGANISATION

There are many different forms of organisation, varying massively in the levels of centralisation that you might find, and the levels of complexity. There is no right answer and different forms of organisation can be made to work. BASF and Exxon are diametrically opposite to INEOS in that they are highly centralised, and yet they work well – they are both large and successful companies.

I have a pathological aversion to matrix-oriented, centralised organisations. I like simplicity, accountability; no-place-to-hide, direct, clear organisations. We operate a federal structure with a tiny head office.

A federal structure means that each business is fully responsible for all its functions – IT, HR, communications, banking, legal, tax, etc. Head office simply has one senior exec for each of these functions to ensure a sensible level of consistency across the group. We expect individual business functions such as IT, for instance, to share best practice across the group, which they will do by regular meetings – say, once a quarter. They must always look for what is best for their business. We have no interests in jealousies, reluctance to share or behaviour that doesn't extract best value for INEOS. It needs team players who behave like owners. Politics stand out a mile and simply aren't tolerated.

A federal structure ensures that communication from the top descends directly into the organisation without filtration through head office. It means that a feeling of ownership propagates in each business. CEOs and boards are fully accountable for their business success and strategy in their entirety.

For me the federated structure really is the difference maker in INEOS. I worked for Mobil Oil and BASF prior to INEOS, and never felt completely in control of the business with so many services and costs coming in from head office. In INEOS, we have the ability to control all the levers of the business to focus the business in the right direction, and also to control all the costs of the business to meet our objectives. You truly get to act as an entrepreneur vs. other business structures. – Kevin

It also means that the delegation of responsibility and authority that we gives inspires poeple, and for those that stay they step up to the mark and thrive on it. – Jonny

It means that in our minds we own the business and run it and care for it as if it's our own. – Paul

It means management must own an idea from cradle to grave, which instils a level of focus, ownership and understanding that is lacking in many of our competitors. – Rob

Each business with its own bank accounts, legal structures and very limited functional oversight allows for clarity of costs and purpose through everything that we do. And we do this while maintaining a strong corporate governance. – Mike

Once the shock of being 'INEOSed' was over (corporate credit cards cut in two, delegations rolled right back to board level, laser focus on costs, etc.), I could start to see a simplicity in the business model which was supremely satisfying. – John

The separate (federal) business structure combines with a genuine board responsible for performance. Many companies run a 'business unit' structure but they aren't really fully responsible as they don't have all the levers under their control. Much is 'outsourced' to internal (and indeed external) functions within the wider company. – Simon

As to organisation, it's lean; communication lines are short and decision-making is quick. As a result, the strategies of businesses are clear and uncomplicated. People are rewarded for pushing the boundaries. – Ian

INEOS's very limited head office function, separate businesses running independently from each other and the board empowered to make decisions, is very powerful – and drives ownership. – Franck

PEOPLE

Business starts and ends with people. Running a business requires an endless stream of decisions, and a few critical decisions on the way. People make these. And the success of the business depends on getting most of these decisions right. Not all, but most.

I could tell you that success in chemicals is down to having world-class assets at world-class scale in the world's key markets. Which it is, of course. But really that is stating the obvious. The clever bit is getting to this point. I have long said that buying the world's most expensive football players is not difficult. You just need to be able to read a newspaper and write a large cheque. *Finding* the world's best players of tomorrow is a much tougher ask, and creates much more value – and, for that matter, satisfaction.

So, getting back to people. And another football analogy. Why do football teams win at home more often than away from home? The pitch is the same size, as is the ball, and grass is grass. It is simply proof in my mind that the disposition of people – the atmosphere, the psychology – affects performance. At INEOS, I believe we do have a supportive environment. We thrive on challenges. We enjoy a laugh. We get a buzz from success. People work hard and play hard. And why shouldn't they? It gets the best from life. On the back of this positive energy INEOS has prospered enormously, as have many of the individuals who work here.

SAFETY

Safety comes first in INEOS. And it's not just lip service. We hold some twenty board meetings (ExCos), one for each subsidiary, each month, that both Andy and myself attend. The first item on the agenda is always safety. Not just personal safety, but process safety, too.

We operate in a potentially hazardous industry. We deal with materials that are flammable, explosive and toxic. We operate at high temperatures and high pressures which exacerbate risk. Intense attention to safety is our licence to operate. Nothing may come before this priority in our industry.

It is mandatory for each board in INEOS to report key safety metrics each month. The detail is such that Andy and myself are aware of the safety performance of each and every business down to details, which means *any* overdue maintenance inspection, *any* loss of containment (i.e. spill), *any* recordable injury to a person, *any* HiPo (high potential incident), *any* major alarm activation, *any* transport injury or contractor injury. This is very granular detail in a business as large as INEOS.

We have seven life-saving rules in INEOS, including no smoking on site, that persons working at height must be tied on, no consumption of alcohol and no safety interlocks to be disconnected without authorisation.

We have a simple overarching rule here, too. If you break a life-saving rule, you will be dismissed. They are there because they save lives, and so we are black and white on this matter. We also have a site RED list. These are sites that are not operating at our required safety standards and therefore carry a risk we believe is unacceptable and has to be fixed. If the site cannot fix them, and they are given time, they will be closed down, because safety comes before profit and money.

Every company has the equivalent, but in my experience they don't enforce them. They typically create the rules with great fanfare and glitzy promotion. Then someone breaks one and they create a 'three strikes and you're out' rule. If it's a life-saving rule, why would you allow someone to create the potential for fatality three times before you escort them off the site? – Simon

Many companies have a strong focus on safety, but many limit that discussion to personnel safety. One of the aspects that I'm most proud about is that we have a discussion in every ExCo about process safety as well – High Potential incidents, inspections, Losses of Containment, asset care and integrity – and other items to ensure that we are maintaining the plants and equipment to the standards that we have established. It is critical to not just the safety of our employees and our communities, but it is our licence to operate and ends up being good business as well. – Mike

For a newcomer, the approach to safety and operational performance was demonstrably superior to the companies with the glossy brochures, because it was clear from the owners down that this was the number one priority. – Graham

Not many companies would have had their owners visit an asset, declare it unacceptable, instigate a programme and then, in the space of a few weeks, roll it out across the whole company, at the same time making it a bonus metric. I could see this either never being something that a chairman of other companies would be interested in or, if they were, it would go off into a central function that would spend a year developing something then another year implementing it! – Simon

ACQUISITIONS

We have made many acquisitions over the years, large and small. And they have contributed to much of our growth. But we have broken the mould, or at the very least challenged the mould, so to speak, in that 80 per cent of our acquisitions have been successful. Maybe more. Conventional wisdom would say that, typically, 80 per cent of acquisitions fail. Forecasts become inflated, prices get frothy and not enough rigorous analysis is carried out. The main reason for failure, though, is that the buyer wants it too much.

INEOS is happy to pay a fair price. We are not what are known as 'bottom fishers'. If it's fair then both buyer and seller get a sensible deal. On occasion, the price will inflate due to strong demand, at which point we will bow out. Or it may be that when subjected to rigorous analysis all is not what it seemed to be, or the Sword of Damocles is hanging over its head in some form. Again, we will retreat to the sidelines.

Having the strength to walk away from a deal is helped by

having choices. We look at lots of deals. I remember from my venture capital days the phrase 'the more deals you look at, the better deals you do'. This gives you better perspective and less tendency to get wedded to a transaction.

In our early days, commodity chemicals (most petrochemicals) were generically unpopular in the public markets because of their cyclicality and the analysts' inability to forecast quarterly results. Which meant they (the analysts) didn't look good! In reality, commodity chemicals give a good return over the cycle. But sometimes you have to wait a bit. Today, the markets are a little more sophisticated. As a consequence, in the past, transactional prices for these businesses tended to be modest as the buyer spectrum was constrained. And thus it came to pass that for many years we mopped up unfashionable, unsexy, commodity and bulk chemical businesses for attractive, or at the very least fair, prices.

More recently, we have looked to oil and gas deals, as the chemicals arena has become overpriced and oil and gas prices have slumped with a falling oil dominance. To give some perspective of quantum here, we have bid on $20 billion of both chemical and oil and gas deals in the last three years.

Deals are seldom easy. There is no perfect world. Often the challenge will be in finding appropriate finance, particularly as we wholly debt-finance. We have never sold down equity. How do you create quasi-equity that the banking community can rely upon? Another common pitfall is price. More often than not, there is a gap between the vendor's aspirations and our valuation. There are sometimes ways to bridge this gap using vendor loan notes, earn-outs and the like. Creativity plays a large part in solving these puzzles, and few companies have been more creative than INEOS. While we may not always be successful, we don't like to let a small thing (!) like equity or price gap get in the way of a good transaction. You will hear about some of these creative solutions in the following chapters – the ICI Chlor facilities to buy EVC, the shotgun in INEOS Nova, the two-step acquisition process in Styrolution and INOVYN, the Oxide equity bridge to buy Fluor and Silicas, and several others.

Having acquired a new business, we roll out our tried-and-tested procedures. We give a friendly welcome to the new people. We generally allow 100 days to change the organisation structure to direct reporting lines. We have an 'INEOS tool kit' which introduces new delegated authorities, fixed-cost reductions, safety reporting, financial reporting and IT systems, plus a myriad of others. We look for opportunities to expand the assets at modest cost. We encourage business teams to come forward with growth ideas. It has been done so many times that it runs fairly smoothly, because people know what to do. And we don't mess about. On day one we are straight in and start to make changes. It seems to work!

The absence of large departments providing central support functions also reduces the risk of 'analysis paralysis'. By this I mean the endless circle of analysis and re-analysis that can either prevent an idea from getting off the ground in the first place, or mean that once a decision is made, it is made too late to be truly effective. We make decisions based on fundamentals and underpinned by a strong understanding of the basics of our business. This means that we are comfortable making decisions on an 80/20 basis, which allows INEOS to decide quickly, out-manoeuvring our competitors when we need to. – Rob

Indeed, the insurance industry firmly believes that acquisitions are always high risk to the performance of the acquired company – we

have finally got through to them that we are actually the opposite. Every acquired business improves under our watch. – Simon

We look at ALL opportunities! – John

INEOS has used the same business model for twenty years, which focuses on key elements such as buying good-quality assets no longer strategic to their parents, running them better, then expanding them. The acquisition deal process has been honed over the years, e.g. ensure sufficient cash flow to raise debt; there's money in defining working capital. – Jim

We know how to acquire businesses with a great M&A team, and know what to do with new businesses when we get them. We set our businesses up to be cash positive at BoC (bottom of the cycle), which enables us to trade through even the most severe crisis. It was testament to this INEOS mantra that during the crisis years of 2008–10 INEOS had no mass redundancy programmes, unlike many of our peers in the industry. We work hard at unfashionable businesses for many years with the unwavering belief that they can be successful. I could think of no better example than INOVYN, a business once unloved by ICI and taken on by INEOS. It is now one of the top performers in the group. Who would have thought it?! – David

Rapid assimilation of the deal/opportunity and speed of decision is key (i.e. never go frothy – aka 'strategic' – and stay comfortable to walk away from deals). – Bill

In the end I think the core of our success has been to break the normal 'rules', in that 80 per cent of our acquisitions have been a real success as opposed to the opposite for most companies. This is due to a combination

of both buying well (unfashionable assets from blue chip majors) and then delivering substantial performance improvement (tool kit, overhead simplification, management empowerment and smart debottlenecks). Also, we have (at least until recently!) stayed loyal to our core petchem and polymer patch, where we have vast experience. – Andy

RISK

Risk can be avoided. But then very little happens. So we don't. Avoid risk, that is. But if you accept risk, you need a clear head and an appetite for rigour. Rigour is my favourite word in business. You need to understand risk, weigh up risk and take a view. Don't let the trees obscure the wood. Don't get paralysed with analysis. Get your head around the big picture, don't endlessly chase unimportant details. Be prepared to step up to the plate.

Every deal or major capital project entails risk. It is unavoidable. And it is not for everyone.

We are quite collegiate when we make a deal. We generally reach consensus and then we collectively share the risk. We don't have a blame culture. Some deals go well, some less well. The ones that go less well we work on and keep working on. Two of our most successful businesses today, Styrolution and INOVYN (both approaching $1 billion of profit), started with poor deals. They are testaments to the philosophy that if you have a problem child, often it can be nursed back to health either by TLC or by creativity, or simply by perseverance. Don't despair. Don't give up. Plug away. Persevere. And it may bear fruit.

In 2005, we acquired Innovene (BP Chemicals) from BP for $9 billion. We had two months to carry out due diligence. We were not allowed to visit a site or meet an executive. It became one of the biggest deals done in corporate history at the time, and it was done at breakneck speed. But we always felt we had a handle on the risk. World-class businesses, a good and honest owner, a well-trodden path (we had acquired from BP before) and high-quality people. We were right, and it was a transformational transaction for INEOS. We quadrupled in size overnight. But it was not for the faint-hearted.

And the move to bring shale gas from the USA to feed our European chemicals base was similar in scale. Financial commitments exceeded $10 billion. Again, it was transformational. Again, we were right. Thank God!

It is often said that INEOS is an entrepreneurial company. The dictionary defines entrepreneur as 'someone who takes financial risk in the hope of profit'. In INEOS, we do more than hope. We have to 'know'. – Paul

PRIVATE COMPANY

Not only are we a private company, but the ownership has never spread beyond the three partners. It is extremely unusual to find a company the size of INEOS that has not had to sacrifice some equity to finance a hard-won transaction. One of the things I love about debt is that you can always pay it back or exchange it for other debt if you don't like the debtholder. Equity is an entirely different matter. Not only do you have no rights to redeem it, there is also no set price. Once equity has been sold, you should consider it gone for ever.

Being private, apart from being entirely in control, confers a number of advantages. For one, you are not subject to the whims of the public markets, which are often driven by boys in short trousers. Our drive into petrochemicals, in the early years, would have been frowned upon by those learned analysts, some of whom were yet to shave, as would our more recent foray into oil and gas.

Heaven forbid if we had intimated an interest in replacing the Defender or buying Belstaff. We are free to make long-term decisions. The capital cycle in chemicals may take up to five years, from planning through engineering and build. The analysts hate that.

Outside shareholders add complexity, they have their own objectives, insist on governance and non-execs, and slow down the speed of decision-making.

We have not been as effective when we have had outside shareholders, e.g. Acrylics, INOVYN and Styrolution. – John

Retaining 100 per cent ownership has only been possible by judicious use of the debt markets and therefore a willingness to accept higher risk – e.g. leveraging Oxide to support the funding of the Fluor/Silicas/Phenol deal or leveraging the whole of INEOS Group to acquire Innovene.

People often ask me whether we plan to take INEOS public. I can think of no place I would rather *not* go, including the South Pole (which, while enormously uplifting on arrival, was preceded by fourteen days of ice-strewn abject misery). Retaining our private status has unquestionably been one of the secrets to success. The freedom to make quick decisions, to make long-term decisions, to make bold decisions, to make contrary decisions. The non-execs would have had kittens with us!

When people ask me what difference being private makes, I tell them that January 1st is the day after December 31st. That's not to mean that we don't have targets and goals (I certainly don't want to give you that impression!), but that we're not beholden to someone on Wall Street or in the City. If we want to do something that makes sense long-term (or even short-term – say, a working capital/EBITDA trade-off), it's a simple conversation. Being private also allows us to greatly streamline the financial reporting and investor relations aspects of the business, which eliminates a huge burden. – Mike

We have had consistency of management, leadership and vision from the top, which has enabled the business to have a clear strategy over many years, building on the successes and learning from the failures. We've avoided new leadership coming in and trying to take INEOS in directions where we might not have been so successful. – David

Stability of leadership is critically important for an organisation, and the stability that Jim, John and Andy have provided is an extremely key element of our success. With that stability comes a consistent strategy and approach to the company. The stability that we have in INEOS has extended into the specific businesses, especially ours in O&P USA. We have been able to develop and implement our strategic approach over these thirteen years, and I think that has been reflected in our performance. – Mike

STYLE

How do you describe 'style'? It is a very subjective concept. INEOS does have its own style. It has surfaced more noticeably in recent years and it is distinctive. Much of the influence, I suspect, descends from the top, but not all. It reflects some of our core values, such as our distaste for pomp, for arrogance, for bullying, for bullshit and for flowery presentations.

Conversely, we like a 'contrarian'. We like creativity. We like unpretentious and supportive leaders. We appreciate grit, character, going the extra mile, pulling the stops out when needed. We don't eviscerate managers for making a mistake. We expect them to learn from it. We encourage team players, doers, hands-on clear thinkers and communicators.

We are comfortable with irreverence, non-PC talk and people who speak their mind. We expect good manners and encourage humour. It is often said that we are a large company that feels like a small company.

All this 'influence' distils down to a style. It's difficult to describe in words, but I particularly love the quote from Jill, who oversees HR for INEOS.

When you wake up in the morning and you want to go to work, when you achieve more than you thought possible as an individual and as part of a team, when you blink and it's the weekend and you look back on the week and can't quite believe how much you have done and how much fun you have had, when you admire and mutually respect your colleagues and consider them to be your friends, then you know you are in the right job in the right company … Well, most of the time! – Jill

There is an esprit de corps in INEOS seldom seen elsewhere. While the press focuses on ridiculous speculation or angles, it never captures the pride that people take in working for INEOS. – Ron

People know very well what we stand for, what we aim for, what we fight for – day in, day out – without heavy or lengthy statements as in BP times. Since 1998, INEOS has been clear and concise about what we want, aiming high and never falling short. In all aspects of our business, from safety over reliability and efficiency to markets and innovation. – Hans

The largest small company you will ever work for – this is the best way I can describe some of the culture that we have managed to maintain

despite our exponential growth. It has a close, family feel with a relatively small number of people at its centre. Everyone is supportive and we all know each other well. There is no large corporate HQ full of non-value-adding people. – Graeme

INEOS is a very large-scale, world-class company, with a small-company feel. – Jill

Northern grit. Roll your sleeves up and get stuck in. Work hard. Get to the point and don't bullshit. No airs and graces. A lack of politics – it just wastes time and energy and does no one any good. We have a common goal to be successful, so let's help everyone get there. – Graeme

Indeed, at INEOS we continue to explore and improve; we are never complacent. Year after year people are keen on knowing what is going to happen, willing and hoping to take part. New ideas are welcomed, challenges accepted, employees triggered, young people encouraged, risks calculated, bold decisions taken. – Hans

SPORT

Long ago I used to draw a parallel between business and football. I had no problem with players that were robust and vigorously competitive. I had no problem being clattered by a player who was intent on getting the ball. I *did* have a problem with the dirty player, the nasty player or, indeed, the half-hearted or moody, temperamental player. You see similar characteristics in business. People in INEOS need to be robust, generally honest in their dealings, tenacious and committed.

Sport, health and wellbeing play a large part in life at INEOS. We have a general view that people who are fit and healthy are happier and more productive. We encourage each site to provide gym facilities and coaches. We run health and wellbeing classes. Some sites run yoga, stretch, spinning and fitness sessions. We have a director of sport and fitness who has reached two Olympic 1,500m finals, John Mayock. We take it seriously.

We have a graduate scheme where all graduates at the end of their three-year programme are invited to spend a gruelling week in Namibia running marathons in the desert, climbing mountains and cycling enormous distances in the heat and dust. It challenges them. They learn about themselves. They learn about teamwork. It bonds. They test themselves to their physical and mental limit. It's not for everyone, and it's entirely optional. It's not a race. Girls and boys alike opt to have a go and so far, most have returned with the glow of accomplishment and pride at having achieved what previously would have been thought impossible.

All INEOS sites and communities have turned into sports addicts, running for fun, cycling the Tour de France, skiing in no man's land, or just climbing flights of stairs at the office. It makes INEOS a most desirable workplace for young and old. It keeps us focused, creative and – most of all – unique in our sector. – Hans

Most companies have some form of a health and wellness program, but INEOS is the only one that I know of that backs this up with actions and attitude. Taking an hour out of the day to work out is not merely tolerated, but wholeheartedly encouraged. – Ron

With the company proactively supporting the health and wellbeing of all staff and being so sports-enthusiastic, a very special team spirit and drive is created across all businesses – not least among all the

young employees who are so crucial for the future success of the company. In this context I remember discussing business strategy during a marathon run – concise arguments help to save energy…! – Gerd

PET HATES

We all have these. And it always helps to get them off your chest. So here are some of mine!

I hate bad manners with a passion. There is no excuse for it and I cannot abide it. There is a lovely example in Switzerland where children are still taught good manners and respect from an early age at school. If you stop at a zebra crossing in Switzerland, whoever is crossing, whether young or old, will always acknowledge and say thank you, without fail. This is no longer always the case in the UK.

Do it right. Don't do half a job – be it analysis or painting pipework. Take pride in your work, which, whatever it is, is important, otherwise you wouldn't be doing it, and do it to the best of your ability. Too many times I have seen chemical plants that are uncared for, litter-strewn, with painting unfinished and rusty pipes. It's one of my hot buttons and has been a malaise I have observed many times.

I am not a fan of consultants, particularly strategic or market consultants. If management need outside help to figure out strategy – which is their primary responsibility, after all – then you have got the wrong management.

And probably top of my list is the use of the 'I' word rather than 'we'. Generally business accomplishments reflect a team effort, seldom just an individual. So why would you ever use 'I'? To me it sounds a trifle arrogant, but maybe I'm getting cranky in my old age!

WRAP-UP

Let me finish, if I may, with a final range of quotes from INEOS execs. After all, they have lived through this first twenty-year phase of INEOS, and have done most of the work.

Arguably it is also easier for them to say how it is, rather than me, since I risk sounding pompous!

INEOS is restlessly eager to take on the next challenge, creative in overcoming it, intolerant of untrue talk, nonsense and fussy procedures whilst doing it, willing to trust its business teams to get on with things in the meantime, and demanding of excellence in whatever it does. – Pete

To my mind, one of the keys to success was having a chairman who didn't know when things were impossible, or claimed not to; and a set of senior managers who didn't want to tell him they were impossible (or didn't dare). So, they tried to make the impossible happen, and to their surprise (and maybe the chairman's, too?), it turned out it wasn't so impossible after all. – Chris

I used a phrase to introduce INEOS at the last insurance market day: 'Relentless Improvement'. I think this sums us up very well, whether we are talking about safety, reliability, operations, fixed costs, capex, risk, EBITDA or growth. – Simon

Relentless drive and ambition. Creativity, solution-finding. Never take no for an answer. Ask the questions, and take the paths others daren't. Truly entrepreneurial. Work hard, play hard. It's an important balance. (One of Jim's quotes I always remember and use: there's never time to go for a run, so you just have to go.) Permanently challenging, which maintains interest and excitement. Little hierarchy. No committees. Nowhere to hide.

For us, it's personal. For competitors, it's just a job. All driven by tone and example from the top. – Jonny

Put it all together, I still get excited going into work each morning. – Ashley (who has just hit sixty!)

The best place to work is a growing company that still has the potential to surprise its employees! – Bob

I do think INEOS is a fun place to work. Sure, there are many, many things that you just wouldn't see anywhere else, but that is what marks INEOS out as different and I think attracts and retains the people that make it work. – David

Humour. Humour is a big and very important part of INEOS. – Andrew

There are a number of reasons that INEOS continues to be successful:

- *The culture of ownership and pride remains, particularly among the leadership teams.*
- *Consistent messages from INCAP (INEOS Capital) ensure that every employee knows what's important and what is expected.*
- *The bonus system keeps everyone laser-focused on what makes their business unit successful.*
- *There is a total lack of bureaucracy. People can focus on what adds value and do not waste time on minutiae.*
- *Decisions are made quickly and efficiently. This must be the most pragmatic company in the world.*
- *People want to work at INEOS! Hiring new employees is becoming easier as our reputation grows.*

- *The sports and fitness culture is fabulous. I love showing people pictures of elevators that say 'lifts are for losers' and explaining trips to Namibia. It's inspiring!*
- *People are rated and rewarded based on results not politics.*
- *There is a unique, progressive, non-stuffy culture at INEOS; people are free to be themselves, encouraged to grow and excel.*
- *Our employees are very proud of their company and genuinely want to work for INEOS.* – Bob

INEOS Capital – Jim's fingerprints are everywhere (that is positively meant!). Quite amazing how that has happened considering the number of different heritage businesses that today represent INEOS – how strongly Jim, John and Andy's principles and beliefs reach most corners of the businesses. Jim's (our) uncompromising priority of safety, health and environment policy (SHE). The focus on cash generation and growth in our businesses. Transmitting these priorities so clearly across over 180 sites and more than twenty countries is very well done. – Sebastian (who joined just a few months ago)

As to people – in my experience senior managers in INEOS are very exceptional people who see themselves as normal, and treat people accordingly – contrasting with other organisations who have a lot of very normal people who see themselves as exceptional. – Iain

Unfaltering drive, the appetite to grow, ambition. – Bill

None of this would have given such exceptional results without the inspirational leadership of the core team. Such leadership is the key to unlock all the potential and to drive the businesses forward. An outstanding twenty years. – Gerd

For over a dozen years, whenever I finish an ExCo meeting, I call my wife and tell her I still have a job. A bit tongue in cheek perhaps, but it is part of the INEOS ethos which I think makes it so successful: employees are given a clear set of objectives, the resources and flexibility to deliver on those objectives, and then are held accountable for their delivery. What a simple but refreshing approach to business! What an exciting way to motivate your employees and attract those who want the challenge of being held accountable for what they can deliver. And yet it seems as rare as fairy dust that one finds other companies being driven by this simple ethos. You can learn a lot about a company's culture by the reputation they acquire in the industry. Time and again I have heard comments relayed over a beer or before a business meeting that the INEOS reputation is of a company that 'always seems to be one step ahead of us', 'can take decisions in hours and days which would take us weeks or months', 'is good at motivating and keeping their employees'. – John

No ivory towers or executive floors
Just a leadership team with open doors
Many execs don't have an office, or door
Just a desk, sometimes shared, on an open-plan floor
So what is the secret of INEOS success
Buying unloved assets, sometimes in distress
Providing vision, leading from the front
Straight talking, sometimes a little blunt
Always supportive, focused on delivery
Challenged teams growing in ability
A clear sense of fairness, recognition and reward
One thing for sure is no one is ever bored
To work for INEOS is like cramming several careers into one
Fast paced, continual learning and above all a lot of fun. – Jill

ACKNOWLEDGEMENTS

Generally, endeavours such as the writing of a book are team affairs – and this is no exception. Ursula, whose name decorates the front cover, is a little-known author largely because she has never written a book before. She is an INEOS graduate. She is twenty-eight years old with a penchant for writing. I rather bravely invited her to pitch in and get writing despite her youthful years. That said, Shakespeare was hard at work by the same age… Her sentences can be a little long for my liking on occasions, but that's probably because she studied archaeology at Cambridge. Her ability to write 'really' long sentences doubtless explains why she came top of her year. Levity aside, she has worked intensely hard on the book. And 'chapeau' for that. At the opposite end of the maturity spectrum sits Jim Dawson, at seventy-three. Of all the people I have met in my short life, Jim has accumulated the greatest volume of knowledge. He has an insatiable thirst for enlightenment. He has proffered scholarly and sage advice throughout this project to both the writers and researchers, and with his Oxford chemistry training has maintained factual accuracy when the going got tough – or technical!

The two researchers – David Leppard and Anna Reynolds – put a huge stint in at the beginning and created the bones of the story. But for them there wouldn't be a book. Thanks also to Laura Grant and Gary Haywood, who painstakingly proofread the book, one from California and one from Oz. Oh, how the world is shrinking.

Finally, I can't miss this opportunity to thank Andy Currie and John Reece, my close colleagues and co-owners for the past twenty years. INEOS wouldn't be where it is today without their insights, loyalty and, frankly, hard slog when it matters.

As for me, I just breezed along in the team's wake and got my name on the cover!

Jim Ratcliffe
April 2018

CHAPTER 1

IN ANOTHER LEAGUE

Britain's largest private company, international chemicals and energy giant INEOS, is not a household name. In fact, it is not known well – or at all – to most of the general public. And yet, INEOS is, quite literally, a partner in everything we do. One of the final bastions and still a beating heart of UK manufacturing, the INEOS family of companies provides the chemical building blocks for everyday life. It purifies 90 per cent of the UK's drinking water, supplies the raw materials to make everything from LEGO to medical equipment, develops specialist materials for future technologies, and touches almost everything else in between, on an international scale. This quiet giant rules an unglamorous yet fundamental realm of business, operating on the fringes of our consciousness but firmly embedded in every aspect of our lives. Throughout its meteoric rise, and increasingly today, the company is disrupting norms and remaking attitudes and economic realities in Britain and far beyond.

INEOS founder and majority shareholder Jim Ratcliffe, along with co-partners Andy Currie and John Reece, are no better known, though the $60 billion per year business they created in just two decades is the stuff of business school textbooks. There is a story to be told here: the biography of a world-class British business rising from obscurity and bouncing to the brink and back, a saga of strategic deals, misfortune, near misses and dogged triumph. Ultimately, though, the story is about people. About the rise of an unassuming and perhaps unlikely team with a canny combination of vision, intelligence, integrity, humility and steady competence in the face of recurring high stakes. A team that, together, created a lean, entrepreneurial, expanding business quite unlike any of its kind.

INEOS had a relatively modest beginning. Founder Jim Ratcliffe was a chemical engineer by training, who had fallen by fortunate accident into finance then venture capitalism in the early 1990s. Having become restless in his deal-making role at US firm Advent International, he was eager to manage one of the business investments he brokered long-term. Aged thirty-nine, during his fourth year at Advent, he spotted a suitable opportunity: a speciality chemical business BP had listed for sale at £37 million. Putting a personal contribution of £140,000 into the deal, and risking everything he and his young family owned, Jim pursued plans to buy the business. Armed with a chemical engineer's training, a London Business School MBA and a natural sense of profit potential, with an as-yet-untested risk orientation, he worked alongside then business partner and mentor John Hollowood, backed by Advent, his employer. This was the first of Jim's high-risk moves, and the start of his journey to self-made billionaire. In the course of the deal, Jim met Andy Currie, then working for BP, who was a fellow northern grammar-school boy with disarming business nous. The two would become close friends and lifelong business partners and, just two years later, would float the newly formed company, named Inspec – International Specialty Chemicals – at a value of £164 million.

In 1998, after acquiring Shell Fine Chemicals and other assets, Jim bought a significant petrochemicals plant in Antwerp from BP and, in the process, sold the balance of the Inspec business to British chemical company Laporte. On 5 May that year, he created a new company to hold the Antwerp plant, which was named INEOS and would lay the foundation for his business future. Two years after its auspicious birth, INEOS's winning leadership trio was complete with the addition of John Reece, joining from leading accountants Price Waterhouse, as the INEOS numbers magnate and a perfect complement to the team.

The early 2000s were an extraordinary growth period for INEOS. The three partners acquired one business after another, using leveraged finance (debt) as their unusual main source of funding, rather than selling their own equity. It wasn't until 2005, however, that INEOS transformed itself into a major player in the chemicals industry, when it acquired the Innovene business from BP in a move that tripled its size overnight. Innovene was BP's huge petrochemicals business, spread across nineteen countries and employing thousands of people. A classic 'unwanted asset', Innovene no longer met BP's growing financial ambitions, due partly to its cyclical nature, and Jim was immediately able to spot its value. Buying such cast-offs and turning them around would become a recurring theme throughout the INEOS journey.

When the $9 billion deal finally closed, the petrochemicals industry was instantly remapped, and the other bidders, all much bigger than INEOS, were left stunned. Jim quickly set about giving Innovene the soon-to-be-typical INEOS makeover, stripping out layers of senior and middle management and focusing on the core business. His attention then turned to Grangemouth, one of two major integrated oil and petrochemicals sites acquired in the Innovene purchase and a strategically important but suffering asset. At the centre of Scotland's petrochemicals industry, the plant included two gas crackers that transform ethane gas into ethylene, which is then converted to polyethylene, an important plastic. Grangemouth is also home to a crude-oil refinery, supplying petrol and diesel for filling stations across most of Scotland, Northern Ireland and the north of England. (Today it employs over 1,400 people, comprises 8 per cent of Scotland's manufacturing base and exports goods worth £9 billion a year.)

Grangemouth was a wholly new and difficult business case for the team, and the site was heavily influenced by the trade union Unite – the most powerful in the UK. The union dominated the workforce and had almost complete control over how the site was run. During a strike in 2008, Unite won an easy early victory against INEOS, costing the company £100 million at a time when Grangemouth was increasingly loss-prone. A painful first lesson in industrial relations, this rhetoric-filled showdown was all the more challenging because it was the first event to bring the name INEOS, and Jim Ratcliffe, to wider public attention. The situation would take another five years to resolve.

In the meantime, the global financial crisis brought INEOS to its knees. After the global banking system meltdown, the price of oil plummeted, and international demand for petrochemicals products, including plastics, evaporated, as hundreds of factories closed. INEOS's leadership did everything they could to reduce costs and increase cash flow but, in the end, there was nothing to do but stand by as the order book emptied and the business faltered. Jim and finance director John Reece had to convince the banks that INEOS wasn't about to go under. The company was still generating cash, but it had some strict banking covenants in place that, if breached, could threaten its existence. The team had to fight hard to convince the banks to allow existing management to run the business, rather than letting the banks take over. The market value of INEOS bonds plummeted to around ten cents on the dollar – the financial markets were clearly voting on an INEOS collapse – but they hadn't figured on the determination and focus of the INEOS team. On the brink of tripping a crucial banking covenant, INEOS was forced to renegotiate its debts at a cost of some €804 million, and the restructuring plan still wasn't enough to guarantee survival. In the heat of the struggle, the last viable option was to trim the corporate tax bill. As a result, Jim and the team requested a deferral from the then Labour government on a £350 million VAT sum. Inexplicably, their request was denied, against a backdrop of Labour-sponsored bank bailouts. In response, the team decamped to a new headquarters in Switzerland in 2010, to save a lifeline £400 million in tax in the Canton de Vaud near Geneva over the next five years. Business-as-usual became increasingly international.

As INEOS slowly recovered, however, the lingering Grangemouth issue resurfaced. With North Sea gas in decline, and the continued cost of high salaries and employee pension contributions – amounting to 65 per cent of salaries – Grangemouth slipped ominously from profit to loss. By 2012, the plant was haemorrhaging £10 million every month. Ten thousand direct and indirect jobs were at risk if it folded. What followed was one of the most bitter disputes in British industrial history: the union rejected Jim's bid to save the plant by ordering a wage freeze and pensions cuts and, instead, launched an all-out strike. With Unite resorting to contemptible intimidation tactics, and the attention of then Prime Minister David Cameron and Scottish First Minister Alex Salmond nervously on the case, days of high drama were played out in the media. Ultimately, with little but grief to show for its efforts, Unite backed down to accept Jim's rescue plan. The incident has since remade industrial relations on the site, and changed the course of British union politics for good.

The future of Grangemouth secured, Jim then began his most ambitious project to date: taking control of INEOS's own energy supplies, amidst an unforgiving global market. Having watched the discovery of shale gas transform the US economy with cheaper energy prices, INEOS quickly saw its US operations making up two thirds of the company's profits, despite having just a third of the assets. The renaissance seen in the United States inspired Jim's vision for the UK's own manufacturing revival, based on the pragmatic recognition that the only way to beat them was to join them. In an increasingly competitive global market, the best means for the European chemical industry to stay afloat, and the manufacturing sector as a whole to do the same, is through globally competitive energy pricing. This is a battle only just beginning, and with a long way to go.

As a first step to stimulating Europe's own shale gas industry, still unexplored in the region, Jim seized on the concept of transporting gas from America across the Atlantic. Never before attempted, this became one of the biggest gambles of Jim's career. It was also an imperative, and the only way INEOS's European chemical plants would be able to continue competing with their

US and Middle Eastern rivals. The INEOS boss envisaged a plan to build a 300-mile pipeline from the prolific Marcellus shale fields of Pennsylvania to a then almost derelict port at Marcus Hook on the Atlantic coast, carrying ethane as both feedstock and energy supply. Here, he would revive a vast deep-water terminal to support an entirely new fleet of ships capable of transporting 40,000 barrels of gas every day (800,000 tonnes a year), at -90°C, across the Atlantic in all weathers, to supply gas to INEOS's European operations. In scale and ambition, the plan was unrivalled – and its success has reshaped INEOS's fortunes, redefined shipping technology and rewritten the rulebook for competitors in the company's wake.

Although the technology required to transport ethane at this scale had not yet been invented, it was brought from vision to reality in just six years. A partnership brokered with Danish gas carriers Evergas, who could not only match Jim's ambition but also provide the skill to realise it, led to eight new ships being commissioned, which have now been built near Shanghai. These boats were redesigned from the keel upward, becoming the largest, most advanced and most flexible gas carriers in the world, with the capacity to run on the very ethane they hold – a world first for energy efficiency. Named 'Dragon Ships' for their scale and the national symbol of their birthplace, each boat requires more than one million man hours for 5,000 people to construct, with the first two launched in early 2015. This remarkable feat has now become a new norm, with INEOS's transatlantic 'virtual pipeline' running at full flow and competitors already riding the wave.

The momentous arrival of the first Dragon Ship at Grangemouth in September 2016 signalled a new era of prosperity for the site, allowing it to maximise capacity and return to profit-making status overnight. It marked the end of austerity measures, and a new era of long-term growth and investment. It was, however, only the beginning of Jim's shale ambitions. While the vast discrepancy in gas cost between the US and Europe makes the elaborate US import system profitable, the next logical step and ultimate goal for Jim and the INEOS team is the stimulation of the UK's own domestic shale revolution – a project which is only at the earliest stages, and fraught with new challenges. It is a controversial undertaking, to say the least – and one grounded in Jim's and the team's respect for hard science, rigorous engineering and sound business logic. By the end of 2017, the company had acquired government licences to explore over 1.4 million acres of prospective gas fields on the UK mainland and, while the technical challenges of realising this project are thoroughly surmountable, the battle to secure public trust in and support for the venture looks likely to be long-running.

Meanwhile, in addition to developing onshore energy extraction capabilities, Jim and the INEOS team have been applying what they do best – turning around unwanted and unfashionable off-cast assets – to breathe new life into the North Sea. In an era when most of the big offshore explorers have reduced activity there, in a market seen as stagnant at best and moribund at worst, INEOS has planted itself as a top-10 player with ambitions to bolster the failing industry and strengthen energy security in the UK. In 2017, as Danish oil and gas company DONG sold its fossil fuel-related assets to focus on renewables, Jim and the team added the business to its now burgeoning portfolio, seeing a profitable and inevitable need for bridging the energy supply gap to keep the lights on and the factories humming until the renewables dream is on its feet. For Jim, this is not only an opportunity, but an obligation.

From petrochemicals producer to energy company, the ever-expanding INEOS project, now matured, shows no sign of stopping – and its drivers are a long way from slowing down. A lifetime of mastering these complex domains has neither sated the appetite nor depleted the energy of Jim and his team – and the mega-company is evolving into new markets and even bolder plans as it slowly becomes better known. From the shadows of the fundamental, yet unfashionable, industrial world, Jim has eschewed retirement to combine his well-honed business convictions with his avid personal interests in projects lying firmly in the public eye, ushering in a new era of INEOS, and of British business to boot. In 2016, perhaps Jim's bravest venture yet was announced: the creation of a new British car company, to bolster the British automotive industry with a 'spiritual successor' to the much-mourned discontinued Land Rover Defender. Code-named 'Projekt Grenadier' after the British pub in which it was conceived, the plan to reinvent the original Defender came to represent not just a passion project but a bold business opportunity. As Jim envisioned it, the new INEOS 4x4 would fill a broad gap in the market for the rugged, old-school vehicle Jim admired and relied upon throughout his life on adventures in Africa and beyond. As this project progressed, INEOS also walked unannounced into the fashion world, buying iconic British brand Belstaff, and has since bought its first football team, Lausanne Sport – the oldest in Europe. Most recently, INEOS has partnered with Olympic sailing champion Sir Ben Ainslie in a bid to bring the America's Cup trophy back home after a 167-year absence.

It is a great virtue of a private company, Jim often jokes, that neither a master plan nor slide-by-slide logic need be explained, much less justified, to the public – and it is exactly this enigmatic governance that makes INEOS so fascinating. Beyond confident assurance that growth is both continuing and thriving, few employees know the compass bearing of the next venture. Deals evolve day by day, and the company seems to define and redefine itself with unusual fluidity. The INEOS trio's business methodology is, however, quite clear: turn loss-making acquisitions into profitable ones, and increase margins in those businesses that are already making money. Of course, all game-changing businesses succeed because their leaders 'think outside the box', take risks and make bold decisions – these are the defining principles of entrepreneurship everywhere – and it is an approach INEOS perfectly exemplifies. INEOS's particular success has, however, resulted from the marriage of this methodology with a distinct management style, creating a thoroughly unique company culture.

The fact that the top managers and owners of INEOS are one and the same works to winning effect. Jim, John and Andy are often asked by industry peers and business journalists why they prefer to keep the company private – why don't they cash in with a public offering on the stock market? The answer is always straightforward: they don't want to, and they don't need to. The commodity chemicals business is a highly cyclical one; historically, and still today, oil and gas feedstock prices have been extremely volatile. Demand for plastics, in cars, planes, consumer goods and beyond, can also fluctuate wildly with global spending. There are ups and downs to every industry, certainly, but the commodity chemicals business is more cyclical than most, and it struggles to win the loyal trust of public markets with no view towards the mid- or longer term.

Under the constant gaze of institutional investors, picky analysts and the financial media, most publicly listed companies are hostages to their own dividend policy. Shareholders such as pension funds and unit trusts buy into big companies as much for the regularity of their pay-outs as for growth. Violent downward plunges in commodity prices can doom even the largest FTSE 100 company, causing share prices to plummet and dividends to be cut or suspended. No FTSE 100 board enjoys the fallout, which can often lead to a management shake-up, while a privately held company need not fear the views of any 25-year-old City analyst. Analysts, though they may never have run so much as a sweet shop, hold the power to trash a listed company's share price, cause it to sell valued assets, and even prompt a hostile takeover. INEOS's owners are unwilling to cede such power to anyone, much less a business neophyte. Owners of private firms ultimately sell for three main reasons: to retire and cash in, to finance acquisitions or to pay down debt. The INEOS trio are now in their early to mid-sixties, but the word 'retirement' does not appear to feature in their vocabulary. If they need finance, they have mastered the art of leveraging the debt markets. For the foreseeable future, a public sale is not on the cards.

With Jim at the helm as company chief, John Reece as the master of numbers and Andy Currie heading up operations, the three-way partnership has rooted itself in a doctrine of six enduring principles, which guide the process of assessing, acquiring, rewiring and running their every venture. These 'toolkit' principles, roughly summarised, are as follows:

- FIND orphaned or unwanted assets. (The success of a deal is in finding the right raw material to work with.)

- FOCUS on the fine detail of financial numbers. (Rigorous accounting sounds logical and essential, though the forensic levels applied by John Reece and his finance colleagues are rare.)
- FIXED costs management. (Tightly control all the variables you can, to create a lean and resilient outfit.)
- FEDERATED business model. (Accountability and responsibility in an organisation nurtures new ideas and bespoke efficiencies.)
- FOOTPRINT maximisation. (In the chemicals industry, maximising capacity – debottlenecking – is fundamental to efficiency and profitability.)
- FIVE years to double EBITDA. (A bold baseline aim to double Earnings Before Interest, Taxes, Depreciation and Amortisation serves to bring into the family only the most promising of offerings – and drives visionary management with challenge.)

Of course, taken individually, not one of these principles is original – or unique to INEOS. Most companies use one, two, or even three of these tools as they seek to maximise operating margins. But few repeatedly deploy all six as a combined methodology. None do so as effectively as INEOS.

Naturally, everything starts with the first principle – finding the right business to buy, and at the right price. Jim has traditionally sought out big multinationals that, due to new leadership or market conditions, have taken strategic changes of direction. These include companies like the exploration and production wing of DONG, the Danish oil and gas firm, which in 2016 decided to concentrate solely on wind energy and offload its North Sea oil and gas units. Similarly, BASF in Germany was wanting to exit cyclical chemical businesses when it sold INEOS its polystyrene interests (Styrolution). Jim and the team certainly have an eye for moving against the grain, scouring the global horizon and looking to pick up these frequently unloved and underappreciated parts of big rivals. The price has to be right, of course. Often, after a period of rigorous bargaining, they would secure the prize at a winning cost, sometimes at 30–50 cents on the dollar. There are notable reminders here of the workings of Warren Buffett, the US investment guru, and one of Jim's great business heroes. Buffett's most famous rule is this: buy a great company at an attractive price and, if possible, hold onto it for ever.

With the bold goal of doubling EBITDA every five years, the prospecting and pricing process is honed even before the other core management principles are brought into play – the first one being rigorous accounting. At the very root of INEOS's methodology is a fine-grained, forensic focus on the profit and loss numbers and cash flow of each and every part of each and every business. Chemical plants comprise a multitude of complex interlinking processes. They constitute a carefully orchestrated chain of production that runs from delivery and storage of oil and gas feedstock through refining and cracking, manufacture, and then finished product storage and distribution. Each link in the chain must run efficiently, or else any kink or bottleneck in the process passes the inefficiency forwards. This is true for the financials, too. INEOS has honed its own 'granular' accounting system to track every dollar, tracing profit and loss among the maze of processes that run daily on its sites. Though fully logical, it is perhaps remarkable that many complex enterprises of this size don't manage cost with the same approach. As just one example, in the course of buying Innovene from BP in the landmark deal that catapulted INEOS onto the chemical world stage, finance guru John Reece noted that BP managers had no clear system for detailing which of the nineteen sites across eight countries comprising its huge petrochemicals division were making profits and which sites weren't. Detail, then, is everything, and INEOS's EBITDA figures speak for themselves. Less than €1 billion in 2009, the figure grew to €1.7 billion in 2010. By 2015, it reached €4 billion, and was on track to be €6 billion in 2017. Little surprise that Jim has been nicknamed 'The Alchemist'.

Once the maze of numbers has been untangled, the INEOS team applies the rigours of fixed-costs management, the significance of which Jim had learned during seven years at industrial conglomerate Courtaulds. Fixed costs are those that do not fluctuate with production or sales volume; they include the cost of headquarters, factories and other fixed assets like docks, among which are rent, rates, dock fees and utilities. One vital element of fixed costs is what accountants call 'supervisory salaries' – the substantial pay rates and perks paid out to swathes of junior, middle and senior management, and it is here that INEOS's lean management philosophy almost literally pays dividends. In a market as cyclical as commodity chemicals, fixed-costs management is fundamental to survival during inevitable downturns, and to maximising top-of-cycle benefits for profit and reinvestment. Maximising site productivity, too – known as footprint maximisation – is a powerfully simple principle based on the economy of scale, which acknowledges that a chemical site is only maximally profitable when running at full capacity. Such a state is often in flux, and peak output is achieved by rigorous processes and equipment management, close technological development monitoring and tightly managed debottlenecking projects. At the micro and macro scale, every operation matters.

As operations chief, it is Andy who specialises in identifying and then removing production bottlenecks. Antwerp, the site of INEOS Oxide, is a prime example. When Jim bought the plant in 1998 as the founding purchase for the creation of INEOS, the plant's output of ethylene oxide was an estimated 150,000 tonnes annually. Andy says that its previous owner, BP, had not really focused on maximising its footprint. By giving more authority to onsite managers and encouraging them to come up with ways of improving processes, removing bottlenecks and expanding the business, Antwerp was transformed into a key profit centre. After several years of debottlenecking, output gradually rose to 450,000 tonnes a year. The plant is now operating at maximum capacity. Similar processes have occurred with all INEOS's new acquisitions, and are an ongoing element of site management.

Discussing the company's early purchases of off-cast ICI divisions, the Degussa phenol business, and then BP's Innovene, Andy Currie remarked: 'We learned that we could run them with a pretty simplified model that we were comfortable with. That differentiated us.' But this belies a more remarkable management approach and value set embodied by the three owners, which runs through the veins of every INEOS unit – a culture stemming from the federated business model, but certainly more than the sum of its parts. From a shrewd business perspective, INEOS's federated structure is lean, fast paced and supremely effective.

Rather than running overlapping functions from a central INEOS core, replicated within each business unit, Jim, John and

Andy devolve control of each business to its own CEO – encouraging full accountability. This is both efficient for decision-making and empowering, enabling managers to think creatively and act effectively through direct relationships with the top team. INEOS is rigorous not only in selecting the right people for this business model, but also in creating the conditions for those people to thrive. Jim describes it simply:

> Like all things in life, success depends on having the right people involved – and they need an organisation that supports them and an entrepreneurial approach, with accountability, a lack of committees, and the freedom to make key decisions. It suits some people but not all. People in INEOS do behave more like owners than employees, and I think that has helped to generate a spirit of entrepreneurship. We want them to think beyond their job description.

Bill Reid, head of the company's mergers and acquisitions team, concurs:

> Entrepreneurship, at least within INEOS, can be summed up in four words: speed, risk, drive and fun. Speed of response to the opportunity, a willingness to take risks, a strong drive to continuously push the company forward, but also to have fun in an environment where INEOS Capital [the centralised management of the INEOS family of businesses] entrusts us with a great deal of responsibility at a very early stage.

As Jim learned while at Exxon at the start of his career, the idea of a network of broadly autonomous business divisions, incorporated in their own right but run like a federation of independent states under 'federal' leadership, was alien to most big corporations. Many of the industry's goliaths had grown into huge corporations over a period of decades. As a consequence, they had slowly, but inexorably, encumbered themselves with hierarchy and bureaucracy. The ultimate symbol of corporate success, the company HQ, was the focal point of corporate power: the bigger the better, regardless of the balance sheet. In contrast, a federated business model like INEOS's does not require multiple management layers anywhere in the corporate chain – Jim fully believes that bureaucracy 'suffocates businesses'. INEOS is famously headquarters-lite – and the three self-made billionaires who oversee it do not surround themselves with the traditional accoutrements of corporate status. There are no swanky private offices staffed by legions of assistants, diary secretaries or speech writers; to the contrary, the INEOS system is simple, unadorned and effective and it starts at the top.

Not surprisingly, then, Jim's office at INEOS's London HQ is a relatively compact four metres by three, filled with photos of family and remarkable adventures. Noticeably spare, the only clue that this space is home base for the UK's most successful businessman is a desk in the open-plan corridor just outside, often stacked high with documents and books, where Jim's personal assistant Christine sits when the team are in London. A warm and phenomenally efficient person who has worked with Jim for over a decade, Christine's diverse role is much more like that of a chief of staff, organising board meetings and coordinating the constant flow of communications between Jim and the top team. Like Jim's, the offices used by Andy Currie and John Reece are equally unobtrusive. Andy, who co-leads one of the biggest companies in the country, doesn't find the need to have a full-time assistant. When business contacts first try to call him, they are often surprised that he picks up the phone himself. While he draws in help to manage his travel arrangements, this assistant, a shared resource with others, neither keeps his diary nor gatekeeps his calls. The down-to-earth Doncaster-raised former grammar-school boy is famously friendly and pragmatic – and insists he doesn't need an 'interceptor', despite the occasional inconvenience. He's grateful for Caller ID, however, 'so I know who is phoning. If it says "number unknown" it's probably some tout trying to sell me tickets to Wembley.'

Modest it may be, but the INEOS system is far from soft. Stripping out the fat from an acquired company's headquarters ultimately means cutting swathes of existing management jobs – and keeping only the best. The three owners have joked that there is perhaps a seventh 'F' to complement the six principles in their toolkit: 'Fit in, or find another job.' As in many successful companies, character fit is fundamental – and Jim states that key attributes for employees are 'grit, rigour, humility, good manners and social skills – preferably with a touch of humour'. He detests bullies and cheats: 'The type of player I like is honest and robust. I don't want people at INEOS who are devious, slippery or arrogant – these guys go at the beginning, they just don't survive.' Managers deemed good enough to stay are subject to further executive cost-cutting – what the company calls 'non-manpower' cuts. Corporate credit cards are removed, and low caps are placed on the spending authorities allocated to senior managers. Money must be spent as if it is one's own – thus there are no chauffeur-driven limousines of the sort associated with some FTSE 100 executives. Jim, naturally frugal himself, usually walks to work or, on occasion, might take a taxi, a small luxury for a man who is now worth billions.

Though working life is no-nonsense, employee development seems to be built into the day-to-day 'business as usual' operations throughout INEOS, with individuals given high levels of responsibility, accountability and support to voice their ideas. While not enshrined in formal HR policy, the strongly held fundamental values dear to Jim and his team percolate throughout the system, with character valued as highly as competence. According to Jim, 'Firstly it is about courage – you must have the courage of your convictions. It is easy to keep your head down and not be noticed, but if you are going to make a difference you need to stand up for what you believe in, put your head above the parapet, and be prepared to be shot at once in a while. It is about being proactive, rather than becoming a victim of circumstances.' A man relentlessly driven by challenge, Jim relishes the opportunity to test and grow his employees far beyond creating a formal, bureaucratic structure.

Proactivity and challenge are in Jim Ratcliffe's blood, to a frankly unusual degree. As is perhaps typical among the leaders of many fields, his drive is not solely channelled into his business life but feeds into, and draws from, several other passions – and none of these is more fundamental than his commitment to sport and adventure. According to his mother Marie, Jim has been a master of the 'work hard, play hard' mentality since childhood. As a youngster, as soon as he got back from school, he would do his homework and then rush outside to kick a ball around no matter what the weather. As he got older, his appetite for regular exercise grew – a 10-kilometre run every morning became part of his daily routine. Much later, curiosity as to his mental and physical capabilities – and no shortage of self-discipline – evolved into a penchant for endurance sport, as he built up from multiple marathons to ultramarathons, cycling trips to Tour de France-esque feats, and, even at the age of sixty-five, an Iron Man triathlon, recognised as one of the toughest endurance events in the world. Formerly top of geography class at school, for Jim, this endurance drive is melded with a love of adventure and travel – a united desire to explore the world and his own limits. It is this passion that equally characterises and defines his unique management style.

Nowadays, Jim's own personal adventure challenges have found their way into INEOS – firstly drawing keen senior managers along for the ride and, more recently, reinventing the 'team-building' model for his international graduate employees. No clay pigeon shooting in Dorset or paint-balling in Surrey for this cohort of intended future leaders. In May 2017, Jim accompanied twenty-nine (almost all) of his company's third-year graduate scheme intake to the Namibian desert, where for six arduous days they ran, hiked and biked over 350 kilometres in blistering 40° heat. For most of the team, this was the first time they had travelled to remote Africa – to Africa at all – or even outside of their home countries – and it was certainly the first time any of them had undertaken such a gruelling physical challenge. With many never having run or mountain-biked before, the company supported the international group with training and preparation to take them to the start line, via marathon events that would ordinarily be once-in-a-lifetime feats in themselves. The rugged remote desert scenery – and particularly the view earned at the top of the 2,800-metre-high Brandberg mountain – would prove unforgettable for the team, though the ultimate take-home for all was a transformation in lifestyle and self-belief. For Jim, this was not simply a holiday, but an exercise in professional and personal development: 'Part of the INEOS philosophy is to encourage people to take on more. It's remarkable what people can achieve when they turn the brakes off in their heads.'

It is perhaps because of the core leadership's passion – and the inevitable fact that INEOS has become such an all-encompassing focus of their lives – that this spirit of striving is offset by fun. The element of INEOS culture which perhaps stands out most obviously to outsiders is the pervasive atmosphere of informality, beyond the company's rigorous and rightfully obsessive safety rules. This informality percolates from the top down, with the leadership having none of the airs and graces often associated with the top brass at a Fortune 500 company. Jim, Andy and John are unstuffy, no-nonsense northern businessmen. Like any busy tycoons, they do not suffer fools gladly. But it is regularly remarked that they treat work colleagues with equal respect, regardless of seniority or status. Jim's mother Marie described the most important thing, apart from his work ethic, that she and her husband Alan had sought to teach Jim: 'To have pride, and be proud of the way he treated others.'

This informality is on display during even the most serious of board meetings. Typically, the company holds a week-long series of meetings – Executive Committees, or 'ExCos' – for all of its twenty or so companies once every six weeks, and these are casual as well as thorough. For a change, each July these meetings are held in a hotel in Cap Ferrat on the French Riviera. There is no standing on ceremony as the financial, technical and operational challenges of each business are thrashed out by participants clad in T-shirts and Bermuda shorts, nor a shortage of good-humoured fun as the state of the union was reviewed. The informality is no less prevalent at INEOS's increasingly renowned parties, such as its 'Back in Britain' opening of its Knightsbridge HQ, or its many (federally organised) Christmas celebrations – the latest of which has resulted in the permanent installation of a baby grand piano alongside the first-floor desks in London. Jim's style is perhaps eccentric, certainly original, and runs throughout the family of businesses by virtue of remarkably close involvement with all.

Perhaps ultimately key to its success, there is one central paradox lying at the foundation of the INEOS project – its management structure, methodology and culture is ultimately balanced on a critical axis of safety and risk. Due to the very nature of the chemicals industry, alongside the core responsibility of managing some 18,500 employees, Jim's first and fundamental priority is safety. The company runs huge machines, many the size of Harrods, which each contain thousands of moving parts and process complex chemicals. Malfunction or misuse threatens injury or even death. Thus, for Jim, safety is a mandate from which everything else follows, and it is the first subject he discusses at every chief executive meeting. Unusually for a company chairman, he demands that even the smallest accident involving employee personal injury, down to a cut finger, be reported directly to him, every month, in a detailed presentation. Citing the Deepwater Horizon disaster, which came perilously close to destroying BP, he claims: 'We are in an industry in which getting something wrong means the whole company can go under.'

By 2017, INEOS's safety record, continuously improving for

Jim aged two years old in 1954 standing on the cobbled streets in Failsworth, Manchester, where he learned to count by adding up the chimney tops he could see from his bedroom window

The first Ratcliffe to go to university – Jim (centre, front row) as captain of Birmingham University's Chemical Engineering football team

Jim and his university classmates using slide rules, before calculators were commonplace

Cologne, the largest INEOS site in Germany

INEOS Chocolate Bayou, Texas – one of the largest crackers in North America

Antwerp, Belgium – the birthplace of INEOS

Grangemouth, Scotland – the INEOS petrochemical site and Petroineos oil refinery sit at the end of the Forties Pipeline System on the Firth of Forth

Lavéra, France – the INEOS petrochemical site and Petroineos oil refinery supplying products to southern Europe

Jim appears on BBC *HARDtalk* to discuss the post-Brexit economy and his plans for British shale gas exploration

Signing a joint venture deal in 2011 combining the strengths of INEOS and PetroChina in the refining business

Jim and Andy talk tactics at the 2009 investor meeting

John Reece speaks to investors during the 2009 downturn

London, March 2009 – Jim stands before hundreds of investors to ask for their support on a refinancing plan to save INEOS from collapse in the financial downturn

Jim accompanies his third-year graduate employees on an endurance adventure in the Namibian desert, May 2016

INEOS moved to Switzerland in 2010, taking over the Cadbury office in Rolle, between Geneva and Lausanne

the past decade, is now best in class – and ironically far better than that of the office-based insurance industry. Seventy per cent of the company's sites were fully accident-free in 2017, and the improvement drive is relentless. The challenges are particularly difficult for a company such as this, because it is continually buying new organisations with management and staff who often have a history of operating in different safety environments. 'It's an immense amount of work,' says Jim. 'But INEOS has now got to a point where it is setting a benchmark for the industry across the world.' From safety, too, comes reliability – a safe plant is also a reliable plant, one that keeps operating efficiently twenty-four hours a day, seven days a week. Naturally, this also makes a more a profitable plant. Safety, reliability and profitability all go hand in hand.

Within such a safety-focused culture, the assessment and management of risk is king. And it is this relationship to risk which, in the business domain, also pervades the mentality of INEOS's owners. Personal health and safety is sacrosanct, but, in the abstract world of business, 'you need to accept some risk', says Jim. 'There comes a point where you have to gamble.' Risk-taking, of course, must be carefully calculated. As Jim explains: 'The name of the game is to think of all the "what ifs" early on and to test them as far as you are able with the information available. You cannot think of everything, and you cannot eliminate the risk entirely, but you can certainly reduce it.' This attitude is scaled up to the biggest deals, such as the landmark purchase of Innovene from BP, which had to be done without visiting a single site or speaking to a single manager, and down to the smallest deals, a process that has been well honed over years by INEOS's leaders. The power of intelligent risk-taking, creating the conditions for good luck and hard work to take root, has defined the high-stakes life and growth of INEOS so far – and is what makes this company such a dynamic one to watch. At twenty years old, still precocious perhaps but fully out of adolescence, INEOS and the risks being taken in its unpredictable expansion are likely to keep bystanders on the edge of their seats for some time to come – and the players fully preoccupied.

CHAPTER 2

THE ADVENTUROUS ENTREPRENEUR

When James Arthur Ratcliffe was growing up in the 1950s, he spent hours looking out of his bedroom window. Beyond the gloomy rows of terraced council housing, his gaze would settle on the huge rectangular red-brick mills, with their iconic chimneys silhouetted against the grey Lancashire skyline. Born in October 1952, in Failsworth, a former mill town half-way up the Oldham Road from Manchester, Jim always had the industrial revolution in his blood. Two hundred years ago, his home town had been at the epicentre of that revolution. The introduction of the Spinning Jenny, the first fully mechanised process to allow the mass production of textiles, had put Manchester and Oldham on the map. From a collection of small market towns and rural villages, the area had been transformed into a northern powerhouse that had made Britain the workshop of the world. The cotton mills of Oldham have long since closed, and many have been demolished. Others lie derelict, decaying relics of Britain's grand industrial past. The survivors have been given a new life, converted into modern, waterfront apartments or shiny new office blocks. It was a fitting, and formative, start for a boy who would become one of Britain's most successful industrialists.

The chemical industry had filtered into Jim's consciousness from his earliest years. When he was nine, his father Alan secured a job running a company that made laboratory equipment, whose customers included ICI, then the biggest chemical and manufacturing company in the country. The significance of this for young Jim was more of a geographical one, though, with the job requiring the family to relocate 100 miles across the Pennines to Hull on the Yorkshire coast. Jim had not been born into a line of professional privilege; Alan had left school at fourteen and apprenticed as a joiner, making doors, window frames and worktops, while Jim's mother, Marie, worked in the gas accounts department of the local council to support the family income. A close-knit family, they taught their two sons, Jim and Bob, that hard work and self-reliance were the keys to getting on in life, and supported the growing boys' education and interests as far as hard graft and limited means would allow.

Jim was successful at school, being one of the few local working-class children to pass his Eleven Plus exam. This allowed him to win a place at the grammar school in Beverley, the oldest state school in Britain, and one of the best in the north of England. It was a ten-mile bike ride from the family's new home through the green fields of East Yorkshire, and on to the pretty market town with its cobbled streets and ancient minster. Beverley Grammar put huge emphasis on qualifications and Jim studied hard, taking a total of sixteen O Level subjects. With a broad range of interests, he was in the top quarter at most, but exceptional in geography, and took a particular interest in art and painting.

It was science and his gift for maths, however, which proved to be his natural field, and would lay the foundations for his future success.

Numbers, of course, meant money. In his INEOS years, the canny numerical skills of Jim and future business partner John Reece would prove key to acquiring and turning around undervalued off-casts of corporate giants such as BP and ICI, generating substantial profits. Almost obsessively detailed financial assessment would become core to Jim's business philosophy. As a teenager, however, his early entrepreneurial spirit was channelled more modestly, through the Saturday jobs encouraged by his parents. His first, as a delivery boy on a local greengrocer's van, wasn't glamorous. His often-grumpy boss drove the delivery van around the streets of Hull, with Jim upfront, jumping out of the passenger seat to deliver boxes of produce to doorstep after doorstep. Jim claims the contact with customers and the thrill of a sale had motivated him even then – but the more fondly remembered role for the football-fanatic youngster was working as a Golden Goal lottery ticket seller at Hull City Football Club. In 1966, the year of England's famous victory over Germany in the World Cup final at Wembley, Jim would stand at every Saturday home game in the entrance tunnel selling tickets to arriving fans. 'The money was really good,' he remembers. He wore his team's kit, got a free seat – one of the best in the ground – and loved it.

Earning pocket money with his hobby was just the beginning of an eminent journey, and Jim's somewhat exceptional drive and industrial interests manifested themselves early. Despite studying hard at sixth form for A Levels, in chemistry, physics and maths, he found time in his late teens to set up a school Industrial Society, the first of its kind at Beverley. While many of his classmates were soaking up the Swinging Sixties, spending spare time at the concerts of the Beatles, the Rolling Stones and the Who, Jim was engaged in the somewhat more mundane task of organising visits for career-minded sixth-formers to local manufacturing and industrial plants, including BP and ICI; touring their sites and talking to staff and managers. Was it all work and no play? Certainly not. But Jim had perhaps slightly larger aspirations than his contemporaries. 'There's no question, I definitely had a bit of the entrepreneur in me when I was seventeen,' he recalls. 'I used to think I would rather like to become a millionaire.'

The late 1960s witnessed an unprecedented rate of technological change that had huge implications for industry and trade, and for the debate about the country's economic future. The development of computers, the discovery of North Sea oil, and the manned moon landing were the result of tremendous advances in science and technology. The age of austerity that followed the end of the Second World War was finally over, and the British economy had grown exponentially. Unemployment was low and living standards were rising – and the rest of the world was growing fast, as well. America, parts of Europe (such as Germany) and the Asian powerhouses of Japan and Singapore were on the rise. The novelist C. P. Snow had set off a debate in 1959 when he claimed that the political and social elites who ruled Britain were ignorant of science and engineering. That, Snow argued, made them unfit to govern in a world where technology was transforming other economies.[1] Four years later, Labour leader Harold Wilson warned, in a now famous speech, that if the UK were to survive amidst the growing global competition, a 'new Britain' would need to be forged in the 'white heat' of scientific revolution.[2] Wilson's speech was a call to arms for UK industry and manufacturing. It also highlighted a long-running discussion about the role of science in the country's life that is as relevant today as it was more than fifty years ago.

Against this backdrop, Jim became the first ever Ratcliffe to go to university, choosing chemical engineering as his vocation. Top colleges were keen to pick the brightest science students, while big companies like BP, ICI, Shell and Unilever had an insatiable demand for promising graduates with a good BSc. Jim's plan was simple: get into university, secure the degree, and head into a stable career with a heavyweight employer. In early 1969, during his final year at Beverley, Jim received offers to study a three-year Bachelor of Science degree from Imperial College in London, and from the universities of Leeds and Birmingham; he chose the latter. His parents were incredibly proud, though he remembers his first day at Birmingham as more of a failure than a triumph. Walking along the corridor of the chemical engineering department to find a group of new students crowded around a noticeboard, he found his name fourth from the bottom on a strangely organised register of his ninety-nine course mates – it was a table of A Level grades. He had barely scraped in.

Jim's choice of chemical engineering was a pragmatic one, chosen by process of elimination. Having pursued the sciences, he knew early that he never wanted to specialise in pure chemistry, maths or physics, preferring to combine these disciplines with some more practical, real-world application. Engineering appealed and, of the four types of degree on offer, chemical engineering was chosen 'simply by default'. Mechanical engineering was out of the question – 'I was useless at anything mechanical. I had no interest and I didn't want to get my hands dirty,' he recalls. Electrical engineering was also a non-starter: 'I never really understood electricity at all. We used to have people who could wire up their own radios at school, but I wasn't switched on by that.' There was civil engineering, 'but I was just not motivated by buildings'. Chemical engineering ended up being a strategic choice for a man who'd become one of the world's most successful chemical industrialists. At the time, however, its appeal to Jim was more immediate.

While the study of polymers, monomers and the like appears inscrutable and utterly dull to outsiders, in reality, it is all about uncovering the dynamics of how the world works. It explains everything from fluorinated drinking water, to gas and electricity for hot showers, to how LEGO blocks are manufactured. The chemical engineer designs the industrial processes to make the foundational chemicals and raw materials that are transformed into items such as plastics, paints, textiles, medicines and mobile phones – almost everything essential to daily life. Peter Atkins, one of Britain's most distinguished chemists and authors, put it this way: 'Without the chemical industry, the world would lack colour. We would live in Stone Age conditions, underfed, dressed in skins, without the many devices that ease our lives and entertain us. Our lives would be short and painful.'[3]

During Jim's time at Birmingham, the three big petrochemicals giants, Shell, BP and ICI, almost guaranteed a job to candidates with a good degree in the subject; those with some relevant work experience were especially sought after. At the end of his second year, undergraduates on Jim's course were encouraged to find temporary work placements and, in the summer of 1972, Jim took up a six-week post at the giant BP Chemicals plant in Saltend, Hull. His job was to map out the complex spider's web of pipelines and valves in the company's speciality oil business, giving him an intimate understanding of the complex physical make-up of a chemicals plant. It was a chance encounter during this summer, however, that had a more lasting effect on his future career – a chat with a BP colleague, a chemical engineer-turned-accountant, who encouraged Jim to explore the business rather than the purely technical side of manufacturing. 'You should open your horizons,' Jim was told, perhaps through applying his talent for numbers.

Jim's summer internship paid off, and he was offered a job as a trainee chemical engineer at BP's Saltend plant during his final year at Birmingham. Relieved that he could now skip the drudgery of the graduate recruitment 'Milk Round', he completed his studies in June 1973, receiving a respectable upper second BSc degree. His plan to move straight into a promising job after college did not, however, run quite as smoothly. On 1 August 1973, Jim arrived back at BP Saltend, a slightly nervous but newly minted chemical engineering graduate, then just twenty-one. He was full of anticipation for what he believed would be a long and successful career at one of the world's biggest petrochemicals companies. But he was fired just three days later. Forty-five years on, Jim still remembers the bombshell encounter in his new boss's office. 'I have got some disappointing news for you,' his manager announced. The company had just read the results of Jim's medical examination, a supposedly routine measure which Jim had undergone months earlier, on first being offered a job. The tests showed Jim had a history of eczema. Though the skin condition was mild, BP's doctors feared it could be exacerbated by some of the toxic chemicals handled at the site. 'We can't risk training you for the next five years only for you to develop a reaction to them,' the manager explained.

Jim was predictably shocked, responding: 'You could've told me before you hired me. I didn't apply on the graduate Milk Round, because you offered me this job months ago.' Recalling his earlier talk with the accountant colleague on placement, Jim thought on his feet, and suggested a trainee accountant position instead. Though the idea was considered, the HR department couldn't seem to find a single post suitable for the new starter. Down on his luck, Jim returned home crestfallen, with his career plans in pieces. Of course, as he recalls now, there was an element of poetic justice in store for him thirty-two years later, when INEOS bought BP Petrochemicals in a $9 billion move that transformed the giant into the success it is today – 'I did finally get to work for BP Chemicals. But only after I bought it.' At the time, though, the Ratcliffe family had moved back from Hull to Bolton, north of Manchester, and Jim, with little income and no savings, was down and out and living at home.

Advised by his father that working harder than everyone else was key to getting on in life, he ended up taking a temporary job on a construction site, while he explored how to reset his derailed career. Two months of hard labour helping to build a mortuary at Manchester Medical School were offset by hours scouring job ads and sending out his CV, until eventually he got an interview for a job at Beecham Pharmaceuticals – the company now owned by GlaxoSmithKline and known for its cold and flu relief products. Though not the size of BP or ICI, the company was still among the top 100 British firms, and one of the largest in its field – a solid place to restart. Beecham's headquarters were, however, in Worthing, West Sussex, a seven-hour, 275-mile drive from Jim's Bolton base at a time when the major linking motorways had yet to be built. On arriving for his interview,

Jim candidly shared his BP troubles – only to be told upfront that Beecham sometimes had a similar problem with penicillin dust, a recognised skin irritant. Hiring Jim as a chemical engineer would be an irresponsible move. Yet again disappointed, Jim drove the long journey back to Bolton in his reliable VW Beetle, arriving home hours later thoroughly depressed.

This time, however, luck was on his side. Jim's backup interest in accountancy had been noted – and the potential for a trainee position explored in house – even as the rejected interviewee pondered his future on the road home. By coincidence, the firm's chief accountant, a man called Tim, was also a chemist who had suffered from allergies. By the time Jim had shared the news with his parents, the phone rang for him. With apologies for missing him earlier that day, Tim was keen to meet him for a second interview. Rising at the crack of dawn the next day, and driving the seven hours back to Worthing, Jim was offered an accountancy post on the spot – the character fit which finally kickstarted his career. It was a bleak time in Britain by September 1973. The IRA were bombing London, there had been a miners' strike, and the country, under the Conservative Prime Minister Edward Heath, was about to enter a period of power cuts and a three-day working week. The global economy was stalled by an oil crisis. For Jim, however, things were looking up. He found a natural affinity with accounting, and a dedicated mentor in Tim, studying hard to qualify as an accountant. He took a home study course with the Rapid Results College, sitting his first exam within six weeks, and was fully qualified within eighteen months.

His grades were strong for the most part, winning As in cost accounting and economics, though he barely limped through office management with a mediocre C. His real education, though, was through Tim, Beecham's top accountant, who took Jim under his wing. It was here Jim learned the core of accountancy, where the cash book is king. The lifeline of a business was tracked through this simple system; on one side, the system records cash received, including accounts receivable and cash sales, and on the other, it records cash paid out such as accounts payable and expenses. The balance sheet, the profit and loss statement, and the statement of cash flows charted the pulse of a business, and were learned with intensive scrutiny. From Tim, Jim learned the fundamental tools which would go on to underlie his phenomenal success with INEOS – the management of variable and fixed manufacturing costs, labour costs and sales and overheads. A fully fledged accountant with a chemical engineer's training, after four years at Beecham, Jim had mastered a rare mix of skills.

Ready for his next challenge, Jim took a management accountant role at Esso, part of ExxonMobil, interpreting the financial results of the world's biggest oil and gas company. Based in Victoria Street, London, the job was well paid, and offered immediate career status within a heavyweight American multinational. The work didn't ultimately stimulate him, however, and the prospects were unexciting. It was clear that, in such a large company, Jim would have to spend years climbing the corporate ladder to reach what he deemed 'a proper job' – one which gave him genuine control of his own business unit. His brief time there was, however, invaluable in sowing the seed of his future tenets on how to structure a business.

At Exxon, Jim witnessed a diffuse and overlapping chain of command, where many executives and staff reported to one boss as the head of their business unit, and to a second boss at headquarters. In business school jargon, this was the 'matrix' model of management. He found that, amidst the multiple tiers of lower and middle management, it was often difficult to establish in each business unit exactly who was responsible for what. There could be two or three people with overall responsibility for a unit's operations and, consequently, for its success or failure, and they often weren't working side by side. Each unit was accountable to its own leader, but also to a head office with its centralised head of research, head of production, head of sales or head of finance. Jim perceived that such an overlapping chain of command created a culture where individual unit managers did not always perform at their best, because someone else shared part of the responsibility for running their business, and with that the costs. It meant less empowerment, less accountability, less incentive for staff and managers to go the extra mile and achieve the best results and, ultimately, less reason for a talented manager like Jim to stick around.

Conversely, other companies, such as Courtaulds, where he next moved, operated a federated structure – where staff reported in a direct line to just one executive at the head of each business unit, who was consequently directly accountable for everything they did. As Jim notes: 'Some people love this challenging environment, and others shy away from it.' For Jim, it provided the perfect conditions to succeed. He adopted this model later at INEOS, giving his chief executives full accountability and responsibility. 'You are responsible for producing the product and for selling it. You are responsible for raising your debt; you're responsible for your own IT, and you're responsible for all your own legal contracts and any legal actions you have to take. You are also responsible for your own HR and for your own safety,' he explains. 'If you are successful, there is no questioning who achieved this, and if you are not, there is nowhere to hide.' It's a high-stakes system, designed for survival of the fittest.

From Jim's perspective, however, Exxon did have one very good thing going for it: every year, the company paid for its most promising rising stars to study at business school. As at Beecham, Jim was identified early on as a great potential talent and, in 1978, was offered a place on the scheme, with a choice of prestigious international schools to take his two-year master's in business administration (MBA). He eventually settled on London Business School (LBS), one of the best institutions of its kind in the world, and grafted hard to win a place on the competitive course. The first hurdle was the Graduate Management Admission Test (GMAT), an extended multiple-choice examination which tested reasoning and mathematical skills, designed by Harvard Business School and since adopted at Chicago, Wharton, Stanford and London. The maths part was no problem; numbers had long been Jim's speciality, and he cruised through with 97 per cent. Verbal reasoning was a different story, however; his paltry mark of just 37 per cent nearly destroyed his chances and left him a mere twenty points above the minimum acceptance level. As with Birmingham University, it was another close call: 'I must have been bottom of the year on 520, so I absolutely just scraped in.'

For a grammar-school kid who had spent most of his life in the North and the Midlands, Jim's two years at LBS were a revelation. He was still only twenty-six and, compared to most of his new classmates, had led a relatively sheltered life. He had been on holiday, of course, including hitch-hiking in Europe, but he had seen nothing of America, Asia or the Middle

East. At LBS, Jim met ambitious, engaging and intelligent young high-fliers from all over the globe; an eclectic group of future business leaders for whom LBS was a nursery – a training ground for eventual entry into the highest levels of corporations around the world. He seemed to thrive in this new environment, and drew inspiration from the world-renowned teaching staff who steered his interests. Among them were Paul Marsh and Richard Brealey, specialists in corporate finance, and Andrew Likierman, a world expert in measuring business success. Jim felt a particular affinity with Likierman, who grew up in a family textile business in Manchester. Nearly four decades later, in 2016, when the now Professor Sir Andrew Likierman, dean of LBS, accepted Jim's record donation of £25 million to help redevelop its new campus site, he surprised his former student by remarking that he remembered him, though he admitted he never could have guessed that Jim would end up where he is today. 'You are the most successful person who has ever come out of London Business School,' he noted, as the two men, once teacher and pupil, shook hands for the cameras.

By the end of his course, Jim was fascinated by corporate finance, analysing a company's assets and liabilities, and the concepts of debt and equity, risk and return. Leveraged finance, the art of borrowing money to invest in new businesses, held a particular draw. Ultimately, Jim claims, good business sense is fairly simple, coming down to rigorous analysis of the numbers, an assessment of the level of risk, and the decision as to whether the anticipated return is commensurate with both. His overarching takeaway from LBS sounds disarmingly simple: 'It is all about money, and the numbers. Money and generating equity return.' He had, of course, mastered many technical learnings, such as the Black and Scholes model, but, in the end, each decision rested on the risk/reward analysis. His two years there played a vital part in developing one of the two halves of Jim Ratcliffe: the industrialist-turned-financier. 'The two bits of me which had to be put in place before I did my first deal when I was forty were my industrial experience and my financial experience,' he explains. 'One of the main things I learned at London Business School was the finance side. That's a critical part of my DNA.' The young boy who got a kick from earning pocket money at Hull City FC was now equipped for the world of deal-making.

In the summer of 1980, when he left LBS, eyes now opened to a new world of business, Jim decided not to return to his old job at Esso, something he saw as a backwards step. Repaying over £10,000 of course fees back to his former employer, he found a new job with industrial conglomerate Courtaulds, an old English business tracing its roots to the start of the industrial revolution. It was also, perhaps, the predicate for Jim's meteoric rise. The firm's reach was vast, manufacturing everything from Gossard ladies' underwear to Peter Stuyvesant cigarette filters, and even anti-fouling paint for yachts. The key draw for Jim, however, was that the company gave him a chance to run a business of his own; Courtaulds had over a hundred of them. In seven years at the company, based in the Midlands, Jim would rise to become business manager of the Non-Woven Fibres business and then head of Advanced Materials. The jobs were not in any sense glamorous, but gave him a solid schooling in the realities of manufacturing economics and savvy business management. One of his jobs involved selling 40,000 tonnes a year of the fibre that makes cleaning wipes known as J Cloths, as well as surgical dressings. With sales of about £40 million a year, it was an enormous responsibility, and he thrived on the challenge.

Jim's time at Courtaulds provided valuable schooling in business people, as well as core business principles. Responsible for the success or failure of an entire factory, he learned to handle difficult players as par for the course. 'If you didn't sell 40,000 tonnes, the factory shut down. The customers weren't always very nice to me. But it was real-life stuff.' He had one particularly difficult customer, the chief buyer of the Dutch arm of Johnson and Johnson (J&J), the American consumer products manufacturer of medications and first-aid supplies such as Band Aid. With over 25 per cent of its non-woven sales, the firm was Jim's biggest customer and he had to fly to the Netherlands every six months in a bid to persuade them to renew their account. Before Jim could even discuss prices, the J&J manager adopted his regular negotiating tactic of pulling something uncanny out of his bottom drawer. On one occasion it was a broom; another time it was an old boot. The J&J executive would say: 'I found this in your fibres. What have you got to say about that?' One day he pulled out a used condom. Holding it aloft with tweezers and rubber gloves, he growled: 'I found this in your bale of fibres. Why should I buy your shit rather than the nice stuff the Germans or the Scandinavians want to sell me?!'

As well as tough negotiating, this was also Jim's first lesson in the gulf that sometimes existed between the quality of German manufactured goods and those in Britain. He found it endlessly frustrating that the Germans, with their now-stereotyped rigour, meticulous attention to detail and consistency, were much better at producing high-quality goods than the British, who in the 1970s and '80s always seemed to lag behind the industry standard. This very discrepancy in quality is a bugbear for him to this day – and he claims that lifting the standards of UK manufacturing and its subsequent reputation is a big part of what drives him to focus on the highest possible standards at his own company. These lessons weren't always hard won, however; Jim got on naturally well with his boss, Sipko Huismans, a colourful Dutchman with a South African background, whom he saw as a mentor and a role model. 'There was a little bit of a maverick in him,' Jim remarks. 'He was a go-getter and a fantastic salesman. He could sell ice cream to Eskimos.'

Jim's numbers mastery, now put into real-world practice, was his biggest takeaway from Courtaulds, and his time there underscored the importance of a keen focus on the management of fixed costs, such as supervisors' salaries, freight and rent rates, to keep business buoyant. While variable costs, like raw materials and basic labour, fluctuated with volume of production and the worldwide commodities market, fixed costs could be more easily predicted and managed. In the face of fierce competition in the textiles market from low-cost, Far Eastern competition, Courtaulds needed a tighter grip than most on its fixed costs to avoid going under. Its margins under intense pressure, it had to shut down scores of factories as it was forced to cut production and product prices. By necessity, then, it never had a big head office staff. And, from that, Jim learned to question the headcount of a team: do we really need that many? Can a function of twenty still operate with fifteen, or ten, or five? This principle is clearly visible in the lean operations of INEOS today.

In 1987, fully settled and thriving in his role, Jim took a not unexpected phone call from a head hunter. It was an American venture capital firm called Advent International, looking for someone to run its chemical and materials portfolio in London and worldwide. Jim had been recommended by a mysterious supporter, and the opportunity was too good to miss. The Boston-based private equity group specialised in buyouts and equity investments for growth and was one of the largest US players in the burgeoning new venture capital scene. The outfit was young and dynamic and employed many Harvard MBA graduates, focused on investing in private firms or buying out public companies to delist them. It was a new world for Jim, far from his now-comfortable business management sphere. In private equity, cash for acquisitions is typically provided by pension funds, insurance companies or wealthy individual investors, and is used to fund management buyouts, finance new technology or simply take a stake in an existing company by expanding its balance sheet. Advent had just received $20 million from Monsanto, the US drugs and chemicals company, to invest in a range of 'new frontier' businesses in the chemicals and advanced materials sector. It needed someone to run the fund and had heard about Jim's unique combination of experience and qualifications. Here was an ambitious young man in his mid-thirties who had learned at Courtaulds how to run a £40 million turnover business, while also being a qualified accountant with a solid grasp of finance, a degree in chemical engineering and an MBA from one of the world's leading business schools. A promising match.

It was a stunning offer, too. Advent proposed a salary of £90,000, with a £25,000 bonus, compared with the £37,000 a year Jim was earning at Courtaulds. The package was worth nearly £250,000 in today's money, and came with a brand-new company BMW 535i to replace his Vauxhall Cavalier. Beyond the material gains, though, the career opportunities seemed limitless.

Venture capital firms were endlessly investing in potentially profitable and exciting new businesses, and were a perfect vantage point from which to survey the field. Jim had, by now, a strong sense that he might soon be ready to break out on his own venture. 'I had always wanted to do something by myself,' he recalls, looking back on that phone call. Feeling more than a little guilty about leaving Courtaulds, which he had come to consider his professional home, he took Huismans out to lunch and told him about the job offer. The gallant Dutchman appreciated Jim's candour, and encouraged him to accept. Only several years later did Jim discover that the head hunter who had tipped off Advent to recruit him was, in fact, Dr Norman Wooding, then deputy chairman of Courtaulds. 'Isn't that outrageous?!' Jim laughed.

His five years at Advent, between 1987 and 1992, were a steep learning curve, the first twelve months in particular. Private equity is about doing deals, and it is cut-throat. You get fired if you do bad deals; you get fired if you do no deals. But Jim had never done a deal in his life. At this stage, he knew nothing about valuation techniques, warranties or legal agreements. On his first day, he was simply given an office and told to hit the phones. There was no training. His peers and superiors were busy, and they had little time to guide him. With typical understatement, he recalls: 'Private equity was a new world to me. I knew absolutely nothing about it. I didn't have the tools in my armoury but just had to get on with it. I sweated a lot, but I survived. Quite extraordinary, really, when I look back.'

Needless to say, this final stage in his entrepreneurial training came naturally to Jim, and he came to savour the stress and exhilaration of the deal-making chase. The money was great, the people interesting and, best of all, for a man getting used to success, it was an unpredictable challenge. On a deal-by-deal basis, he was able to play with the boundaries of what he and others thought possible. Beyond command of financials and a well-honed instinct for operational efficiency, Jim's time at Advent finally nurtured in a professional capacity one of Jim's lifelong personal drivers – his pursuit of 'grit' and adventure. It's no revelation to draw parallels between the curiosity, discipline and dalliance with risk required in the fields of sport and exploration and that required in the world of venture capitalism, or entrepreneurship at large; this is the creed of an entire generation of corporate motivational speakers. Jim, however, was becoming a textbook example of unbounded ambition long before this became a cliché.

Fit and active as a youth, and captain of the university chemical engineering football team, Jim's passion for extreme adventure was first stoked in his late twenties, born of bravado among his driven friends at London Business School who produced a 'list of manly challenges' that, like most of his grand schemes, he says, was dreamt up in the pub. The list included windsurfing across the Channel, climbing Mont Blanc, and taking part in the Paris–Dakar Rally, an eclectic set of goals, mostly abandoned as the group became enmeshed in corporate life. The ideas lingered, however, and some were ticked off, some were dropped off, and plenty of other challenges were added as inspiration struck. Manifesting itself decade by decade throughout his life, Jim's quest for pushing the possible was galvanised at the Advent juncture of his career, but formed a steady core of his character and 'extra-curricular' life.

Jim's first notable feat was Mont Blanc, an original on the 'manly' list, undertaken with naïve confidence with his friend

Tony Loftus in 1995, which almost ended in disaster. As they climbed towards the 4,810-metre (15,800-foot) summit of the highest peak in the Alps, the pair got into serious difficulty and Jim ended up marooned. Tony had to drop out due to altitude sickness, and Jim, rather foolishly, decided to complete the climb alone: 'It was slightly irresponsible. I was in my early forties then, and you're invincible in your early forties, aren't you?!' On reaching the summit, it was eerily empty, and the group of climbers he'd been following had simply vanished. He later found out that they had all gone to a rescue hut near the summit, called the Vallot. 'It was very unusual because normally in August there are a hundred people there, but I was the only one.' Everybody else had set off with a guide except for Jim and Tony. 'My guide was Tony Loftus, and he reckoned it was a piece of cake getting to the top. He said we'd just follow the crowd, but then he had to bugger off back down.' Jim took a photograph of his rucksack and ice axe lying in the snow on the summit, his only memento of the climb, and quickly discovered why the other groups had abandoned their summit attempts.

At these extreme altitudes, the weather can turn in a moment, and the winds had started to gather pace up to 100 kilometres per hour. Jim still had to descend the infamous Bosses Ridge, which drops off thousands of feet on both sides, and is intimidating enough in calm weather. 'People say that if you fall off one side, you end up being buried in Italy; you fall off the other side, you end up being buried in France. And if you're roped together and your partner falls off one side, the only way to survive is to jump off the other.' With visibility in the oncoming storm reduced to a few metres, Jim took the wrong route down the ridge towards the Italian border. When finally aware that he was lost, he was forced to dig a shallow hole in the snow to gain some shelter and wait, with no food supplies left to tide him over. 'Unfortunately, Tony had all the Mars Bars so I didn't have anything to eat. I was completely ill equipped.' On trying to call mountain rescue, he found signal was down in the storm and decided to take what was likely a life-saving risk to turn back on the upwards climb, with the hope of finding the route down. Back at the Bosses Ridge, he miraculously encountered a guide leading other failed climbers to safety. He spent the night in the Vallot rescue hut with them, at -30°C, underdressed and underfed: 'I didn't have enough clothes, had no food and was completely exhausted. It was the most miserable night in my life.' The next morning, with the sun out, he walked safely back down, frustrated but undeterred – there were other extremes still to follow.

For many years, fatherhood and family life, alongside fitness pursuits and hard business grind, kept Jim's attention from more extreme endeavours but, as his two young sons Sam and George grew older, his penchant for pushing his physical limits resurfaced with verve. Realising he was spending 'too much time behind a desk', he began planning a trip with old friends and his boys, which back then seemed the challenge of a lifetime – to trek the 'final degree of latitude', a distance of sixty brutal miles, to the North Pole. In April 2009, Jim and a team of eight, this time with a guide, set out on an expedition dubbed 'Two Feet on the Table' – a phrase used by naval officers to mark the crossing of the Arctic Circle.

The team was an eclectic one: fit, driven and similarly drawn to the lure of the extreme. Accompanying the three Ratcliffes were Chris Cecil-Wright, a former army officer and yacht broker to the rich and famous; Adam Carey, a doctor and nutritionist for the England Rugby Football Union; Fred Wadsworth, also a doctor; and ski instructors Jeannot Jolie and Henri Thurier. Their guide was veteran explorer Doug Stoup, who is described as a 'Californian man-mountain'. Some of the team were taking on the trek for charity, others simply for the challenge. Setting out from Ice Station Barneo, a floating ice camp north of the Norwegian archipelago Svalbard, on 13 April 2009, they encountered average temperatures of -40°C and metre-high ice formations as they pulled their supplies by ski sledge. The weather was brutal. Jim's youngest son George recalls how they finished up with eyes swollen from the intense UV light and the roaring winds. There was nothing about the scheme designed to be comfortable but, as luck would have it, the ordeal was brief. The ice they were walking on was drifting towards the Pole, enabling them to complete the ten-day trip in just three. By the time they had arrived at the Pole on 17 April, they had smashed the record for the fastest men ever to walk the 'last degree'.

One pole leads to another, it would seem, and two and a half years later, in December 2011, the group decided to complete the 'set' by walking to the South Pole. Jim insists that this was never the original plan – 'it just happened' after a speculative email received a universally enthusiastic reply. 'Clearly, no one had learned anything from the last trip,' he jokes, though it would turn out to be a far more dramatic ordeal than the first quest. A plan formed to walk the last 100 miles of Ernest Shackleton's unfinished 1909 journey to the South Pole, guided once more by Stoup. Not seeking to make any further records, they aimed instead to arrive on 14 December 2011 – the 100th anniversary of the day Norwegian Roald Amundsen became the first person to reach the South Pole. From the outset, things were tough, with their rickety DC3 airliner struggling to land on the uneven ice for its first nine attempts. The atmosphere was tense, flitting from foreboding to celebration.

The team were dropped 88 degrees south – virtually the exact spot where the explorer Ernest Shackleton had been forced to turn back on his famous 1909 expedition. Back at temperatures of below -40°, with unstable ice beneath them, the team this time had the additional challenge of 2,800-metre altitude, which, due to lack of oxygen at the Pole, feels like 3,500 metres anywhere else. As sickness set in, the going was slow, at just over one mile per hour – and the daily goal of ten miles became increasingly remote. By day six, the health of Adam and Chris had deteriorated to the point where they could no longer pull their sledges, with Jim and his sons distributing the weight among them to push the group ahead. The next day, emergency rescue services were called to recover a severely deteriorating Adam – a rescue that took over twelve hours, fraught with broken-down vehicles and delayed aeroplanes.

With pace picking back up but morale at an all-time low for the reduced team, Jim's diary for the following day reads: 'My lips are cracked and sore, my nose is peeling from the frostbite two days ago, and my frozen thumb awoke me last night. I'm getting quite mad and tired.' After almost two weeks of bleak, white landscapes and gruelling pacing, however, they finally came across tracks in the snow of the Norwegian anniversary expedition, and spotted black specks of the Pole buildings on the horizon. At this point, they were fourteen miles away and 'the pull from then on remained brisk, as our goal was almost within our grasp.' Finally arriving at the South Pole within twenty-four hours of Amundsen's arrival 100 years before, Jim recalls: 'It was one of the most exhilarating feelings I can ever remember experiencing.' Because of the significance of the anniversary, Jim and his team weren't the only ones there – the Norwegian Prime Minister, Jens Stoltenberg, had turned up to make a speech, and there were a couple of TV crews. Jim took the opportunity to introduce himself and, surprisingly, the PM was quite familiar with INEOS, which had sites in the country: 'We had a good chat about the company and our ten-day trip from Shackleton's turnaround point, and then we took a few photos.' To this day, Jim claims the South Pole expedition was the toughest thing he has ever done.

That's not for want of trying, however. Further adventures, endurance events and personal bests have followed, in defiance of age and apathy. For his sixtieth birthday in 2012, he surprised colleagues by taking a three-month sabbatical to travel around Africa. Joined by twelve friends, including sons Sam and George, Jim decided to ride a motorbike off-road on a round trip from Cape Town via Mozambique, Zimbabwe, Zambia, Botswana and Namibia, and then back to the South African city. The goal was to cover 10,000 kilometres in 100 days. Looking back, Jim says: 'I can only claim ignorance got me to Africa on a bike. I had little conception of the magnitude of the difficulties that would face us, but it seemed a good idea at the time, despite having never ridden a motorbike off-road before.'

The whole idea seemed pretty glamorous at first, and the bikers looked the part. Jim called it 'that Marlboro cigarette look', with the dusty clothes, beaten-up boots, hair awry and cool shades, all set off against a rugged landscape. They were all clad in leathers from Belstaff – the company he would buy in 2017 – and driving BMWs. Everyone was given a nickname, including Jim, who was dubbed 'Buspass', much to the amusement of his friends. 'The name was clearly not my choice. I don't use buses,' he says, deadpan. It was no jolly, however; Jim broke three bones in his foot, ordered a ski boot to be flown out to the middle of the African desert, and continued in determination. For the remaining weeks, he rode wearing the boot for protection, in the extreme heat, while the rest of the team picked up nine broken bikes, and a couple of near-fatal injuries. Still, Jim describes the trip only with fondness: 'It was a true adventure with your mates. It doesn't get better.'

Three years later, in June 2015, the same group plus a few new recruits set off on their next adventure, calling it Africa 200. Again, it was a 10,000-kilometre journey, predominantly off-road on BMW 800s, but this time they gave themselves just thirty days to complete the route from Kenya's Mount Kilimanjaro to Cape Town on the South African coast – succeeding with fewer dramas than their debut. In May 2016, engines were abandoned for human power, as a yet-further expanded team of intrepid friends and family joined Jim to run, cycle and hike 600 kilometres through the Namibian desert to its rugged Skeleton Coast, the trip which inspired Jim's unorthodox graduate team-building challenge. Such trips continue, and show no sign of ceasing, as Jim devotes his out-of-business time to a seemingly endless variety of challenges, catching friends and family in his wake. This is life lived at full capacity; 'one should, if one can, try to maximise the number of days that are unforgettable'. Often out-enduring team mates less than half his age, he is a tough leader and an embodiment of grit – and described by friend Jim Dawson as 'the fittest and most adventurous CEO in Britain'. For a man this driven, a self-determined life project was, after his early business training, inevitable – and it was this sense of adventure that first lured him from venture capitalism to strike out on his own.

It was with a mind to speculate on emerging opportunities that Jim first accepted his job at Advent International, though his role there was simply to chaperone private equity from one purchase and sale to the next. Itching after five years to adopt one of these promising projects as his own venture, he finally emerged as a fully fledged entrepreneur as he neared forty, a late starter by some standards, but rich in experience. After almost twenty years of setbacks, good fortune, hard work and eclectic experience, the manufacturer-financier came to set off on his biggest gamble yet – acquiring the company which would become INEOS.

CHAPTER 3

THE BIRTH OF INEOS

Like so much of the INEOS story, the company's conception is a tale of luck, common ground and friendship. In 1991, tasked by Advent to find promising purchase opportunities in the fine chemicals sector, Jim was handed a fortuitous connection – successful chemist-turned-entrepreneur Dr John Hollowood. Originally from Liverpool, Hollowood had set up his own chemicals business, Fine Organics, in 1977, which he'd sold to Laporte for £8 million. Feeling listless in retirement, he was looking to invest again and, on receiving a call from Jim, jumped on the train to London, and back into the game. When they met at Advent's offices, John recalls that they clicked immediately: 'We got on very well. We are both Lancastrians. The only thing we disagreed on is that Jim supports Manchester United, and I support Liverpool.' Together, they began scoping dozens of companies and, in the spring of that year, found exactly what they were looking for. It was a facility owned by BP – the very company that had sacked Jim so unceremoniously at the outset of his career nearly twenty years before.

The petrochemicals giant was looking to sell one of its

subsidiary businesses, BP Fine Chemicals, which manufactured niche speciality chemicals for lubricants, coatings, plastic packaging and fragrances. It owned two plants, one in Carshalton, south London, and a second in Hythe, Hampshire, and wanted to merge them. The combined outfit was valued at £37 million. Jim and John thought this was a bargain, with huge potential, but they didn't want to take it on for Advent alone. It was time for Jim to take a personal stake, with his new business partner alongside. Proposing to step in as CEO, with John standing as chairman, Jim believed the deal could launch him into a new epoch of his career. Nothing about the BP acquisition was straightforward, however. BP had only ever done deals with big-name competitors like Shell and Exxon, and knew nothing about Advent International, let alone its ambitious young deal maker Jim. 'I had to go to BP and swear over my mother's grave that I could raise £37 million,' he remarked. To help him with the task, the would-be entrepreneur brought along Bill Teasdale, a senior accountant from Price Waterhouse, to his first big BP meeting: 'I managed to persuade Bill to perjure his life away and explain to BP that the money was as good as in the bank,' Jim joked.

In 1992, Andy Currie was working as the commercial director of BP's Carshalton site. Quiet, friendly and unassuming, his affable northern demeanour concealed a first-class brain – and a comprehensive knowledge of chemistry. He had an upbringing similar to Jim's: raised in a small, semi-detached house in Doncaster and attending Mexborough School, the local grammar, while his father worked in purchasing for the National Coal Board. An exceptional student, Andy had won a place at Cambridge University studying natural sciences, graduating with a first-class honours degree in 1977. From there he went straight into a job at

BP Chemicals' plant in Hull, the very same BP facility at Saltend where Jim had done a six-week student internship in 1972, and been fired from the following year. Four years younger than Jim, their paths had not crossed, and he would spend a further fifteen years working for BP on the more conventional track Jim had initially intended before they finally met.

That first meeting occurred under challenging circumstances. At the time, Andy's Carshalton site was making about £4 million a year. Its management team was small, with just four senior staff, comprising Andy, Derek Warner, Gary Corsi and Chic Fell. Andy remembers that, on the day they were told the site was due to be sold, 'a rather tough American guy' called John Robinson was sent down to break the bad news, pulling no punches. 'As subtle as a brick', Robinson told the team their fate, and instructed them not to bother applying for alternative roles in BP. Advised to now engage with their new CEO Jim Ratcliffe, all of a sudden the future of the site was in new hands. 'We knew that, as soon as they closed down Carshalton, the slimmed-down sister business [at Hythe] was going to make ten or twelve million, which is exactly what happened,' Jim explained. 'You were going to have this business which took the same level of turnover, at only half the cost. BP hadn't fully recognised the impact of that on profitability.' On top of that, Jim could anticipate further costs which could be trimmed, and Andy was won over, optimistic about sales growth.

Jim's immediate respect for Andy became the beginning of one of Britain's most successful business partnerships, and the two new colleagues believed they could succeed in turning the site around. They worked on the forthcoming deal for a year and a half, thrashing out the details with Rod Wilson, BP's famously hard-nosed chief negotiator. His style was brusque, on one occasion telling Jim: 'You couldn't organise a piss-up in a brewery. You're useless' – though Jim ended up growing fond of him. 'It was just because I was young. He was hard as nails.' By the beginning of September 1992, after an arduous eighteen months of meetings, negotiations and late nights, the necessary money was in place and a promising deal with BP was finally on the cards. Four venture capital firms were funding the investment – Advent put in £10 million, HSBC private equity contributed £3 million, and Charterhouse and Candover put in £2 million each.

Of the individuals involved, John Hollowood invested £250,000, with Andy Currie adding an extra £30,000. But Jim's was the biggest gamble. He staked every penny he owned, even remortgaging his family home to raise £140,000; 'I put all my chips on it. So if that had gone down, I'd have been in a mess. But those were the old-fashioned days of venture capital.' The venture was a bold one, and almost a disaster. On Wednesday 16 September 1992, 'Black Wednesday' as it is now known, the Bank of Scotland, the primary lender on the deal, called to back out of its commitment. The financial markets were unravelling.

Less than two years earlier, Britain had joined a pan-European currency agreement, the Exchange Rate Mechanism (ERM) – part of a wider scheme to integrate Europe's economies more closely. It had committed the British government, then under Margaret Thatcher, to broadly track other major European currencies, especially the German Deutschmark. Now under pressure from prolific selling by currency traders and an economy in recession, the British pound began to fall perilously close to the bottom of its permitted range, and not even a Bank of England rate hike from an already high 10 per cent base rate interest to 12 could halt its downward path. Forced by the ERM to intervene further, the Bank announced it would be raising rates to 15 per cent, while John Major and his panic-stricken government watched the crisis escalate. This day of drama was the most significant moment to date in the history of Britain's membership of the EU, and would only be surpassed by its decision to leave the organisation altogether twenty-four years later. As the saga unfolded, lenders everywhere started to react – and the Bank of Scotland announced to Jim that it was calling off its support for the deal, as the proposed venture's business model could no longer handle such unexpected rates.

It was a painful blow. John Hollowood's answer was simple: exasperated, he took a plane straight to Barbados that afternoon. 'He just buggered off,' Jim quipped. Having already made several millions on his sale of Fine Organics, he was affluent enough to walk away with minor wounds. Jim, however, was now in a far more difficult predicament. 'I was completely shattered.' He didn't have a job, and the chances of Advent taking him back were slim, while personal financial disaster loomed as he and Hollowood were liable for major fees and costs. In those sobering few hours on the afternoon of Black Wednesday, Jim walked alone to St Paul's Cathedral in the City of London to take in the news and contemplate his future: 'I was forty years old, had a wife and children, my house was on the line with the prospects of no job, and one and a half years was wasted.'

It was during this dark hour, as Jim's options looked shot, that one of the greatest strokes of luck to steer his career would intervene. That evening, the Chancellor of the Exchequer, Norman Lamont, appeared outside the Treasury in Whitehall to announce that Britain was going to leave the ERM. The following morning, the Bank of England base rate reverted to 10 per cent. Still very high, it now matched the cost of borrowing defined in the original Bank of Scotland deal, and the bank called to reinstate its interest. Jim immediately called Hollowood, who jumped on a plane back from Barbados, and within seven days their purchase of BP Fine Chemicals was complete. A new enterprise was born – and the first of Jim's own. Named at the eleventh hour, it was dubbed Inspec, for 'International Speciality Chemicals', and Hollowood became executive chairman with Jim as his CEO. The board was completed by Gary Corsi, made financial director, Andy Currie as sales and marketing director, and Derek Warner taking control of operations. For Advent, it was the biggest investment they had ever made, and they profited more from this deal eighteen months later than any other to date. As Jim left the firm, CEO Doug Brown paid him a back-handed compliment: 'You were always a bit too nice for venture capital.' 'Some people will find that rather curious,' joked Jim. He was a shrewd leader even then.

With Jim and John at the helm, Inspec went straight to work on transforming the business's fortunes, and within a year had already bought two American companies. It paid $20 million for Allco Chemical and $17 million for Imitech, which supplied a special insulating foam called polyimide to the US Navy. A deal every six months set a fast pace for growth, and meant that Inspec was soon producing products ranging from synthetic lubricants to speciality acids. In 1994, after less than two years of work, Jim and John floated Inspec on the London stock exchange. 'You remember the numbers,' said Jim. 'We paid £37 million for the UK business, and we floated it for £164 million.' Management shares went up by a factor of 198. Jim had made a paper profit of nearly £28 million in only eighteen months.

The process of going public and raising interest among prospective shareholders was no easy task. Jim, John, Andy, Derek and Gary had to give dozens of presentations in the UK and overseas, sometimes making the same speech more than thirty times. The predictability began to take its toll, and the slog of it soon became farcical – every time Andy referred to a 'thin lacquer layer', his colleagues at the back of the room collapsed into fits of schoolboy laughter. Once the public pitch had finally succeeded, the board stayed in place, and had their five minutes of fame on the front page of the *Financial Times* company news section. Jim had been cut out of the leading photograph, though, to the bemusement of the team – a fitting metaphor for the quiet rise to prominence that was to characterise the budding billionaire.

Growing in renown, Inspec soon added a couple of heavyweight non-executive directors to its board, among them Julian Sheffield, the chairman of Portals, the accredited Bank of England banknote security paper manufacturers, and Sir Charles Tidbury, the former chairman of Whitbread who had been knighted by the Thatcher government. Those Inspec days were fondly remembered. The board worked hard but had a lot of fun, and they would regularly invite financial analysts from London to join them on corporate hospitality 'jollies'. One of these was the 1994 'Round the Island' sailing race circling the Isle of Wight, which was preceded by an overzealous evening session in the local pub. Strolling back in the dark, a senior executive from BASF, the German chemicals giant, walked straight off a nearby jetty, disappearing under the water to the bemusement and amusement of his companions. Jim instantly dropped to his knees, stretched out his arm and fished the man out. 'I had an inappropriate laughing fit – the guy could have died. He was white as a ghost,' recalls Gary. It was this culture of grounded humour combined with bold ambition that attracted further talent to the team, including current INEOS head of mergers and acquisitions Bill Reid, joining in 1995. Having previously worked at BP's Grangemouth site and then ICI, the young Reid embodied the ideal technical and entrepreneurial skillset for the growing business, drawn in by the fact that 'Inspec was a clearly driven company, with high ambitions'.

These ambitions were by no means shy and, on 5 May 1995, Inspec made its most significant purchase to date. It bought the Hythe plant's sister petrochemicals facility, which BP still owned in Antwerp, Belgium, for £84 million. This sideways leap – moving from speciality to commodity chemicals manufacture – would turn out to be the best deal Jim ever made, eventually enabling him to launch his international chemicals empire. The port of Antwerp is second only to Houston, Texas as the largest concentration of chemical plants in the world, and BP's vast facility there turned out to be a hidden gem. The Antwerp facility's commodity chemicals were distinguished by their bulk production from basic feedstocks, such as ethylene and propylene, derived from oil and gas – a business proposition quite distinct from the speciality chemicals domain where Inspec now comfortably sat.

To an industry outsider, these two branches of industrial chemical production are not readily distinguishable, and this is because consumers typically engage only with their end products. Speciality chemical end uses are, as the name suggests, specific, and include adhesives, cosmetic and food additives, cleaning materials and construction chemicals used in a variety of settings – domestic, automotive and aerospace. In contrast, commodity chemicals are a broader class, used directly and indirectly in almost every form of manufacturing industry, with each chemical having a range of different applications. Their most famous use is, perhaps, plastics and, produced at high volume, these 'bulk' chemicals touch every aspect of our daily lives. From a manufacturing viewpoint, these two industrial branches could not be more different; speciality chemicals are more stable and suited to public markets, while commodities are cyclical in terms of supply and demand, tied closely to the price of their oil and gas feedstocks, and often flirt with low margins, widely seen as a risky business to invest in. This was BP's view in making the decision to sell off its Antwerp assets in 1995. Despite producing 125,000 tonnes per year of ethylene oxide, a bulk commodity chemical used to make materials such as plastics, polyester fibres in shirts and soaps, the Antwerp site was deemed ultimately unprofitable. At the time, most similar companies were likewise focusing their growth on speciality chemicals. Jim and his team were unconvinced by the trend, however: 'I'm not interested in whether it's a commodity or not. Just as long as I think it's going to make loads of cash over the business cycle.'

Moreover, Jim was attracted by Antwerp's sheer size: 'This was a proper big, BP-built petrochemical facility.' The single site occupied 500 acres – almost the footprint of the City of London – and employed over 400 people, making it one of the world's biggest. Andy Currie saw that BP had underrated it as a business and, as he anticipated, Antwerp became a true money spinner, eventually tripling its capacity to 400,000 tonnes of ethylene oxide per year. Its growing profitability allowed Inspec, and subsequently INEOS, to mortgage it to raise key loans. As well as a valuable production asset, Inspec inherited a capable leadership team at Antwerp, including Andre Desutter, Paul Nauwelaerts and manufacturing and operational maestro Tony Verrijckt, who would later join the company's main board and stay until retirement. The early days of business travel between the plants was, however, anything but smooth. For the first meeting the Inspec board attended in Antwerp, Jim chartered a small plane from Southampton to fly them there: 'We were bouncing over the North Sea in a paper-thin Piper Cherokee. We were all suffering,' remembers Gary Corsi. After that, Corsi and John Hollowood began taking the long route to Antwerp via Heathrow in a commercial jet, leaving Jim and the rest to the dubious comforts of a private twin-propeller aircraft.

By no means abandoning speciality chemicals just yet, in 1996, Inspec bought the newly off-cast Fine Chemicals business from industry giant Shell, which had sites across the UK, the Netherlands, France, Germany and Chile. It was another major bargaining process, with Jim personally negotiating the $300 million deal with his opposite number at Shell, the highly experienced Jim Dawson, who sat on the Shell Chemicals board. A few years later, Jim Dawson would move to become a key non-executive director at INEOS, and still remains an *éminence grise*. Inspec's steady upward rise wasn't to last long, however. In the autumn of 1997, macroeconomic events intervened once more to reshape the course of Jim's career. A crisis of confidence caused by economic woes in Hong Kong and other Asian economies led to a 'mini crash' in global stock markets by October, and share prices in London dropped so low that Inspec's advisers began to worry. 'They told us we should sell Antwerp,' remembers John Hollowood. Jim and John were advised that, if they sold off the commodities business, raising much-needed cash for Inspec, its share price would likely double overnight. It was a crossroads of crisis and opportunity.

It was at this roadblock that Jim then took the most momentous decision of his life – proposing to buy the Antwerp facility for himself, and form his own company to run it. The single site was already turning over $200 million a year, and he knew it had great future potential. 'Effectively, it was a management buyout,' explained Jim. 'But people hadn't heard of MBOs in Belgium back then.' Getting Antwerp out of Inspec was not easy. Jim had to raise the cash in the form of a new high-yield 'junk' bond, a type of high-risk security that was becoming increasingly popular in the debt market, and he hired a private jet to travel for a fundraising trip across the USA. It was a high-octane adventure – at one point requiring an emergency landing when the jet cabin filled with acrid smoke-scented fumes. Amidst the hectic schedule, Jim discovered a true passion for the salesmanship involved in raising leveraged finance: 'I remember jetting around America telling everybody how wonderful our high-yield bonds were.'

The £84 million buyout was part funded by Scottish investment house Murray Johnstone, which put in £10 million (Murray Johnstone were subsequently bought out by the management team in 2001). The future management team contributed £1.5 million, and the remaining £72.5 million came from the new high-yield bond. As the analysts had predicted, the share price of Inspec virtually doubled shortly after Antwerp had been sold to Jim, but now the entrepreneur was out on his own for a while. John Hollowood, Andy Currie, Gary Corsi and Bill Reid had stayed on at Inspec, which was acquired by Laporte in September 1998 for £611 million, while Jim walked away with a sizeable windfall of £28 million in cash on handing over his management shares. Andy and Bill were to see out their contracts at Laporte before joining Jim's new venture, while Hollowood finally re-retired and Gary headed into the world of biotech, not returning again until 2005.

The day of 5 May 1998 marked the minting of Jim's new company, exactly three years to the day since his initial acquisition of Antwerp by Inspec. The new enterprise needed a name, however, as the lawyers called to remind Jim just hours before the deal drew to a close. Rushing to the local library, he brought a Latin and a Greek dictionary back to his family home in the New Forest and pored over words with his young sons Sam and George. After the boys had exhausted all the rude words, a more fitting name was suggested – INEOS, stemming from one Latin and two Greek roots. 'Ineo' is Latin for a new beginning; 'Eos' the Greek goddess of dawn; while 'neos' means something new and innovative – together heralding the 'dawn of something new and innovative'. Conveniently, it was also an acronym of 'In Ethylene Oxide and Specialities', a rather more pragmatic name derived from the main products of Jim's Antwerp plant and his portfolio of speciality chemicals companies.

It wasn't until a year after Jim left Inspec that people finally began to understand how much the Antwerp plant had contributed to its profits: a colossal 40 per cent, something Jim had recognised immediately. 'Nobody realised just how much money that Antwerp business made, because they didn't do their accounts correctly. It was a great deal.' Even so, Jim's new central command centre was deceptively modest, and the company's first head office was in a four-storey town house in Romsey, a small market town north of Southampton. Calum MacLean, who had followed Jim from Inspec and would go on to become one of INEOS's top executives, joined Jim's personal assistant

Kate Holmes, Bill, Andy and their accounting assistant Julie Smith in the modest headquarters. Bill Reid recalls: 'The house had creaky floors and nothing in it was straight. We didn't look anything like a petrochemical company.'

As the new business found its feet, no time was lost looking for new acquisitions to bolster it, and the first purchase was ICI Acrylics, the largest Perspex business in the world. Its biggest UK plant was in Darwen, Lancashire, a site linked to the legendary Second World War Spitfire fighter plane. ICI Acrylics had manufactured the Perspex screens for the Spitfire's cockpit, and its location was intended to ward off German attacks. Andy explained: 'Darwen was known as the cloudiest place in Britain, and was chosen so the Luftwaffe couldn't find it.' Offloading the Perspex business was a necessity for ICI, a global chemicals powerhouse that, by the late 1990s, had started to implode. Nonetheless, Jim, Andy and the team could see an opportunity to double the company's earnings over five years, a formula for profit-making that would soon become integral to the INEOS model: 'The business was overmanaged and had complex overheads,' recalls Andy. The team knew that if they could reduce costs by 25 per cent, they could double their profits efficiently. The formula was simple, but it had worked in the past with BP Fine Chemicals, so was likely to succeed again.

The Perspex business had international reach, too, employing over 2,000 people across Europe, the US and Asia, adding hugely significant sites to INEOS's portfolio in areas such as Texas, Thailand and South Africa. The chemicals giant wanted £500 million for it, a sum that Jim initially deemed far too high. A period of fierce negotiation and fundraising ensued and, to finance the deal, the company teamed up with London investment firm Charterhouse, who put up £200 million of equity, while INEOS was left to raise £300 million in debt from a suite of banks. The 'promote' arrangement that was ultimately reached left INEOS responsible for the company's day-to-day management and, in the first of many such christenings, it was renamed INEOS Acrylics, with Andy its chairman. All of a sudden, INEOS was on the chemical world stage, lifting its profile and reach far beyond its Antwerp roots.

Around this time, the INEOS leadership shifted into its final, enduring guise, as accountant John Reece came to join Jim and his trusted lieutenant Andy as equity partner. According to Jim, Bill Teasdale, the senior Price Waterhouse accountant who had earlier advised on Inspec, 'told me to steal him from Price Waterhouse, as in his opinion he was the best accountant in the firm'. Reece, Teasdale's protégé and by now a partner specialising in chemical companies, was a gifted accountant who had spent his twenty-one years since university working his way up the Price Waterhouse ladder, and was ready for a change. He was the perfect fit for the ambitious business – a northerner hailing from Sunderland, he had attended Bede grammar school and had, like Andy, graduated from Cambridge, studying economics. He had worked across the UK, Toronto and Philadelphia, and had an unflappable, understated manner combined with a scalpel-sharp grasp of finance. Joining the two existing owners in 2000 as financial director and partner, he would quickly become the company's numbers guru.

Shortly after John's arrival, the company moved to new headquarters in Queens Terrace, Southampton, before the team's expansion precipitated another shift to the hamlet of Hardley, Hampshire, close to where Jim and Andy lived. This new office was tiny, on the edge of an industrial estate, and had a plumbing company above it. The trio of owners now look back on those days incredulously. 'We used to call ourselves Hardley International,' laughed Andy. Jim Dawson thought 'hardly suitable' was a better description, and this certainly seemed to be the bemused impression of business partners, such as Deutsche Bank executives, travelling from London. 'By then we were a relatively large corporation, and yet we were sitting amongst plumbers with a glass front – a bit like a car showroom. They were astonished,' recalls Andy.

Their humble setting belied unwavering ambition, and, by the end of 2000, the new trio of owners had acquired three further off-cast businesses from a floundering ICI. The three-company purchase took over a year of long, torturous negotiations. To complicate matters, in those days INEOS didn't have any base in London, where ICI was headquartered, so a lot of planning took place in a coffee bar called Richoux on South Audley Street, in Mayfair. The upmarket café had a room at the back where the owners would sit and drink cappuccinos for hours into the night. It became their de facto office. There were two consecutive all-night meetings that never reached a conclusion. 'It was a very miserable situation to be in. It was one of the most painful, long-winded processes I have ever been involved with,' recalls Andy. On the third attempt, in January 2001, the deal was finally completed.

During negotiations, the team was ably supported by Chris Bown of Freshfields, a leading London law firm. Bown was a partner specialising in M&A who was very bright, capable and energetic but also possessed a fiercely combative personality. He was often present during tense negotiations as the INEOS adviser and was generally very effective but could become gratuitous in his approach when discussions stalled. The unforgettable

'As you do not seem to understand, let me now explain in words of two syllables or less' and the equally memorable 'I'll now speak more slowly so you can understand me' were just two of his specialities. Eyes would roll in the INEOS team and a break would be taken to regroup.

Two of the businesses involved in the package were still profitable entities, and therefore relatively simple acquisitions. Crosfield, soon to be renamed INEOS Silicas and led by respected Inspec veteran Brian Foster, produces the chemicals found in most household detergents and has a long history dating back to 1815, when Joseph Crosfield, a northern soap and chemicals baron, set up a manufacturing factory in Warrington. Fluor, which produced fluorocarbons used as air-conditioning fluids in cars and homes, had sites in the north of England in Runcorn, and others in Japan and Louisiana, and was run by the affable and astute Tom Crotty. 'It was on the brink of being very profitable,' Crotty recalls, and though ICI had spent a lot of money on three brand-new factories for the business, it didn't fit in with their plans for the future. Tom and his then CFO, Roger Bell, had begun looking into their own management buyout, but were immediately impressed with Jim and Andy after first meeting them at Freshfields law firm in London and decided instead to join the INEOS team. Tom remembers Roger remarking that he would 'rather be sacked by that guy [Jim] than continue to work for ICI'. Crotty became CEO of INEOS Fluor, the start of a fruitful collaboration that has since led him to the role of communications director for the entire INEOS conglomerate.

Unlike Fluor and Crosfield, the chlorine business Chlor was losing money by the minute. It had made significant profit for ICI back in the 1960s, when the chemical was used in many chlorinated solvents; however, new health and safety regulations had now been brought in banning many of these products. Because chlorine is so corrosive, the equipment on site has to be replaced fairly regularly, but lack of ICI reinvestment in the plants meant that the business was gradually deteriorating. With each visit, Andy told them they had to reduce the price further. 'Nobody else would take it on,' he said. The business had sites across Europe, including Runcorn, Barry and Wilton in the UK, a couple in Germany, including a large site in Wilhelmshaven (once famous as a harbour for German U-boats), and one in Baleycourt, France, near the First World War battle site of Verdun. Many of the most unprofitable units were quickly closed, but Runcorn, the last chlorine production site left in the UK, was still haemorrhaging cash. The plant had an enormous cell room that used as much electricity as the entire city of Liverpool, and was described by the new owners as a 'real dog'. The concept of buying the ICI businesses as a trio gave the INEOS team an edge over the other bidders, though, due to the state of Chlor, each unit was separately funded. ICI offered INEOS a £100 million dowry to take Chlor off their hands and cover the first year's losses while Jim, John and Andy tried to restructure it. They had to act quickly to prevent it from going bust and, with Calum MacLean appointed CEO of the newly named INEOS Chlor, the team ruthlessly applied their now-crystallised toolkit.

It was, however, no simple journey. In the weeks that followed the deal, another problem emerged with the troubled Chlor business. Forty per cent of the chlorine produced in Runcorn was used to make polyvinyl chloride, better known as PVC, a type of plastic used in pipes, packaging and buildings. At the time, ICI had a complicated joint venture with an Italian company called EniChem (ENI) in this field. The JV was called European Vinyls Corporation (EVC) and was actually the primary customer of the Chlor business. It had been floated on the Amsterdam stock exchange in the early 1990s, but was now going bust. 'We realised it [EVC] was going down the toilet and it was our main customer. The fear was that it could take what was left of our chlorine business – which was already in trouble – with it,' explained Andy.

The owners persuaded ICI to let them use part of the £100 million dowry to inject cash into EVC and buy two thirds of the business. The team called it the 'Italian Job'. It wasn't easy; both the chlorine business and its customer EVC had to be restructured. The saga stretched over several difficult years. 'We had to close assets, we had to sell assets. It was a long and stressful slog,' said Andy. Jim doesn't recall the episode fondly. 'EVC was a shocking business. The worst deal we ever did.' Most of the Italian assets were sold to local businessmen, including one to a slightly strange character from Venice for as little as €1. 'He appeared to have no idea about chemicals and used to turn up to meet us in his boiler suit,' said Andy. 'He thought he could transform it, but it went bust about a month later.'

After EVC was saved by the cash injection, ICI's and ENI's shares were each reduced to 16.7 per cent ownership – a third of the total value. But, as Jim, John and Andy saw it, ICI and ENI ended up with one third of something, rather than 100 per cent of nothing. Since then, the business has been used as a platform to build a truly global chlorovinyls business. Bill Madden, the former chief executive of ICI Advanced Materials, was appointed non-executive chairman of the troubled INEOS Chlor in 2000. Like Jim and the team, he was fixated on managing fixed costs, a discipline he had picked up from his own international management experience, and would religiously draw out proportions of such costs against gross margin at every INEOS meeting. If this proportion was too high, above 50 per cent, Madden would demand explanations from the various units, Jim Dawson recalled. These businesses were not turned around gently.

Chlor has undergone multiple transformations since the takeover, and is now known as INOVYN – a standalone, self-funding and very profitable business, and the biggest PVC producer in Europe. Yet only two years ago it was still struggling. 'One of our tenets is that we occasionally get ourselves into deep muck – but we always seem to manage to find a creative way out of the swamp,' said Jim. Meanwhile, across the wider Runcorn site, the transformation from degrading asset to thriving production facility has been total, with the site now supplying 90 per cent of the UK's drinking water chlorination, and priming almost everything we drink from our taps.

INEOS did what it always does when it comes to transforming this batch of troubled businesses – it bought new assets, closed old ones and stripped out layers of fixed costs. 'There's no rocket science here – we're not super geniuses compared to the rest of the industry,' declared Andy. 'It's just that we have a particular technique which is impossible for the big guys to copy. If you start big and try to shrink down, it won't work.' Growth in the early days was not simply made through acquisitions; a lot of investment was organic, made in existing plants. The rescue of Chlor, a heritage site where the chlorine industry was first founded in the 1800s, is a case in point. INEOS was keen to challenge the 'asset-stripping' image that critics sometimes attribute to it: 'We're thought of as these restructuring guys, who just shut things down. But, like with Grangemouth, we have also spent an enormous amount of money saving sites which would otherwise have died,' said Andy.

Even while the extended ICI deal-brokering was underway, Jim and his fellow directors were still out scoping the horizon for other potential acquisitions: 'We were quite young and full of energy. We had a model that worked, so why not keep repeating it?' recalled Andy. So, when an opportunity was presented in 2001 by the German chemicals company Degussa to buy its phenol business, one of the largest producers in the world, the three leaders jumped at the chance. Phenol is a commodity chemical and the main compound in plastic windows and car headlights, and the Degussa business had operations spread across three sites in Alabama, USA, Gladbeck, Germany and Antwerp, Belgium, employing some 700 people. It was a premium offering. This was the trio's biggest financing challenge yet, because INEOS needed to find £350 million to fund the deal, and couldn't raise enough cash using conventional loans. Rather than accept defeat, they came up with an innovative solution: they devised a complex 'burning bridge' deal that allowed them to borrow the money, but gave them only a year to refinance the capital before the debt could be called, prompting the lenders to take control of the company. While the INEOS team were confident their lending banks wouldn't want to run a chemicals outfit, they recognised that, if the refinancing was unsuccessful, the banks would swallow them up. It was another huge gamble that eventually paid off.

By this point INEOS Oxide, the original Antwerp site, had grown much bigger and more profitable, so much so that new debt could be raised against this prize asset, and the site effectively financed the major acquisitions in the early years. This had been achieved mainly by expanding the site's production of ethylene oxide at a remarkable scale. The company would ultimately increase capacity there from 125,000 tonnes per annum in 1995 to 400,000 tonnes per annum today, not only by investment but also through refocusing the business, incentivising management and cutting costs. INEOS managed to raise €1 billion of debt by mortgaging part of its Antwerp asset, and used this towards Phenol, Fluor and Crosfield, too. (Chlor and EVC were separately funded by the ICI dowry.) It wasn't a smooth or pleasant process, though, especially when it came to talking with venture capitalists in a bid to raise additional equity, and the team recall several peaks of frustration as they traipsed from meeting to meeting. One session, with George Soros's capital fund, ended in a standoff, as the preppy young American attending in place of the billionaire investor goaded Jim with accusations of having 'no skin in the game'. Not suffering fools gladly, Jim forced the young executive to admit that he was not in charge of making any final decisions, and walked out of the meeting declaring: 'You're wasting all of our time.' Other meetings were, thankfully, more productive.

After the Degussa deal closed in April 2001, Jim was now running six companies. The INEOS team was honing its unique management method and was intent on nurturing each acquisition in a mode quite unlike that of traditional private equity. As Andy explained: 'Give or take the odd adventure, we focus on one very technical industry and become specialists in it. Unlike some private equity owners, we can't afford to cut costs everywhere, especially in a chemical plant – you'd risk blowing the place up.' The team were in it for the long run, becoming quite at home with their success. And, since each acquisition brought a new influx of executives, the group was finally ready to construct a headquarters fitting their scale. Still based in the New Forest, where the team were raising their families, Jim bought an old Victorian mansion in Lyndhurst, with a plan to build an artfully designed new office. The site of a former nursing home, the mansion had been the residence of the head of British Naval Intelligence during the First World War, but had since become derelict and used for drug-fuelled rave parties. The challenge of securing planning permission was unexpectedly large, requiring Jim and the team to engage with and assure the local community in the sleepy rural village that the international chemicals giant moving in was a neighbourly one. Eventually, a parking-sharing agreement with the Baptist church next door, along with a wood and glass design befitting the leafy surroundings, won the day, and far greater community integration followed later through sponsorship of events, sports teams and support for local charities.

Still, the ambitious core team had no intention of getting too comfortable in their new surroundings and, by 2005, the profitability of four key companies – INEOS Oxide, Fluor, Silicas and Phenol – had improved, opening up fresh opportunities to the still-restless leaders. Because it was making a lot of cash and fast paying down its debt, the company was now in a position to raise substantial new loans. 'We had built up enough equity and firepower to make a transformational acquisition,' said Bill Reid. 'And that was clearly very much Jim's intention at that time.' After seven busy years of growth, the three owners were now ready to move into the big league.

CHAPTER 4

SWALLOWING THE WHALE

Innovene was BP's petrochemicals business, and the fifth largest petrochemical company in the world. It comprised nineteen manufacturing sites across Europe and the US, including an oil refinery and two gas crackers in Grangemouth, a refinery and naphtha cracker at Lavéra in France, a huge petrochemical complex at Cologne, Germany, and one of the largest gas-cracking facilities in North America, at Chocolate Bayou, near Houston, Texas. Employing 8,000 staff, it generated an annual revenue of $22 billion – a business in a wholly other league to young INEOS. In 2004, news broke that it was up for sale. Despite its obvious potential, BP saw Innovene as a financial burden; it wasn't making the level of profits desired, and Lord Browne, the chief executive who had built BP into Britain's biggest company, was keen to divest in order to focus more fully on oil and gas. Browne was planning to float Innovene on the US stock market, but Jim, ready for his next audacious move, made his interest known.

It was an unlikely proposition. By 2005, after seven years of operation, INEOS had grown to an annual turnover of $7 billion and was employing 7,500 people at twenty sites. The proposed deal would increase the company's size by three times and raise its turnover from single-digit billions to a whopping $30 billion almost overnight. As David Anderson, an American industry consultant, put it: 'This was the guppy swallowing the whale.' A private sale was not straightforward, either, though BP director Iain Conn and chief financial officer Byron Grote declared themselves open to the right offer. For BP, this would mean a cleaner, quicker process, because they could receive all the payment for their 'disadvantaged' business upfront; in many ways, the more appealing option. Culturally, however, a private buyer presented an uncomfortable disruption to the norm, and jeopardised the entrenched status and comfortable salaries of existing senior management. Ralph Alexander, the BP director running the business, was managing the initial public offering (IPO) and, along with his thirteen seniors, was heavily invested in a stock market success. The operation was progressing fast, supported by banks Goldman Sachs and Morgan Stanley, and its impending success was unquestioned; a new headquarters for the business had already been acquired in Chicago, and the senior team's new roles were lined up.

Unbeknown to most, however, fierce negotiations were rallying in the background. Jim and his team pitched hard, justifying, in successive presentations to the BP elites, how he, John Reece and Andy Currie were prepared for the big league. Jim and Andy had successfully led a management buyout to form Inspec in the early '90s, and they had since established a winning *modus operandi* of buying unwanted businesses, including some of BP's, and turning them around. They had the growing confidence of investors and, bolstered by Reece's financial expertise, the company was gradually establishing a name for itself in the leveraged loans market. They had a vision for how they might transform this giant, but there was no denying this was an intrepid bid. Jason Meers, a former investment banker at Barclays, recalls: 'INEOS had quite a good following, but this deal was a dramatically different size.' Jim admitted: 'It was frightening – but I could see we'd finish up as one of the world's top chemical companies.' It was certainly a hard sell.

Despite BP's initial lack of enthusiasm for an INEOS proposal, Jim could clearly see the opportunity for profit. It was evident that the Innovene business had suffered from a complex management structure which inevitably led to inefficiencies, and he was raring to turn it around. Months of talks fizzled out, however, and, in an era where the global economy was booming and the markets were in overdrive, the INEOS team were not content to lament and sit still. These were the heady days with the likes of private equity giants KKR and Blackstone doing huge M&A transactions, and INEOS wanted a piece of the pie. Jim set about bidding for several different businesses, at one point having three potential deals running concurrently. One of these was for Basell, a joint venture between Shell and BASF, which, like Innovene, could have transformed the company's status. Basell had an annual revenue of $9 billion, and great promise, but ultimately represented a lucky escape. Uncomfortable about making the offer because it would have precluded any lingering hope of financing Innovene, Jim lost out on the deal at the final hurdle to American business tycoon Len Blavatnik. His private industrial outfit Access Industries bought the company for $5 billion, but Basell went bust several years later during the 2008–09 financial crisis following its merger with Lyondell, leaving what was, according to Bill Reid, 'a bad smell behind it, for the whole of the industry'.

Losing out on Basell was a tough blow for Jim at the time, by then typically used to accomplishing his goals. It didn't deter him long, though, and, as noted by Barclays's Jason Meers, 'INEOS doesn't win every battle, but it tends to win the ones that matter.' Jim carried on pursuing Innovene, even as the public sale looked inevitable. In July 2005, the team made a breakthrough, as a faction of the BP leadership, now close to completing the IPO, were convinced enough of INEOS's competence to resume negotiations. At the eleventh hour, there opened an opportunity, in strictest secrecy, to avoid the public flotation with a private sale. John Reece remembers it being extremely fraught: 'BP was obviously paranoid about confidentiality, because they still had the IPO process running. They didn't want anyone to know they were thinking about selling.' The talks had to be kept secret – if word got out it would cause chaos internally. Apart from CFO Byron Grote, his M&A team and chief executive Lord Browne, nobody at BP knew a private sale was on the cards. There were, however, two other rival bidders in the game, Reliance Industries, an Indian conglomerate, and the ambitious Blavatnik, still on a high from his Basell victory and on a mission to expand his empire. The challenge escalated.

Grote set out the terms and conditions of the deal, and they were brutal. BP wanted a staggering $8 billion for the company, and the deal had to be closed by the end of September, the date the IPO was due to be finalised. A process like this for a business as large as Innovene would normally take months. If Jim was serious about buying Innovene, he would have to act fast, with just ten weeks to raise the money, and the team knew their only option was to refinance their entire business. Jim put Calum MacLean in charge of the day-to-day management of the project, codenamed 'Winchester' after the Hampshire city, and the search for lenders began in earnest. The planning of the team's bid was especially hindered by the deal's clandestine nature; they were bidding blind, not able to visit a single site, and could only perform limited due diligence of their own. The IPO running in parallel was at least a saving grace – due to US regulations, there was a lot of detail about the business that BP was forced to disclose to the public market. The US Securities and Exchange Commission registration was an extremely detailed document aimed at encouraging individual and corporate investors to buy shares in the company, and helped to reassure the banks, including those that INEOS was courting.

The strength of the markets at the time, with investors willing to take more risks, played to Jim's advantage. That said, it was still a colossal bet. If there were any get-out clauses from the lenders, an economic downturn or an oil crisis, the whole project could fall apart, leaving Jim, John and Andy with nothing. Andy knew that, despite the company's track record, it was by no means a done deal: 'We didn't go in thinking it would be a definite success. We had just lost Basell, and a few others had also fallen away.' What did make the company unique, at least in the eyes of the investors, was that it always used debt rather than equity to fund its deals; the management team continued to own 100 per cent of the company, despite making such a series of large acquisitions. This raised the level of risk for them, but assured lenders that they were fully accountable leaders.

The challenge of raising funds was exacerbated by a major obstacle from BP: the stipulation that just one bank should underwrite the entire loan for a private sale. Due to concerns over confidentiality, they also intended to select the bank: Morgan Stanley, the outfit already working on the IPO. Jim fought hard against this – 'You can't ask one bank to underwrite $9 billion, they just won't do it' – and eventually managed to bring on board Merrill Lynch and Barclays, who had worked on his previous deals. Jim had strong relationships with these teams – attested by Barclays' Jason Meers: 'Ultimately, we believed INEOS could deliver what they said they could. It was a big part of our decision to support them.' As things began to take financial shape, however, Morgan Stanley, BP's favoured bankers, started to wobble. It looked like they were about to pull out, thinking the whole project was too risky to justify. With pressure ramping up, the INEOS team worked even harder, with John Reece bearing the brunt of things and holding crisis talks with Barclays. John was working eighteen hours a day that summer, and his colleagues feared he was close to breaking point. At the darkest hour, things suddenly turned, as Merrill Lynch made an extraordinary offer to underwrite the entire deal, quickly followed by Barclays proposing to split the deal in half. Then, finally, Morgan Stanley reappeared – offering for each bank to carry one third, and the deal pushed forwards. Things were not convivial, however; Andrew McCullagh, the lead banker at Merrill Lynch, recalls the usual 'argy bargy' that went on over who was the lead on the transaction: 'It was intensely painful and incredibly irritating. With every deal, in terms of fees, there's always someone who is driving the bus. Placing a bond of that scale in a global context is big news for any sales desk.'

Legal wrangling was no less complex, as the contracts were thrashed out at the company's New Forest headquarters. With the amount the banks were lending so high, chosen lawyers Slaughter and May were spending every hour poring over bank documentation, trying to spot any get-out clauses. Jim was rallying against them, however, pushing towards the tight deadline, and impatient with the details being laboured. His well-known, no-holds-barred negotiation style was already in place as he ran the meetings, bringing legal teams to stunned silence as he set his priorities. In-house general counsel Jonny Ginns remembers a particular impasse over an employment issue, reframed by Jim demanding: 'Is this issue worth $50 million? I've made it very clear if this issue is not worth at least $50 million then do not raise it.' Stakes were incredibly high. In discussions around the sale and purchase agreement, the core legal document that lawyers draft up for a deal, the external lawyers wanted to cover their backs, insisting on hundreds of terms and conditions; Jim dismissed many of their concerns, telling Charles Cameron from Slaughter and May to stop 'dicking around', before abruptly stripping multiple clauses out of the document. This became typical of the firm's unusually fierce deal-making approach, which Ginns describes as a 'slash and burn' attitude to all the unnecessary 'bullshit' that slows up the M&A process. What ultimately counts is the price. Robert Stern, the lead lawyer on the deal, explained: 'There was a genuine worry that if we were difficult in any way, [BP] would just trip over to the IPO – that's what their management wanted. They would far rather be directors of a listed company than employees of INEOS.'

The week before the deadline, the acquisition team received a phone call from Jim confirming that the deal was definitely on. 'I have no idea how he did it,' said Rob Pulford, one of the Merrill Lynch bankers closest to the deal. 'We were all just shocked and delighted because we were providing all the debt on one of the biggest deals ever done. It was amazing.' The race to the finish, seeking to overtake the expected IPO announcement, was fraught with tension, the law and finance teams working around the clock on the final weekend before the expected stock market announcement on Monday. Tired, stressed and on edge, even while on the brink of success, tensions were running high for the INEOS leaders, too. One of Jim's most poignant memories of the period was being deeply affected by news of competitor deaths in that weekend's Great North Run half-marathon, which he'd completed several times before. There was an overarching sense, perhaps, that things could all be over at any minute.

Despite the all-hands-on-deck approach, there was just no way this magnitude of money could be in place in such a short space of time. Interestingly, during the whole process, Jim never once considered changing tack and going public to raise the cash: 'We had learned from Inspec that it doesn't work. We've always owned 100 per cent, and that's what works for us. There are very few other companies that run the same model as ours.' As a result, Barclays came up with an unprecedented and extraordinary solution: they would offer an unsecured loan for the entire amount, for one month. This was, in effect, a 'burning bridge' deal – Barclays would write a letter to BP guaranteeing the entire purchase price upfront, while INEOS would then have one month to refinance the business and pay back the money, or be in default with the banks. Pulford at Merrill Lynch thought this was incredibly risky. It was a gargantuan deal and, by now, Jim no longer risked any of his personal money, using the company as collateral. With few options, INEOS took the offer, a handy short-term loan to get the deal done, on the basis they would negotiate more permanent finance afterwards.

Even then, there was further eleventh-hour contention. BP decided to add into the package two oil refineries that were proving difficult to extract from their petrochemical operations: Grangemouth in Scotland and Lavéra, near Marseilles, France. 'We were now all of a sudden buying two huge refineries, and we knew f*** all about refineries,' recounted Jim. These are not small or cheap operations, with Grangemouth looking particularly daunting; occupying a 1,700-acre site at the end of the Forties Pipeline System on the Firth of Forth, about twenty-five miles from Edinburgh, it refines around 210,000 barrels of crude oil per day, supplying all of the petrol and diesel for Scotland and Northern Ireland, and most of northern England, too.

The addition of the refineries made the deal far more complicated and costly, and it was here the team began to feel the heat of the competition. On the final Friday, Pulford recalls being told they were losing to the Indian bidders, Reliance Industries, who looked like they had sealed BP's support and were prepared to pay extra for the added assets: 'It sounded like we weren't going to be able to win. Jim was very dogmatic, and very intransigent about being forced to do something he didn't want to do, and wanted to keep to the original [$8 billion] price.' Pulford believes, however, that the addition of the refineries is ultimately the reason Jim finally won the deal. Part of the agreement brokered meant that BP would continue to use the fuel produced by Grangemouth in all of its petrol stations in Scotland. 'They cared a lot about who bought the company. It wasn't just about the price of the business; it was also the relationships with BP in the future,' said the Merrill Lynch banker. During the months of negotiations, and even on becoming the frontrunner, Jim didn't once have the chance to meet with BP's chief Lord Browne, despite proposing it. 'This was the biggest disposal BP had ever made, so I suggested perhaps we should have a cup of tea one morning.' The refusal was blunt, and it wasn't until ten years later that Jim actually met Browne. 'Now we get on quite well, but in those days I obviously didn't cut the mustard,' Jim jokes.

The negotiations were abstract, and on a knife edge. With the late addition of the refineries, the final cost of the acquisition was negotiated until the very end, when all other constituents of the deal seemed to be in place. Having intimated that an $8.7 billion price tag might get it over the line, the sellers upped their ask at the last minute, catching Jim fully unawares. He had left the team in London to go on his annual mountain-bike trip in Scotland, and recalls being in the midst of a rather foreboding rainy valley, surrounded by deer, when he received a phone call from Byron Grote. 'It was rather surreal,' said Jim. 'I sat on a rock in Glen Nevis – all the other riders had buggered off.' He was asked to up the sale price to $9 billion and, with little choice, agreed on the spot. 'I didn't tell him I'd just got off my mountain bike, covered in mud and shit.' Inauspiciously attired, he had just made the biggest pledge of his business life.

As word of the successful deal leaked out among close colleagues, others were caught unawares, too. Rob Nevin, who worked at BP at the time and was good friends with Andy from his earlier days with the company, had been one of the first at BP outside the 'secret circle' to hear that Innovene had been sold. He was in Istanbul when he received a phone call from Andy: 'It was an incredibly audacious move. I thought Andy was joking. Where did they get the money from?! It took a while to sink in,' he recalls. Nevin was at ease with his new employers already, however, having considered moving to INEOS years before. There were plenty of others who were due to feel a greater sense of shock. When Innovene chief Ralph Alexander was told the news by BP, he was called to a meeting at head office in St James's Square in London with Jim, Calum MacLean and Grote, with no inkling of what was in store. Grote introduced Alexander to Jim, his new boss, and Calum remembers Alexander's reaction: 'He was gobsmacked, but extremely professional. He asked for clarification.' Alexander then held a conference call telling all the senior BP staff that they had been bought by Jim's firm, and was virtually in tears when he broke the news. Naturally, after months working on the IPO, he wasn't pleased with the outcome; but what upset him the most, Nevin said, was that he hadn't been told: 'It was a bit harsh – but that's business life.' BP had run the IPO option in parallel with the private sale plan and had ultimately selected the better option for their shareholders.

The following morning, MacLean returned to BP with his communications team – which then comprised just one man, Richard Longden – to discuss how they would publicly announce the deal. When MacLean and Longden walked in the room, it was packed. BP's entire press team had turned up, and a sense of panic descended as they worked against the clock to draft a statement. For Calum, this was the moment he realised just how big a deal they had managed to pull off. For the rest of BP, the surprise at the announcement was tangible; BP was one of the world's largest oil companies, and few of its management had even heard of INEOS; those that had saw it as a small European-focused chemical company. It was immediately clear that things were about to change quickly. 'We were a lean, mean, fast-moving barracuda swallowing a whale,' describes Bill Reid. 'The Innovene guys were all sitting comfortably in middle management roles fully expecting to be running their own company and in charge of the show.' Once the announcement had been made on 7 October, Alexander appointed Simon Laker, his then personal assistant (and now group operations director for INEOS), as the coordinator on behalf of Innovene, to finalise the transaction and manage the communications work. Alexander, however, quickly requested to step down; his goal had been to become CEO of a publicly listed company and, after ensuring the transfer was a success, he was determined to move on.

There are mixed accounts of how Jim was first received by BP. It seemed the main worry was whether he could manage a company the size of Innovene, particularly with the additional refinery business. Jim's background as a venture capitalist made some people apprehensive – many assumed his intention was to run the business for a couple of years, double its revenue, and then sell it on to someone else. His manner also unnerved some on first impressions; the first speech he gave to BP employees shortly after the sale had gone through 'didn't exude warmth', according to Nevin. He recalls Jim announcing to his new employees that he didn't use head offices in his business, and that management would base themselves on site. This seemed to create immediate concern among the staff, who were worried about their future and where they would be moved to: 'I can see the wisdom in that now,' says Rob, 'but you sort of wonder whether it was necessary to create that unease so early on.'

Jim and his team wasted no time in overhauling the company's operations and putting new systems in place, which would gradually transform the former BP colossus into an efficient and profitable business. But, from the get-go, both the new managers and inherited employees had to fight to mutually prove themselves. Management presentations were held with the leaders of each division to determine who should be kept on and who they would let go. 'Jim was quite tough and wanted to see how people responded, because he was assessing who he wanted to run these businesses,' MacLean recalls. 'He is quite a hard-arse at times but it's just until you get to know him.' BP had a rather top-heavy, hierarchical business structure that Jim wanted to strip out. At BP, managers were assigned to a geographical region, so, while they were responsible for a large area, in reality they didn't seem to know much of the broader strategic detail. INEOS conversely operates a 'vertical structure' (or 'federated' model), whereby managers need to understand each individual business top to bottom, and this cut out a lot of senior staff at headquarters who were duplicating much of the work done in the individual units. Unsurprisingly, people soon began dropping out.

Calum recalls one of the biggest early issues was that most of the thirteen senior executives working with Alexander had a 'change of control' clause in their contract, which meant that, if BP was bought by another company, they were guaranteed a large payoff if they didn't want to stay with the new owner. 'You had these thirteen senior guys, some of whom we actually wanted to keep, who were all going to get multi-millions to leave,' said Calum. Many were perturbed by the restructured hierarchy. 'Lots of guys threw their toys out the pram.' One senior figure at BP said to Jim: 'You don't understand, I don't report to people!' Needless to say, he didn't last long. Jim called him into an office and told him frankly: 'You say you don't report to anyone? Then you don't report to me.' Eventually, there was only one original Innovene board member at BP who was kept on in a CEO position at INEOS. It was Dennis Seith, who had been one of the executives formerly selected by BP to run the post-sale Innovene. He remembers: 'I had never heard of INEOS, and it definitely wasn't a household name to most in the US. There were very few [management] layers left in the [new] business, and responsibility was thrust upon those willing to take it. Many weren't comfortable with the downsizing and reduction of overheads, or this approach to entrepreneurial accountability in a private sector company.'

Alongside the management overhaul, there were several other points of contention in the early days, as the new governance system took root. BP had been paying around $100 million for Innovene's IT, but Jim wanted the whole company, including Innovene, to spend just $40 million – which is exactly what happened, after no shortage of upheaval. Communication was another point of friction; BP had formerly handled corporate communication in an almost military fashion, cascading from the top, causing a culture clash when the BP staff struggled with new and unaccustomed informality. This also played out in discussion over company policy and internal staff moves, which was all of a sudden more open. 'Coming from a BP world, that degree of informality and casualness was unheard of. If you had something to say, you would have to present it in a great big plan with twenty slides,' remarked Nevin.

The financial governance of the businesses was perhaps the most significant clash, however, as John Reece set to work forensically analysing the new acquisition's financial systems. On asking the Innovene finance directors to explain exactly where they made their profits, they reportedly replied: 'No, we can't do that, John. We just have one central profit and loss – we keep it very simple.' The new owners were equally taken aback by the looseness of financial reporting, as they tried to plan the doubling of the company's EBITDA. One key measurement figure, mis-estimated by a CFO to the tune of some £20 or £30 million, was justified to Reece with: 'Well, in BP we were regularly out by a hundred million, and no one ever noticed!' In the new order, the tides had changed.

The overhaul of the core chemicals business was by now familiar territory, scaled up. Yet the biggest question facing Jim was how to run the two added oil refineries at Grangemouth and Lavéra. Concerned that he might be out of his depth, Jim called upon his old friend and colleague Jim Dawson, the former Shell hand, who was by now a non-executive director on the INEOS board – and Dawson, only half tongue in cheek, sent him a link to a website called HowStuffWorks.com. It is a running joke that the company learned nearly everything it knew about refineries from that website. Bill Reid recalls: 'Refining was a ten-billion-dollar business, but our understanding of it was very, very thin. It's a very different beast to petrochemicals. We were utterly clueless.' Jim directed perplexed colleagues to the website: 'It's all written down there.' Fortunately, the team's understanding of their new facilities grew rapidly, and they applied fresh outsider perspective to planning the operations. Little did they know that, during the next decade, they would become leaders in the oil and gas sector, too, buying up swathes of the North Sea. The industrial learning curve was steep.

Following the deal's close, Jim and Andy spent weeks on an inspection tour of their newly acquired plants, surveying their dramatically expanded company. Jim remembers there being some excellent assets, and other rather ropey ones – but, overall, the insurance value of what they bought was $30 billion. 'We got a lot of kit for our $9 billion,' said Jim. 'An awful lot of our success is based on buying assets at thirty or forty cents on the dollar. It basically triples your return on capital. It's much cheaper than building a new plant.' They were still not financially secure, however, with the terms of the burning bridge loan looming over them. In January 2006, the core team of John Reece, Tom Crotty, Bill Reid, Calum MacLean and senior manager Peter Clarkson set off on a bond-raising trip to the US and Europe, fighting to secure $2 billion in unsecured bonds to cover part of their urgent obligations. INEOS had until the end of the month to obtain that financing before the banks drew in, and the ten-day traipse to Edinburgh, Paris, Zurich, Amsterdam and Munich, followed by eleven cities across America, was exhausting. Several of the pilots had to be replaced, but the pitching team could not slow.

'There was no time for a shower or dinner – it was travel, meet, present, then travel again,' explained Clarkson. The roadshows involved either a one-to-one with a hedge fund firing probing questions, or a larger meeting with a dozen or more organisations, for more general interrogation, and INEOS had just forty-five minutes to pitch. They told the same story to around thirty different investor groups. At a presentation in Chicago, when Reid and Clarkson were at the back of the room waiting for their turn to speak, Reid heard a bagpipe playing faintly in a nearby function room and turned to his colleague to ask: 'Pete, am I dying? I'm hearing the pipes.' The gruelling schedule was successful, however, and the necessary financial deals were made in time to douse the burning bridge. The new INEOS was now a secure player on the world chemical stage, and the team were ready to celebrate as hard as they had worked.

The party held to mark the completion of the Innovene deal was a lavish one, held at Highclere Castle, the inspiration for TV's *Downton Abbey*. Jim was keen to bring together everyone who had worked on the momentous acquisition, and around 200 people, including spouses and partners, filled the iconic venue outside Newbury, Berkshire. It was with great relief that the group came to toast this success – and their readiness to let their hair down had by no means been dampened by the previous months of hard work. The in-house band, which still exists in some guise today, was out in full force – described by Bill Reid, who played bass guitar on the night, as 'all a bit Spinal Tap, and very tongue in cheek'. The night's six-piece line-up included Jim's friend Nick Hayward-Young on vocals, and a number of eminent INEOS figures – Peter Clarkson on 'blisteringly fast guitar', a guest appearance from Chris Tane on lead guitar, and Tom Crotty on sax, with the audience providing vocals on the choruses of 'Mustang Sally' and 'Alright Now'. 'We played so loud to try to mask our incompetence,' recalls Bill, though 'it was all a little high risk bearing in mind we were surrounded by fine Italian stucco plasterwork from the 1700s'. Jim's speech at the event was comical, with Tommy Cooper-style jabs directed at lawyer guests Mr Stern and Mr Jolly. As Clarkson noted, company humour was 'not usually cerebral'. It was a celebration well earned, as the success of the turnaround bore fruit. The boom-time was not to last long, however; the world's financial markets had other things in store.

CHAPTER 5

CRASH

Following the 2005 Innovene deal, INEOS was in good shape. It had focused on paying down its debt and steadily improving its financial security, but markets elsewhere were unpredictable. In America, the housing boom was peaking, and trouble was in store, far beyond analysts' imaginings. During the 2000s, America's central bank, the Federal Reserve, had relaxed its regulatory authority over banks and other lenders and, as a result, scores of mortgage lenders, motivated by the lure of lucrative bonuses, had abandoned their loan standards. Many had stopped asking homeowners for documentary evidence of employment history and income, and introduced more relaxed credit rating practices. This had led to an increase in 'subprime' mortgages, or high-risk loans, being handed out to people with poor credit histories. The mortgages were then bundled up into collateralised debt obligations and sold on to banks and investors around the world. By 2004, the US homeownership rate hit an all-time high of 69 per cent, and the more loans that were given out, the higher house prices rose. The flood of irresponsible lending had created a dangerous housing bubble in America.

Increasingly worried about inflation, the Fed started raising interest rates from mid-2004. Mortgage costs followed suit and, by 2005, hundreds of thousands of homeowners began to default on their loan repayments. By 2006, house prices had peaked and began to drop, under pressure from the tightening loans market. As homeowners started to default, mortgage lenders began to call in the loans, but people often couldn't repay them. The subprime market was about to collapse. In April 2007, New Century Financial, a specialist in subprime mortgages, filed for bankruptcy. Because it had sold many of its debts to other banks, a chain reaction followed, exposing a weakness at the heart of the world's largest financial system.

In August that year, the first signs of crisis in the financial system began to emerge. BNP Paribas, a French bank, told investors they could not withdraw money from three of its investment funds due to a 'complete evaporation of liquidity'. As the contagion spread around the world, the European Central Bank began pumping cash into the banking market, and the US Federal Reserve, the Bank of Canada and the Bank of Japan also intervened. In September, British bank Northern Rock, which relied heavily on the US subprime markets to fund its mortgage lending, called on emergency support from the Bank of England. The day after the news broke, customers withdrew £1 billion – the biggest run on a British bank in over a century. Later that year, the heads of UBS and Merrill Lynch stepped down after revealing huge losses from subprime-related investments.

As 2008 loomed, the crisis worsened. Global stock markets fell dramatically, and the US Federal Reserve was forced to make its biggest cut to rates in twenty-five years in a bid to stop the economy from falling into recession. In February, leaders from the G7 group of industrialised nations announced that worldwide losses resulting from the collapse of the US subprime mortgage market could reach $400 billion. In the same month, the UK government nationalised Northern Rock. In March, Bear Stearns, a major US investment bank, collapsed under the pressure of its imploding mortgage-backed securities portfolio, and was bought by JP Morgan for $240 million. The growing crisis reached a climax in September, when US Wall Street bank Lehman Brothers posted a loss of almost $4 billion for the previous three months. Within a matter of days, Lehman Brothers filed for bankruptcy, becoming the biggest casualty since the start of the credit crisis. Shortly afterwards, Merrill Lynch was saved from a similar fate, only by being taken over by the Bank of America. Within weeks, mortgage lenders across America were closed down. As 2008 progressed, the worldwide credit crunch turned into the greatest recession since the 1930s. Led by the Royal Bank of Scotland, which had to be taken over by the British government that autumn, the UK banking sector, heavily exposed to the subprime mortgage market, was also in meltdown.

For INEOS, the first sign of trouble appeared when the company published its quarterly results in January 2008. As consumer demand for plastic products began to fall, earnings came in lower than expectations. Just as investors started to worry about the company's numbers, an industrial dispute at the Grangemouth refinery at the end of April saw profits plummet further. The two-day strike ended up costing £100 million – considerably more than the £70 million management had forecast. DebtWire would later report that the company had suffered a 32 per cent shortfall in monthly earnings for that month. Jim and his partners were already feeling battered – but they were about to encounter the perfect storm. While the company was recovering from its own internal crisis, the full ferocity of the international credit crunch had begun to bite. The housing market, then the banks, had been the first to feel the blows. But the domino effect meant that ripples felt in consumer industries soon grew into an economic tsunami. As people began to tighten their belts, global growth evaporated. A full-blown recession began. Manufacturing was among the last to feel the crunch.

Being further up the supply chain, it wasn't until September that the company saw hard evidence that it was in real trouble. Returning from their summer holidays, John Reece remembers sitting down with Jim and Andy to go over the books. They couldn't believe what they saw: 'The orders had just dropped off a cliff,' said John. The price of oil had fallen dramatically, which had a direct impact on profitability. It dropped from a peak of $145 a barrel in July to $30 in December, creating a crisis for energy companies. Michael Grayer, then a financial adviser at asset management firm Lazard, was waiting to board a plane at Heathrow airport when he received an anxious phone call from John. The two men had formerly worked together when Grayer was at GE Commercial Finance, one of the INEOS banks. John asked Grayer if he could meet Jim and his lawyers as soon as possible. Grayer remembers the subsequent meeting well: 'Jim was looking worried, and the lawyers even more so. At that moment they thought they were going to lose the company.'

For INEOS, the ramifications of the global crash were potentially existential. Just three years after betting the farm on the Innovene deal, the company was still largely funded by bank debt, all of which was traded. In total, by early 2009, INEOS owed $8.5 billion, funded by a syndicate of 230 banks. As Grayer points out,

Jim was technically bust: the value of his company was worth less than its debt. Under the borrowing terms with its lenders, the company had to pass certain 'covenant tests', similar to a stress-testing performance review. The most worrisome covenant was one that compared company profits with the amount of debt in the business. If INEOS 'tripped' on the earnings-to-debt covenant, the banks were within their rights to ask for their money back. If the money couldn't be repaid, INEOS could go into insolvency. Despite the company's fears about this nightmare scenario, Grayer himself remained optimistic: 'My initial view was that, however bad it was, the banks would only ever want to drive a hard bargain. I didn't see them actually pulling the trigger.'

Nonetheless, with the price of oil low and the order book empty, the banks were becoming increasingly concerned about INEOS. The problem was that ten million barrels of oil were sitting in the refineries at Grangemouth and Lavéra in France. 'Because we carry a lot of oil and oil-related products in our inventory and stock, we made a big paper loss,' explained Reece. That affected the key earnings-to-debt ratio by which the banks judged the company's profitability. In reality, INEOS hadn't actually made a cash loss at all, but the banks didn't see it that way. Meanwhile, the refining business was also running at its lowest capacity. David Thompson, who was head of investor relations at the time, recalls: 'At the end of 2008, our utilisation was so low, some of the chemical crackers were running at just 40 per cent, which was horrendous.' To make a profit, crackers need to be running at 90 per cent capacity. The owners put the brakes on and stopped spending wherever they could. 'We could see it happening, so we got ready for the crunch,' remembers

Thompson. The management team set out on a vigorous cost-reduction programme across the entire business.

Capital expenditure was cut from €750 million to €250 million, and fixed costs reduced by €200 million. There were significant job cuts and a pay freeze. 'It was painful,' said Reece. The group's cash flow received a welcome boost of €190 million from the sale of its Silicas business in August, but even this wasn't enough to reassure the banks, who demanded a financial forecast for the upcoming months. That was impossible: 'We couldn't see forward more than a couple of weeks,' Reece explained. In situations like this, most companies would ask their banks to temporarily suspend their covenants but, because the debt syndicate was so large – one of the largest bank syndicates around at the time – all of the lenders would have to agree. In November, INEOS asked its two lead banks, Barclays and Merrill Lynch, if it could postpone all of its financial covenants for six months. This included a net leverage test, interest coverage test and debt service coverage test for the fourth quarter of 2008. In an interview with DebtWire at the time, John Reece was forced onto the defensive: 'The chemicals cycle is falling into a trough now, which is overlaid by the credit crisis, so our covenants don't match market conditions.'

This delay was offered in exchange for a new business plan, and a four-year forecast by June 2009; the company appointed professional services firm PwC to advise on the new plan. Though it would come at the cost of higher bank fees, the request seemed reasonable enough to the team. The banks viewed it differently. In December 2008, a meeting was held in London with INEOS's banking syndicate, a representative group of 230 lending members, to discuss the company's request for a waiver. Two American fund managers stood up and objected to the proposal. According to CapitalStructure, a financial news agency, one hedge fund manager dismissed it as a 'piss-take', while another said: 'The margin increase just isn't enough to compensate lenders for the additional risk they are being asked to take on.'

US funds represented 15 per cent of the company's lenders, and INEOS needed approval from two thirds of the entire, wider group of 230 organisations for the waiver to be granted. One investor asked pointedly: 'If they are that confident that the business will turn around, why don't the shareholders put in new money?' After widespread pushback, INEOS sweetened its initial offer by hiking senior debt margins by between 1.75 and 2.25 per cent across the board. Tensions reached crisis point when an attempt to stop the vote on the waiver reaching the wider group was narrowly avoided: 'The Americans were blocking, but INEOS will get it through,' commented one lender at the time. Despite the pushback, the majority of the syndicate voted in favour of the new debt terms: 'Blocking the waiver and pushing INEOS into default is in nobody's interest,' said another. Lenders were given just a few weeks to return their vote, and the company eventually carried the day.

Jim, John and Andy had bought themselves some much-needed time. However, they weren't out of the woods just yet. Peter Marshall, an adviser at Houlihan Lokey who worked on the deal, observed: 'It didn't help that they were going to breach again in the following year, so they needed to reset the covenants for a much longer time period.' According to the DebtWire news agency, shortly after the deal had been agreed, some of the US investors requested increased compensation for agreeing to the new terms. Nonetheless, it gave John a vital six months of breathing space to work hard on the books.

The weeks that followed were particularly bleak, not just for the company but for the whole of the UK, which was showing alarming signs of recession. The Royal Bank of Scotland and Lloyds Bank were dramatically saved after the government was forced to buy control of them. Sales for the petrochemicals sector were down 25 per cent in December 2008 compared to 2007. Jim recalls a very depressing Christmas and New Year: 'The lights went out, and they stayed out, because everybody took their money off the table. No one reopened after Christmas – all the car companies, all the washing machine companies. Nobody knew when they were going to start again.' Tom Crotty remembers being dragged around the Christmas sales in London by his wife when he got a phone call from Dennis Seith, a senior executive in the States. Seith was worried. He had heard rumours that LyondellBasell, the conglomerate formed in 2007 by Blavatnik's Basell, was going bankrupt. They were not just a rival but an important customer. They owed INEOS millions of pounds.

The situation at INEOS was no brighter. The company couldn't risk shutting down its refineries and crackers; the shutdown and start-up costs were just too great. Crotty says they had no choice but to keep them going, even though they knew they had no customers for their product: 'We were putting petrochemicals onto boats and just sending them off in the hope that by the time they arrived somewhere we'd have found someone who would be willing to buy them.' Tom recalls a nightmare he had at the height of the crisis, in which a meeting of executives at the European headquarters of one of INEOS's main customers for butadiene (the chemical that goes into car tyres) turned dark. With no cars being sold, the supplier's orders for tens of thousands of tyres had dried up and, to Tom's horror, the boardroom became increasingly black as huge piles of unsold tyres grew to great heights, blocking the daylight outside. In waking hours, too, stress was at an all-time high.

With the banks temporarily off their backs, Jim and his management team began trying to regain some momentum. But, as 2008 turned to 2009 and the global recession deepened, hundreds of companies in the US, UK and the rest of Europe were starting to go under. To Jim, it was beginning to look like INEOS might go down with them: 'You're in this black tunnel with no light at the end of it and you've got no idea how long it's going to last. There were immense debts in banks around the world and nobody could get their head around the potential numbers. We didn't know whether it was one trillion or ten trillion. Nobody knew whether governments could or would bail them out.' January 2009 was rock-bottom, with the company making no profit whatsoever. Jim recalls: 'I always remember that the EBITDA for January 2009 was zero. You can't put up with too many months like that.'

To make matters worse, as Tom and Dennis had feared, US rival LyondellBasell had now filed for bankruptcy, crushed by its $26 billion debts. It was the largest bankruptcy in the history of the chemicals industry, and it put INEOS's own position under increased scrutiny. An article in *Chemical & Engineering News*, an industry news outlet, summed up the fears of a domino effect:

> Industry watchers point to UK-based INEOS as another large chemical company that used leverage – incurring debt based on assets already held – to acquire more assets. Through aggressive financing, its managers built from scratch a chemical producer that is one of the top five worldwide. INEOS has been facing

> the same operating problems that LyondellBasell faces – falling demand and wildly fluctuating raw material and product prices.

John Reece recalls: 'Even though we'd got the waiver from the banks, as soon as that [bankruptcy] happened they all thought we must be next.' From that moment on a sense of alarm set in. The phone didn't stop ringing.

An adviser suggested that INEOS should appoint someone to be the main contact for investors and, in January, David Thompson stepped into his role as head of investor relations. 'There was a whole host of investors who barely knew anything about INEOS because we had never told them anything,' said Thompson. The owners had a complicated business structure that made it difficult for bond investors to model financial results. Thompson remembers a busy period that followed, as analysts came running to him for information. He also had to deal with a lot of negative stories: 'There were lots of emails saying we weren't going to survive.' Bond investors started demanding to know how much cash was actually in the business, what the company's order intake was, and how much management paid themselves. The company was left with no choice but to give them what they wanted. 'We began issuing weekly updates and reports full of information,' said Thompson. 'No one else was doing this, but we were trying to save the company. We had to pull our pants down and go from there.' Even this didn't satisfy some. Michael Baum, an aggressive American investor, was reported to have told the company: 'Unfortunately, you're going to have to do this day in and day out to stop the outright panic that is pervading the market.'

Just when things couldn't get any worse, a long-running spat with an individual in the US over a piece of intellectual property in INEOS's Phenol business came to trial. INEOS had virtually no support in the small-town Alabama courtroom: 'It was a classic scenario of the big foreign multinational chemical company against a well-regarded elderly local guy. Everything seemed to go against us at the same time,' said Thompson. The jury found against INEOS, to the tune of $200 million. And if that wasn't bad enough, due to a technicality in the finance agreements, the award would have led to a financing breach if not for a mad scramble to get the banks to agree to a quick amendment. The case then rolled into a mediation process. For once, INEOS's desperate situation created some leverage – the plaintiff had the option of taking some cash as a quick settlement, or pursuing bigger numbers and risking INEOS no longer being around. A timely newspaper article on the morning of the mediation predicting INEOS's bankruptcy helped them to see sense, and the case was quickly settled. But not without INEOS having to pay out a still-significant amount of money, cash it couldn't afford to lose.

It wasn't all bad news, though. In January 2009, INEOS managed to renegotiate the industry price of ethylene – the main chemical the company produced. Up until the end of 2008, the way the European market worked was that, each financial quarter, suppliers and customers would agree a set price for ethylene. This then became the basis for what customers paid. The difficulty with such a model was that the price of feedstocks going into ethylene – crude oil and gas – changed daily, meaning that, while the ethylene price might be set for three months, the feedstock cost could vary on a day-to-day basis, making it hard to monitor margins. The company had tried and failed to change the system in the past, but this time it successfully persuaded its customers to switch from a quarterly to a monthly price, helping the business to get back on its feet.

In the early months of 2009, Jim and John attended a series of meetings in New York to reassure their US lenders. The pair flew over in Jim's private jet, which, though both hard won and necessary given the company's now-vast international reach, became another source of contention with some of the banks. 'There was a stand-off between Jim and the banks, but Jim is a robust guy,' said Grayer. 'His view was: "If you need me, then this is what it's going to cost."' The banks grew so nervous they created a steering committee. This was a group of seven banks appointed from the total of 230, who between them held 15 per cent of the debt. 'The steering committee was not a lot of fun. They didn't really care about the company,' said John. What made it an even harder pill to swallow was that INEOS picked up the bill. 'It was very painful for us. If you looked at the cost of our debt for the following four years compared to what it would have been if this had all never happened, it was an extra €800 million,' he added.

The steering committee was composed of representatives of Barclays Capital, Merrill Lynch, Carlyle, Alcentra, Eaton Vance, Harbourmaster and Lloyds Banking Group. Once formed, it decided to appoint its own advisers and instructed investment bank Houlihan Lokey, led by Peter Marshall. Accountants Deloitte also came on board with lawyers Sherman and Sterling. Finally, INEOS hired its own advisers, Lazard, to join the group, led by Michael Grayer. Deloitte's job was to tell the banks whether or not INEOS was running out of money, and the management team started preparing weekly reports on their cash flow for Deloitte to review. The prognosis didn't look good.

In March, CapitalStructure reported erroneously that INEOS had been forced to make contingency plans for a debt-for-equity swap, which would have meant the three owners surrendering some, if not most, of their control. One lender noted: 'Fingers crossed it won't come to that. I'd consent to an extension if there is evidence of progress and the level of disclosure is improved. It's much better than it was but they do need to be straight with us on what exactly they are trying to do and how.'

For Jim, John and Andy, a debt-for-equity restructure, in which part of their shareholding was given away to cancel their debt, was the most unpalatable option: 'If you're forced to sell a business in the recession, you're going to get an awful price for it,' explained John. The odds were stacked against them, but the owners refused to give in as pressure built up from all directions. Some of the banks even wanted to own INEOS while Jim and his management team continued to run it. But this was something Jim wasn't prepared to do in the event of his ownership being wiped out. Then, in April 2009, in the midst of it all, Jim simply disappeared. Unknown to any of the lenders, he had gone on a long-planned expedition, spending ten days in the North Pole. 'The banks had no idea,' said Grayer. 'If they had known, they would have been mightily concerned.'

It was Peter Marshall of Houlihan Lokey who eventually put an offer to Jim: 'We said to him that he can still end up being the majority shareholder, but the business will be considerably de-levered because there will be less debt.' But Grayer held a very different view. 'In Peter's mind, he was pulling off one of the biggest restructuring deals in Europe – but it would have screwed over the bondholders with unsecured junior debt,' he remembers. Jim would not allow his junior lenders to be crushed.

Grayer explained: 'We also couldn't guarantee that we would come out the other side with Jim in control. There were a few people hoping it would all go wrong. Jim didn't have any cash – it was all debt – so it soon became a competition for control of Jim's company.' Grayer described the process as a 'game of poker', which ended with Jim declining Marshall's offer.

Marshall was disappointed with the outcome: 'Jim clearly believed in the long-term value of the business and that, over time, he would be able to repay all of the debt and so there was no need for the business to go through insolvency.' Marshall then went back to his clients to ask if they wanted to go down that route anyway – without Jim on board. Fortunately for the three owners, they weren't the type of lenders who wanted to own the business. 'They were more interested in getting their loans back and being compensated for lending the money,' said Marshall. 'If the debt had traded further down significantly, then the answer back would have been very different.'

There was, however, still more negotiating to be done. The lenders demanded increased interest on existing loans. 'They didn't want the house, but, because there was a lot more risk involved, they wanted to get paid more interest,' explained Marshall. The lenders also wanted to make further restrictions on what Jim could do – and wanted to know how much he paid himself in management fees. It was no secret that Jim and his management team paid themselves well. Marshall remembers an uncomfortable meeting that followed with Jim: 'As you'd expect, he turned around and said no.' This is where things got difficult. Jim ultimately knew that Marshall's client, the steering committee, didn't want to own his company. 'On one hand you can't make stupid demands because Jim's just going to say no. On the other hand, if Jim said no to everything, at some point my client is going to say: "OK, maybe I will have his house," and so you've got to try to balance the discussions in a way that my client feels they have been adequately compensated – and Jim feels that he hasn't been abused.'

These difficult negotiations took place at Lazard in the heart of London, with around twenty or thirty people in the room. Jim and John were separated off in another room, and there was a lot of back and forth. Grayer recalls that it was all very odd: 'Jim didn't have a board of directors, he doesn't like outside advisers, and there were no non-executives.' What he did have was Bob Wigley, a very senior executive with Merrill Lynch, who sat in on these meetings giving advice.

Eventually they agreed a deal. The five-year business plan included a proposal to reset all of the covenants, including halving the management fees. Deloitte would also monitor the business's cash flow with liquidity being tested weekly as soon as the covenant reset had been approved. The deal, however, had been agreed only between the company, Jim and the steering committee. The steering committee owned just 15 per cent of the debt. Under the terms of the banks, to reset a covenant, agreement was needed from two thirds of the bank group.

Jim was adamant that he and John should give the presentation in person to the syndicate, but the steering committee claimed such an 'in person' approach was just not the way things were done. They advised strongly against it and tried to persuade Jim to let them make the proposal instead. Jim refused; it was important that they could see he was completely honest and open with his investors. He won his way. Annual meetings are to this day held in London and New York, where INEOS CEOs and

CFOs stand in front of investors to relay the company's financial forecasts.

The meeting at the end of June 2009 took place in Gibson Hall in the City of London. Jim and John had the daunting task of standing on stage in front of 300 banks, all of which had brought along a couple of representatives, making an audience of around 600 people. The stakes were high, and a convincing delivery was imperative. The night before the meeting, John Reece had enjoyed a Bruce Springsteen 'London Calling' concert in Hyde Park, which he remembers inspiring his own, rather different performance. He recalls: 'I thought, if Bruce Springsteen can stand up in front of 30,000 people, I can stand in front of 600. Of course, the difference was that they were pleased to see Bruce Springsteen. These guys weren't pleased to see me!'

He was right. There were people in the hall who didn't like the proposal, and they weren't afraid to make it known. When questions opened to the floor, a banker from US investment firm Avenue Capital spoke up. He was trying to form a blocking group to stop the waiver going through. 'Those guys were quite aggressive. They wanted big returns and to end up owning the company,' said John. Luckily, the majority voted in INEOS's favour, and the struggling conglomerate was bought another temporary lifeline.

As 2009 went on, INEOS's bond prices continued to deteriorate and auditors at PwC said that refinancing talks with the banks had raised a 'material uncertainty which may cast significant doubt about the company's ability to continue as a going concern.' Reports were also surfacing that INEOS was looking to sell Grangemouth to ease its debt burden; Jim would eventually sell half of the refineries business to PetroChina in 2011.

Meanwhile, the scale of the refinancing proposals debated was by now the largest ever for a single company in UK history.

Distressed hedge funds, whose job is to buy up flagging companies and make a huge profit, spotted an opportunity, and pushed for a full restructuring of INEOS. David Thompson received countless emails from investors telling him what to do – all of which Jim ignored. A comment from Baum, the high-profile US investor, stands out in Thompson's mind: 'I give you a 1 per cent chance of getting through this time without an asset sale or new monies.' But Jim and his partners had such confidence in themselves and the business that they ignored all the doom-mongers. They stuck stubbornly to their strategy.

The company's bonds had become very attractive to some hedge funds, John remembers: 'You could buy $100 million of INEOS debt for $10 million, literally ten cents on the dollar. So, if we recover, I'm going to pay you $100 million for something that you bought for just $10 million.' According to CapitalStructure, however, one creditor present at the Gibson Hall meeting said: 'There are potential buyers, but not many are actually willing to buy chemical assets at the moment as they think prices have room to fall further.' Another added: 'Buyers are playing a waiting game.' It was certainly a tense one for all in play.

As the meeting debated whether to simply roll over the plans at higher interest or go for the nuclear option of a full debt-for-equity swap, the running sore of the owners' annual management fees fuelled the fire. Under the proposed new financing terms, the company said it would cut these from €73.5 million to €60 million, but refused to provide any further breakdown. That didn't satisfy most lenders, with many feeling the fees were still too high. It also left some investors irritated: 'It's an emotional issue that people got very upset about,' said one creditor. Others, conversely, recognised the need to incentivise management, especially given the banks' dependence on the three key partners to run the company. 'Ratcliffe's only ace up his sleeve is that he is probably the best man to run the business, but it's a pretty big ace,' one of the participants in the talks involved said. Another lender even expressed concern at the prospect of Jim backing down: 'What would we do if he handed over the keys?'

There were further complaints that the firm wasn't being open enough, which irritated John immensely: 'We seem to have done nothing this year but communicate with our investors,' he said at the time. David Thompson recalls how he, John and Graeme Leask, the CFO of INEOS Group, spent every day fielding phone calls and emails, often having to answer repeatedly what he described as 'stupid questions'. One investor told him: 'You do realise that a quarter of your investors don't understand anything anyway?!'

Despite their bullish tactics, the blocking group struggled to get mass support for a full debt restructuring. According to DebtWire, one lender said: 'We hesitated because they were looking for equity. We don't want lenders to own Grangemouth. We'd rather INEOS carry on trading and was supported through the downturn.' Undeterred, the blocking group led by Avenue Capital appointed their own legal advisers, and pushed ahead in the hope they could get enough support from other disgruntled lenders to stop the deal going through. 'If they got 34 per cent that didn't agree, we could not have done a covenant reset,' said Peter Marshall. It was a tense time.

Eventually, the hedge fund blockers, which owned only 15 per cent of the loans, were forced to back down. One lender blamed their aggressive tactics for scaring off the majority of the bank investors – who formed the main component of the lending syndicate. According to Global Market Intelligence, which published a specialist financial newswire: 'Avenue and Co were too aggressive with what they wanted to achieve, and blew it in terms of bringing those lenders looking to amend the covenant reset on board.' Once again, luck was on INEOS's side. The size of the syndicate was so large that the blocking group simply couldn't gain sufficient traction. Moreover, the majority of the banks just didn't want the pressure of having to run a chemicals business they knew nothing about, when they were already under immense pressure to keep their own businesses afloat. Ultimately, the banks took the view that the value of the company without Jim and his top management would be much less than it was with Jim running it.

The rescue plan was crucially helped by the fact that the business was still making cash – profits for 2008 had been £1.4 billion before an £850 million non-cash charge to revalue its oil inventories. The company managed to convince a sufficient number of hedge funds that they weren't getting to the point of insolvency. 'After a very long and painful negotiation we managed to show them we weren't sufficiently distressed,' said John. The INEOS team had also decided to offer a cash incentive for lenders to vote 'yes' to the bailout, an added sweetener to move things forward. Depending on how many bonds each lender held, they would get a substantial fee for consenting to the deal. When the vote came, INEOS was saved. But, as John remarked, it came at a massive cost. 'It left us with this requirement to pay the banks €800 million in additional fees and interest over the next three to four years.'

In July 2009, John went back to the credit rating agencies with the new deal and asked them if they could rerate the company's debt. The business was under pressure from the banks to repay €750 million within eighteen months. John recalled that the broader economic situation then started steadily to improve: 'The credit markets reopened again in 2010, we sold a new bond, and used the proceeds to pay down some of the bank debt. It relieved a lot of the pressure we were under. We didn't do anything wrong, we just happened to be caught in this economic storm and the price for getting out of that was to pay the banks more money,' John says. Michael Grayer, however, sees another side: 'To this day, Jim and John believe the banks gouged them. Another way of looking at it is the banks could have taken the company away completely.'

Today, INEOS doesn't have such problems. 'One lesson that it taught us was never to get into that position again. The company remained cash positive throughout the economic crisis. It was just one technical banking covenant that tripped us up,' said John. In 2018, INEOS is covenant-lite: it has learned its mistake the hard way.

CHAPTER 6

SANCTUARY

INEOS had barely survived the financial crash – and, by 2009, was staggering to its feet, bruised and in bad shape. Yet the fight to stay upright continued, as the global economy, still reeling, stretched manufacturers to their limits. The deal INEOS negotiated with the banks left it with an exorbitant interest bill on top of the mammoth sums already borrowed, and the company's lending syndicate now included a number of US institutions specialising in distressed companies. 'They would take your trousers off if they could get an extra dollar for it,' remembers Andy Currie. 'We got ravaged.' If the company couldn't find additional cash quickly, it now risked going bankrupt, and the next financial frontier was tax.

The new Labour Prime Minister, Gordon Brown, who succeeded Tony Blair in 2007, had reduced corporate tax rates from 30 to 28 per cent in 2008, in an attempt to get the UK economy back on its feet after the recession. But this effort still didn't bolster many of the country's fragile corporate giants, particularly with changes to tax on profits earned overseas. With competition levels high in a globalised system, it was becoming increasingly unattractive to run a multinational company from the UK, and many companies began to relocate to neighbours with more favourable corporate tax policies. Dublin drew the likes of advertising empire WPP, asset management firm Henderson, and Shire Pharmaceuticals, and Switzerland attracted *Lloyd's List* publisher Informa and the European HQ of tech giant Yahoo!.

For INEOS, in full survival mode, forensic accounting had never been so fierce. Twelve months of fixed-cost cutting had led to the elimination of all non-essential site maintenance, a freeze on salary increases and bonuses, and tighter central management. 'It was the one occasion when the federal model stopped,' said Andy. 'We just sent directives telling people what to do. We had to stop cash bleeding out of the company.' The age of austerity made the work environment fraught for all involved – and the company's leaders were ever pragmatic. Jim recalls sitting senior management down in September 2008 and telling them that the going was about to get extremely difficult: 'We may or may not survive, but it's really important that you don't run around like headless chickens. You've got to man up, be responsible and lead your team.' 'The troops played a blinder really,' remembers Jim. They quickly learned survival was going to mean flight as well as fight.

Cutting back on capital expenditure had its limits and, as the economic environment grew increasingly hostile with no slack left to negotiate debt, John Reece decided to investigate potential leeway with tax. INEOS's refinery at Grangemouth, which had a joint capacity of 210,000 barrels of oil a day, created a hefty quarterly VAT bill on its petroleum sales, sending some £350 million to the Treasury every three months. Now airing the company's distress in the public sphere, a tax negotiation was a highly sensitive solution, though Reece decided he had little choice but to ask the UK government for a six-month deferral on VAT payments. 'We weren't asking for a hand-out, just a modest timing accommodation that would help us get through a very tough patch in the business,' said Jim.

An unusual but not unprecedented request, the INEOS team sought the advice of Michael Tory, a former senior adviser at Morgan Stanley and Lehman Brothers, to make an approach to the government. Tory had worked with INEOS for several years and, having left Lehman at the time of the crash in the autumn of 2008, had set up financial advisory firm Ondra Partners within a matter of weeks, with INEOS as its first client. His contacts within the Treasury quickly facilitated a meeting between Jim Ratcliffe and Gordon Brown's then private secretary, Jeremy Heywood, and, in September 2009, Jim and Michael met with the Treasury to put forward their request. 'The Treasury wanted to help us,' recalls Tory. After a positive meeting, the request was passed on to Downing Street for approval, and Jim and Tory left the meeting feeling relatively confident. When they were invited back to Downing Street a couple of weeks later, however, the mood was different. 'They flat out refused to help us,' remembers Tory. 'They were so cavalier about it and gave no good reason why.'

Tory's introduction did little to alter the fact that the government of the time seemed to have little existing awareness of Jim Ratcliffe or INEOS. To this day, he suggests that had a senior Labour minister sat down with Jim to hear why the government should help a big manufacturing company stay in the UK, they would have been convinced. However, 'they were too focused on other things, like bailing out RBS and Lloyds Bank. Everything was crumbling, the economy was collapsing, and they were very short-sighted.' Of course, the Labour Party has long been perceived as being 'anti-business' in contrast with the Conservatives, partly due to their close historical ties with the unions, and Jim viewed the lack of support as unsurprising confirmation of an anti-manufacturing bias. Remembering the Downing Street meeting with clear discomfort, he concedes: 'It was a bit of a case of "If we make an exception for you, we have to make exceptions for everyone".' Having committed over £100 billion of taxpayers' money to save the failing banking system, it seemed to INEOS strangely misjudged for the government not to contemplate a short delay in a VAT payment to bail out one of Britain's leading manufacturers.

This wasn't the first time INEOS had been refused government support, and it finally crowned the company's frustration with the national valuation of industry. Earlier in 2008, when the markets initially nosedived and its bonds dropped from $100 to $10, INEOS had also asked the government for strategic financial help to secure its debt. 'If we'd had the cash, we could have bought all those bonds for $10 each and de-levered the company,' explained John Reece. Lacking the cash for their own purchase, however, and with predatory hedge funds keen to snap up such bargain bonds, INEOS proposed a unique safety mechanism to the government. Via a complex transaction, it could sell the government the bonds at market value and then reissue them, enabling the company effectively to be supported without an injection of taxpayers' money. Though it seemed like a genius idea, it was vetoed by Downing Street.

Similarly, in April 2009, INEOS asked the UK government

for funding help with a green energy initiative, and was, again, refused. A proposed 'Energy from Waste' plant in Manchester, devised to produce electricity from commercial waste, was very similar in concept to a scheme on INEOS's German Wilhelmshaven site, which had been eagerly supported by state and central governments there, underscoring a deep contrast in national attitudes. Tory remembers that, while the Germans had treated Jim 'like a king', enthusiasm from the UK government at the time was not forthcoming. When a last-ditch meeting at HM Revenue and Customs to request the VAT deferral resulted in a decline 'for technical reasons', the INEOS team resolved to take their business elsewhere. These incidents, recurring and unresolvable, became damning testament to the UK's ambivalence to manufacturing and, eventually, no love was lost in the bid to remain in the UK.

It was a remorseful time – all three INEOS leaders defined themselves as deeply 'pro-British', and Jim had never before lived outside the UK. He was, after all, a Mancunian who loved his country, and that patriotism similarly defined Andy and John. It seemed, however, that uprooting was the only guarantee of corporate survival. 'Had they given us that deferral we could never in all good conscience have gone to Switzerland,' states Jim; but, within months, INEOS was newly headquartered near Geneva.

The search for a suitable relocation destination was a mix of emotion and tax pragmatism. At first they considered Monaco, the sovereign state on the glamorous French Riviera – with a reputation for housing some of Britain's most wealthy expats, including Formula One drivers, celebrities and City millionaires. The likely need to shift the core of the company, including many young families, made this a more difficult option, and it therefore wasn't pursued. Ireland, on the other hand, with a corporate tax rate of 12.5 per cent, made Dublin extremely attractive, but was deemed unsuitable for other reasons – including the weather. 'Much as I love a nice weekend in Dublin, it rains all the bloody time,' said Andy. As for Jersey or Guernsey in the Channel Islands, a popular haunt for tax exiles – 'You can't get your car out of third gear, which is fine if you are retired, but not so much if you've got to run a business,' he remarked.

The best remaining option seemed to be Switzerland. It is geographically well positioned in the centre of western Europe and, for keen skiers such as Jim, John and Andy, it also had lifestyle appeal. Towards the end of 2009, the team engaged the assistance of Swiss banks Credit Suisse and UBS, who gave them a tour of the most popular areas for relocating businesses in the country, segmented into 'cantons' (similar to UK nations, or American states). Each canton is independent and sets its own tax rates (which have to be approved by the Swiss federal government), meaning the range of relocation options wasn't simple. Many other businesses relocating to Switzerland were settling in the German-speaking area, near Zurich – in places such as Zug (home to British chemist Boots and American food company Kraft) and Wollerau, where tennis champion Roger Federer lives – but the INEOS team quickly knew they were drawn to the French-speaking side of the country.

After being offered a competitive tax deal in Zug, they de cided to test whether their advisers could match the offer nearer Geneva, and were greeted with a warm reception by the Canton de Vaud. Nestled on the shores of Lake Geneva, with the country's fourth biggest city, Lausanne, as its central seat, it seemed an ideal choice. For business, it was only a stone's throw from Geneva airport and, for the weekends, only a short drive to the Alps. The Vaud tax office had some key prerequisites in matching Zug's favourable tax rate – keen to attract other manufacturers to the region, they requested that INEOS relocate a minimum of sixty people and create local jobs. INEOS immediately agreed. Securing support from the company's investors was, however, another hurdle.

While INEOS had previously been under a UK holding company, INEOS Capital, in the New Forest, it now needed to put a Swiss top company in place to facilitate a relocation – a technical restructure that would require consent from its syndicate of banks. 'From a bank's point of view, Switzerland is not an attractive place compared to the UK,' explained John. The main reason is one of security: 'Our banks were lending to a UK company with security on the assets, so if anything went wrong they could take us over.' In Switzerland, however, the rules are different. Regulations are not so friendly to creditors, and a bank lending to a Swiss company cannot take control if payments lapse. Instead, the bank has to enter into a one-year standstill agreement if a deal breaks down. 'We had to do a bit of a selling job on the banks to convince them it wasn't only good for us, it was also acceptable for them,' John recalls.

The banks' consent was central to moving forward, and negotiations yet again became tense. Reece and Debra Smeeton, INEOS's head of tax, were required to present the proposal to hundreds of lenders at a special presentation, while a consent paper was then drawn up giving the banks thirty days to respond. The company had a somewhat compelling justification for their shift – based on its projected figures, John worked out that, over the course of five years, the company could save some €450 million in tax. 'We had to go public and say this is good for both us and our lenders, because the financial position of the company is going to be much better.' Even so, a sweetening deal still had to be offered to get the syndicate on board. 'Effectively we paid them to say "yes", otherwise they just wouldn't have agreed,' said John. Because the banks also needed to see how their investment would be affected by transferring to a Swiss holding company, a litany of lawyers and analysts was also brought in. By early 2010, the syndicate had voted securely in favour of the shift, and relocation planning began in earnest.

It was something of a hectic move, with the company required to be in Vaud by the end of the UK tax year, leaving little time for logistics. Firstly, Jim, John and Andy relocated to Switzerland with their families, working in a temporary office in Lausanne on a short-term lease, while the remaining top executives joined them from Lyndhurst over the next six months. Once the lease was up in the Lausanne office in November 2010, they moved into new headquarters in Rolle. This bigger office, which was next door to Cisco, the American telecoms company, had previously been Cadbury's European HQ, while Nissan, Yahoo! and WPP were all headquartered nearby. At the time of the move, Cadbury was being bought by Kraft, the American foods conglomerate, in the now-famous takeover. John remembers the atmosphere was rather hostile: 'Kraft had a Swiss office near Zurich, so they instructed the Cadbury people in Rolle that they needed to move over there.' Some people did want to relocate to the German region, but several didn't, so INEOS inherited a few Cadbury employees, too. After the lease was signed, the owners were invited to meet representatives of their new landlord, and John remembers being passed a business card with a curious English address – Alnwick Castle in Northumberland, featured in the Harry Potter films. It later transpired that the landlord was the Duke of Northumberland, Ralph Percy, who happened to own a couple of offices in Switzerland – and the base quickly became home away from home.

Meeting tax stipulations for the British and Swiss authorities was technical. Individual tax residents in Switzerland can only spend a maximum of ninety days in the UK, and John remembers: 'They looked at things like where your doctor and dentist were based, and your telephone bill. They wanted to know if you had a UK mobile or a Swiss number, and which clubs you were a member of and why.' Meanwhile, to prove to the UK government that they were Swiss-based, all day-to-day INEOS management had to be conducted in Switzerland, and all senior business people had to be based there permanently to take part in executive meetings. John recalls the hardest aspect of the move was having to explain to his staff that this wasn't just for a year or two; essentially, they were asking them to emigrate. 'We were moving the head office from Lyndhurst, and there wasn't due to be any return back there.' Many of the senior staff had lived, worked and brought up families in the New Forest for years, so the move represented a major upheaval.

Jim, John and Andy spent a lot of time working on the relocation package for employees. Switzerland is an expensive place to live, there was a new language barrier, and most people were concerned about the impact it would have on their children, in particular. With Swiss house prices then around three times as expensive as the New Forest, and many native Swiss instead opting to rent, this resulted in a feeling of unease for those rooted in the UK property market – and especially those with families.

'It was a bit traumatic for some,' recalls John. The INEOS owners spent a long time poring over the details of the relocation package, investigating which particular schools the children would feel happiest in, and, by making the deal increasingly attractive, they had around thirty relocated employees by the end of 2010, with more quickly to follow. As they settled in, INEOS and its expats began to build relations with the local community, both in their office village of Rolle and in Lausanne nearby. 'As newcomers to Switzerland and beneficiaries of a competitive tax system we wanted to show commitment to the community and give something back,' said Jim. With the sporting ethos of INEOS senior management ever prevalent in its new setting, the company came to sponsor the Lausanne ice hockey club and local football teams and, by 2017, had acquired the Swiss Super League football team Lausanne Sport.

Just as INEOS was getting settled in its new base, however, life back in the UK was to change dramatically – and somewhat ironically. Only one month after INEOS had abandoned confidence in the Labour government and moved abroad, a general election took place. Winning just 30 per cent of the vote, Labour were drummed out of power after thirteen years, to be replaced by an unprecedented new Conservative–Liberal Democrat coalition. Taking office in May 2010, Tory Prime Minister David Cameron lost no time in overhauling corporate tax policy, and, in a bid to get the economy back on its feet and deter companies like INEOS from moving their assets offshore, Chancellor George Osborne set out staggered rate cuts. Under Cameron's leadership, corporation tax fell from 28 per cent to 20 per cent in the years between 2010 and 2016, and relations between INEOS and its native government became warmer. While their very public move had led to INEOS's owners being portrayed as tax exiles, communications director Tom Crotty recalls a sharp contrast in the way the new coalition government interacted with them. The new business secretary, Vince Cable, visited several of the company's sites, Jim was granted a meeting with Chancellor George Osborne, and INEOS once again felt somewhat appreciated. The concept of return crept onto the horizon.

The Swiss years were an efficient period of earnest rebuilding for the central INEOS management. The owners set about consolidating the business and getting it back on its feet, refinancing debt, reviewing its assets and striking new and profitable deals. In May 2010, the company sold a high-yield bond which allowed it to refinance a chunk of its bank debt and put it on a more stable financial footing. The company also cast off its struggling Italian assets that had formed part of EVC, and closed down a number of irredeemably underperforming sites, including its PVC facility in Barry, Wales. 'We really did a lot of cleaning up in those two years,' said Jim. Finally, in 2011, INEOS's return to fighting fitness was marked by two significant deals: its landmark joint venture with PetroChina, which saw 50 per cent of the refining business sold to the Chinese state oil company for $1 billion, and its new joint venture with BASF, which led to the formation of Styrolution, a heavyweight styrenics business. The Swiss secondment provided the sanctuary INEOS needed to bounce back from the recession even stronger than before.

The return to rude health came far quicker than expected. And, with the UK business climate reviving slowly, too, it wasn't long before the INEOS owners' personal loyalties were backed with business incentive by the new Conservative-dominated government. In response to a Conservative push to attract overseas investment, there was, by 2013, a sudden surge both in the number of foreign multinationals moving to the UK for the first time, and in UK multinationals looking to repatriate their headquarters. INEOS was, of course, among them. With post-recession bank interest rates low, the company's assets performing well across the globe, and a new portfolio of potential UK-based oil and gas projects on the table, the return looked increasingly tempting. In 2015, the British tax office launched a concerted review into companies that had relocated their headquarters overseas to ensure they weren't breaking any rules. 'We had to be mindful not to spend too much time in the UK,' remembers John.

When the 2015 general election saw Labour leader Ed Miliband lose out to David Cameron, who finally won a Conservative majority, the potential for five years of warmer business policy was the final pull home. A Conservative victory had also meant a devastating blow for the Unite union, Miliband's largest financial backer, and Jim's former *bête noire* – and the potential to structure more progressive industrial relations at the critical Grangemouth site beckoned. In 2016, George Osborne announced further corporation tax cuts, to reduce the overall rate from 20 to 17 per cent by April 2020, and the country was competitive on the G20 stage yet again. Repatriation was a welcome move for the INEOS team: 'We'd all done our time,' said Jim. 'Six years is quite long enough.' Though the move to Switzerland ended up saving INEOS slightly less than the €450 million it had originally estimated, that was enough to keep the company solvent through its biggest crisis.

In May 2016, the three owners once again became UK tax residents, along with a handful of other senior executives in INEOS's newly acquired UK oil and gas business. A new headquarters was founded in Knightsbridge, London, and the office became the small global hub of what is a broad-reaching international operation. The company still retains a split identity, however, and many key executives who had left the UK remain in the Rolle office, where most of the company's European operations are managed, just as US operations function from Marina View, an office outside Houston. It is an arrangement that, organically evolving, suits the still-growing company well – pragmatic, somewhat non-conformist, and grounded in strategic financials. As Brexit looms on the horizon, the corporate tax issue will no doubt bring further international unrest while the state of play is renegotiated, but INEOS now seems more secure than ever in its British-international identity.

CHAPTER 7

WIN–WIN

Just as strategic deal-making formed the ladder rungs to INEOS's prodigious growth, strategic deal-making likewise revived the company from the ashes of the financial crisis into a newly ambitious enterprise. Around 2011, as the markets picked themselves up and INEOS's finances had steadied once more, the leading team was on the lookout for ever more ambitious acquisitions. Three of their most successful surges in this new climate came from a new shape of deal – the artful joint venture. Rather than prospecting and purchasing unwanted companies outright, the success of INEOS's spate of joint venture deal-making enabled the company to build bold but mutually beneficial entities with competitor-collaborators, exploring new markets while gaining financial support and expertise. Though not necessarily negotiated as co-ownership in perpetuity, these deals increased confidence and built trust between parties, enabling more complex shifts in ownership to settle sensitively, when appropriate. Such arrangements were fraught with challenges, and confronting new corporate cultures at such close range perhaps marked INEOS's maturation – though its youthful ethos remained steadfast.

One of the first targets for such a bold joint venture was INEOS's European refining business, which the company had acquired from BP as a part of the Innovene deal in 2005. The adoption of the Grangemouth and Lavéra refineries brought over 400,000 barrels per day of refining capacity into the INEOS group, and propelled INEOS overnight into the position of the largest independent refiner in Europe. This brought significant new challenges to the company, on multiple levels – the scale and complexity of these physical assets, the magnitude of the working capital management task, and the voracious appetite of the assets for capital investment. The refining business in Europe, and globally, enjoyed some decent margins by historical standards between 2005 and 2009 and, during this period, INEOS focused on integrating the new assets into its business family, as well as driving better performance across the board – on costs, safety and environmental, commercial and financial performance. Management also established some critical partnerships in these years, including an oil trading partnership with Morgan Stanley and a technical support partnership with Shell Global Solutions, to ensure that the right specialist support was at hand to optimise operations.

Overall, the business was in good – and still improving – shape as the financial crisis unfolded. Still, INEOS recognised that the refineries had greater potential, which could be realised by a joint venture with the right partner. Such a partner would, ideally, bring to the table deep technical refining expertise, access to a broad oil trading network, and financial capacity to enable reasonable funding with a commercially optimal level of working capital. A handful of possible candidates were identified, and a process to review interest was kicked off in 2009. Exploratory discussions were held with several suitable and interested parties over the year, and one company emerged as the most likely potential partner to deliver the synergies being sought – the Chinese state-owned company PetroChina. This long-established giant had the attributes INEOS leadership were seeking – a large refining asset base and associated technical expertise, a global oil trading presence and solid financial backing, linked to the Chinese government. They had also expressed a strategic objective to expand their refining and trading interests in North America and Europe, so a refining joint venture was of clear mutual benefit.

Despite the neat fit for both parties, progress on deal completion was slow. PetroChina required significant detailed due diligence to be completed, including multiple physical visits to the assets by their experts, while it didn't help that the market had suffered in the wake of the financial crisis. Both parties at different times held out to push their priorities forward, and the negotiations were subsequently protracted, punctuated at times with silence. Most fundamentally, it took time for the two parties to get to know each other and their respective cultures – though, over the extended negotiations, key relationships were established between individuals on both sides' management teams, and at the highest level between Jim and the senior PetroChina executives responsible for the deal. With trust came partnership, and the joint venture, named Petroineos, was formally established on 1 July 2011.

This JV valued the refining business at over $2 billion, and was a significant step forward for both INEOS's and PetroChina's strategic European interests. The two refineries remain strong assets within the integrated refining and chemical sites at Grangemouth and Lavéra, and still generate growing synergy value with adjacent chemicals assets. On the commercial side, a standalone trading office has been established in Victoria, London, and the JV now has a fully independent supply and trading team that has optimised integration with PetroChina's wider global trading network. The move was, by all accounts, a win–win for both parties, and testament to the value of enduring joint ventures when partnerships are carefully built.

Meanwhile, INEOS's 2011 Styrolution joint venture was a game changer for the company within the chemicals sphere, creating a successful template for similar later collaborations. BASF, INEOS's long-standing competitor (and the largest public chemical company in the world), was looking to sell off its struggling global styrenics business, which had sites across the US, Mexico, Korea, Singapore, India and Europe. INEOS had existing styrenics sites in the US, Canada, India, Thailand and Europe. It was not a small opportunity – with combined annual sales of €6 billion, this would be the world's largest styrenics company, the size INEOS had been before the Innovene acquisition.

The polystyrene and acrylonitrile butadiene styrene (ABS) that BASF made had numerous end applications, including yogurt pots and food packaging, medical and laboratory equipment, white goods, children's toys such as LEGO, and lighter, more fuel-efficient car parts, but the global market was, since the early 2000s, in a long-running downturn. The business had fallen into ill health. Being a cyclical commodity, the business would typically have a good year followed by a bad one, and such volatility made it unattractive to a public business playing in the equity markets. Despite being one of the largest styrenics players in the world, BASF was coming under increasing pressure from analysts to sell this entire division. 'You have to toe the line or you'll get abandonment by your shareholders, and you'll get taken over or your share price trashed,' explained Andy Currie. For an entrepreneur like Jim, less sensitive to stock market fluctuations and more focused on growth in the long term, this commodity operation was far more attractive – and a worthy acquisition.

This wasn't INEOS's first foray into styrenics. It had bought BASF's US polystyrene business in 2005, and continued to acquire other styrenics operations, becoming a steadily bigger player. Kevin McQuade, who had been with BASF since 1992, joined INEOS and, in 2005, became part of another 50:50 joint venture deal, this time with Nova Chemicals, based in Canada, operating sites across North America and Europe that formed INEOS Nova. McQuade became CEO. When the financial crisis hit in 2007, the styrenics business BASF had been keen to offload was knocked sideways and was unable to find a buyer at such a tumultuous time. In 2008, an interested INEOS started discussions with BASF, although it was clear buying the business outright was not an option. Jim quickly spotted an opportunity for a deal that could work for both parties – by forming a joint venture between BASF and the existing JV INEOS had formed with Nova, both companies could rationalise capacity, make savings and create synergies. 'If one plant is running at 50 per cent, we could shut that down and run other plants at 100 per cent. You don't need two of everything,' explained McQuade. By consolidating IT, HR and other overheads, new efficiencies were found, and a promising proposal was put together.

As always, there were a few hurdles to jump. Three holding

companies were involved in this new joint venture, because INEOS Nova was already itself a JV. Partner Nova had, after the initial deal with INEOS, been acquired by a company called IPIC, which was wholly owned by the Abu Dhabi United Group (ADUG), a UAE-based private equity company that also owns Manchester City Football Club. With BASF and INEOS primed and keen to strike a deal, the ADUG played hard to get. 'We wanted to take things on to the next stage, but they were being very difficult and holding up the negotiations,' recalls Andy Currie. It soon became clear that the joint venture could not go ahead if the ADUG was involved. 'Their inability to make decisions threatened to stop the deal in its tracks,' said Jim. In a bid to break the deadlock, Jim decided to carry out what is known as a 'shotgun deal', capitalising on a clause in their joint venture contract allowing either party, at any point, to make an offer to buy the other out. The recipient would have ninety days to accept the offer and take the money or say no and buy the other out at the same price. Of course, the ADUG could have bought INEOS out and done a deal on their own with BASF. 'It was a high-risk strategy, even in our terms,' explained Andy. 'If you lowball bid, you'll get wiped out. If you bid too high, you pay too much.'

'Jim made a pretty bold decision,' said McQuade. It is the first and only time in INEOS history that a shotgun deal was carried out. It was a tense ninety days over the summer of 2010 and, even on news of a positive outcome, a final deal with BASF rested only on trust. Prior to pulling his 'trigger', Jim had spoken with Martin Brudermüller, then CTO of BASF, and they had agreed, over a handshake, that BASF would complete the deal if INEOS were successful. There were no legal guarantees. Jim believes, however, that such risk-taking in the name of trust and personal relationships has been fundamental to his business success to date. 'One of the reasons Martin thinks highly of INEOS is that we put all of our business at risk on the basis of a handshake,' Jim said. 'That doesn't happen very often.' When the Nova side came through, and both INEOS and BASF bosses honoured their word, the finer details of the styrenics joint venture began to take shape. It took a year for the deal to come together, and in 2011 the new Styrolution business was formed, headquartered in Frankfurt, Germany, at BASF's request.

In the three years from 2011 to 2014, the Styrolution business doubled in profit, an outcome neither BASF nor INEOS could have achieved on its own. Today, the company spends €200 million less on an annual basis than it did in 2011. This is a staggering cost saving, achieved by cutting the management structure in half, closing a few plants and consolidating services. Being such a lean company also protects the business against unpredictable cycles. When the market is doing well, commodities surge and the company makes huge profits; conversely, in a downturn, INEOS dials back costs and endeavours to continue making money at the bottom of the cycle. 'We don't worry about top of cycle, because if you are profitable at the bottom, you sure as hell profit at the top,' Andy explains.

All this was, however, a shrewd stepping stone to full ownership for INEOS. Within the deal, as is fairly typical, there was a potential 'call' option, meaning that, after a certain length of time – in this case three years – INEOS had the option to buy BASF out. Various accompanying clauses in the contract addressed business valuation at such a juncture. Three years on, by October 2014, the global market had improved, Styrolution was doing well and, sitting in on board meetings, Jim and team could see it had potential to grow even further. Meanwhile, BASF made no secret of the fact that it now wanted to focus more on speciality chemicals, so, with the timing lining up neatly, Jim used his 'call' card. It was a profitable exit for BASF, as Jim had predicted, with almost €1.6 billion paid for their stake, and the company 'ended up much better off than if they had sold it three years before', noted McQuade. As a longer-term investment, it certainly has been fruitful for INEOS. Using the INEOS team's rough valuation method of multiplying annual EBITDA by five or six, the company is worth around €4.5 billion today.

Styrolution continues to find savings even now. Headcount has been reduced by about 15 per cent – in 2017, Styrolution had 3,200 employees across sixteen plants globally – and, as margins have improved, the business is entering new markets. It is not all savvy strategy, of course – demand for the polystyrene, ABS and other styrenic polymers INEOS produces has increased in recent years, mainly in the automotive industry, where the trend for better fuel efficiency in cars has been a welcome gain. Nowadays, Styrolution works with all the major automotive companies, including Audi, Volkswagen, Mercedes, BMW, General Motors and Ford, and is proactive in developing new and innovative technologies. Styrolution is growing organically, opening new factories in Texas and India, and looks well set to ride out future market fluctuations.

The Styrolution deal set a precedent for ambitious win–win arrangements with competitors and provided a template which Jim and the team went on to replicate shortly after. When Solvay, the Belgian chemicals giant, was looking to break from its own joint venture with BASF, a PVC-producing company named Solvin, INEOS saw a window of opportunity. At the time, Solvay was the second largest PVC producer in Europe, and another public company looking to reduce its involvement in the cyclical commodities market after being a major player for decades. When Solvay's CEO hinted in a mid-2012 speech that the company might not be a long-term leader in the industry, Jim and team were paying attention and, within a matter of weeks, a new proposal was forming.

INEOS had existing PVC heritage, beginning when Jim bought the chlorine business from ICI in 2001, renaming it INEOS Chlor. After subsequently buying Chlor's main customer, an Anglo-Italian company called EVC (soon named INEOS Vinyls), the two units had been fused five years later into the successful outfit INEOS ChlorVinyls. Chris Tane, who had transferred from ICI in the first deal, was made ChlorVinyls CEO in 2006, and continued to bolster the business by purchasing similar players, including a Norwegian chlorvinyls business called Hydro Polymers for €600 million, as well as the chlorvinyls business of a Belgian company called Tessenderlo Chemie for €110 million. This rapid acquisitional growth meant that, by 2011, INEOS ChlorVinyls was the biggest producer of PVC in Europe, with a 20 per cent market share. The business employed 2,500 people across nine sites, with turnover of around €2 billion.

INEOS's decision to join with Europe's next biggest PVC producer made great business sense to the team, and the resulting enterprise, now named INOVYN, has become one of the company's most profitable deals to date. It was, however, one of the most challenging and long-running negotiations in INEOS history, not surprisingly. To combine the two largest PVC producers into one collaborative enterprise created significant issues in the face of EU competition law and, at a number of junctures during the painstaking deliberations, the deal threatened to collapse as the competition authorities imposed ever more onerous conditions. Though talks began over dinner in July 2012 between Tane and Solvay senior Jacques Van Rijckevorsel, just weeks after the CEO's fateful speech, no official joint venture was born until three years later, in July 2015.

This extended timeframe resulted both from EU legal issues and from other challenges between the parties themselves. Initially, Solvay wasn't convinced that sufficient synergies existed to make the merger worthwhile. For it to work, INEOS would have to quantify the benefits. This couldn't be carried out in typical fashion, however, because the two companies were competitors in the same market. As a result, a third party, Boston Consulting Group (BCG), was brought in to conduct a blind study on the potential of a proposed JV. The two companies were similar in size, though geographically INEOS had greater reach in northern Europe, and Solvay in southern Europe. Because of the spread, there wasn't much scope for merging sites, but there was potential for cutting back transport costs. Solvay was producing in Spain and selling in the UK – and the JV could certainly streamline that operation. BCG also estimated there were €100 million worth of savings to be made by merging head offices, finance, IT and other central functions. The distinct overlap of presence in Belgium and Germany, however, would be an issue getting EU approval. 'Putting the number one and number two companies together was bound to raise some concerns,' said Tane. INEOS and Solvay sought a wealth of legal advice on competition clearance and, although there was no question it would be difficult, with some asset divesture in the mix, the endeavour was deemed doable.

Negotiations properly began with debating how much each party was to put into the JV. As well as its European sites, Solvay was building a Russian plant and owned the majority of shares in two Thai and South American businesses – but it was quickly decided that only the EU assets would be brought into the partnership (the South American and Thai units have since been sold on). Next, the two sides needed to decide how long the arrangement should last – Solvay wasn't ready to exit the market completely, so their intention was for the JV to be a long-term project. The teams decided on a call option similar to that in the Styrolution deal, but, in the first version of the contract, Solvay had stated their intent to be involved indefinitely. By the time the second contract was drafted, Solvay had reduced this to a maximum seven years. In the third and final contract, this period had been cut to a fixed term of three years, after which Solvay would exit the JV with a final payment based on the financial performance of the business during the JV period.

A first stumbling block was the issue of proportional shareholdings. 'We were adamant from the start that the maximum split we would accept was 50:50,' recalls Tane. But Solvay viewed their business as more valuable than INEOS's, and wanted to own the majority of the new venture. The line of argument was a valid one; though INEOS had a similar number of sites, turnover and people, it was carrying €1 billion worth of debt, whereas Solvay was debt-free. This became a critical part of the negotiations. INEOS stuck to its guns, however, and Tane refused to back down to anything less than an even split. Once again, being a private company played to INEOS's strengths. 'We could just shrug our shoulders and walk away from the deal,' said Tane. On the other hand, Solvay had committed to it – their

CEO had stood in front of his shareholders and made a public announcement.

The competition clearance issues were, in contrast, far beyond INEOS's influence, and technically complex. After two years of negotiations, the European Commission stipulated that the merger could go ahead only if INEOS divested two thirds of its existing chlorvinyls business, so that the company wouldn't overly dominate the market. EU competition clearance comes in two phases, and most cases (95 per cent) clear in phase one. Following formal application, there is typically a three-month investigation period, after which a company is told whether clearance has been granted. If not, a more challenging and intrusive phase two process begins, with a timescale of six months or more. This was not the first time INEOS had found itself here – INEOS's 2007 Norwegian chlorvinyl acquisition process had also run on extensively after a first refusal, and Tane recalls that 'one of our advisers said I had achieved a record as the only CEO to go through a phase two twice'.

The Commission sent INEOS and Solvay several requests for information as they pulled together the case, some more taxing than others. 'If the deadline is not met, they stop the clock and make a public announcement that you have failed to deliver,' explained Tane. It was a frenetic, and intrusive, process. Tane remembers when the Commission requested to review every single one of the companies' emails relating to ethylene – the main material used by Solvay and INEOS – in just ten days' time. INEOS and Solvay had teams of people working through the nights and weekends to pull this and all other information together. 'It was unbelievable, and put extreme stress on the organi-sation to keep the day-to-day business running,' said

Tane. Meanwhile, meetings with the Commission were continuing to take place. Tane attended some twenty-eight meetings in Brussels; his deputy on this project, Stuart Collings, went to twice as many.

By the end of phase two, the Commission would impose what they call a 'remedy' measure for a deal to go ahead, or give clearance. A remedy is effectively a compromise offered by the company to persuade the Commission to green-light the deal, usually involving divesting capacity (i.e. selling off assets). In INEOS's case, the Commission instructed Tane as to which geographical regions should be reduced in coverage, and the scale of the necessary reduction. In particular, the Commission wasn't happy with the supply overlap in the Benelux/German region. The main problem with remedies is the uncertainty they create, because 'they [the Commission] can't give you the answers, you have to work out the solutions for yourself and then offer them up,' explained Tane. Inevitably, negotiations went back and forth, prolonging the process even more.

It was a particularly intense time. Tane half-joked that his marriage almost fell apart after he cancelled and rescheduled an important family holiday to make a mandatory Commission meeting, only to be told the meeting had been rescheduled again. When he eventually made it to the holiday, he spent the entire time on conference calls from Cape Town. It was during this trip he was told the deal couldn't go ahead: 'They gave me the worst news you can imagine – they didn't agree with any of our arguments, and wanted more remedy offers.' Tane and Collings returned to Brussels for more meetings, hoping to reach some sort of agreement, and each session took place on a Friday afternoon starting at 1 p.m., requiring a 4 a.m. start from Runcorn. The pair would arrive in Brussels to be told yet more bad news, and then would spend Friday night sitting in the airport. Tane described it as 'the most difficult time of my career'. All the while, Tane could never be certain the deal would come through in the end.

The Commission's eventual solution was not an easy pill to swallow. INEOS would have to sell off the entire business they had acquired from Tessenderlo, along with its chlorvinyls site in Wilhelmshaven, Germany, and had just six months to find a buyer. Selling a business with a turnover of €1.5 billion in such a short timeframe seemed an impossible task, particularly when most chemical companies were trying to exit the PVC industry, not get into it. Against all the odds, and with literally days to spare, INEOS found its buyer, a business called Vynova, owned by ICIG, a private company based in Germany. With that single divestment (ultimately approved in May 2015), INEOS would create the second largest PVC producer in Europe, and its own competitor. Finally, at the last minute, the Commission threw in one more tough condition. INEOS would have to divest part of its main chlorine plant in Runcorn into a joint venture, ideally with the same buyer to whom it was selling its other assets. 'It was the final twist of the knife,' recalls Tane. Backing out now was not an option. The INEOS executive had to grit his teeth and give in.

During the six months it took for the Commission to approve the transfer of the Runcorn plant, the INEOS–Solvay joint venture was put on hold. INEOS and Solvay were unable to make any decisions about the business, which meant many people were in the dark over whether they would still have a job at the end of it. It was extremely bad for morale. Finally, in July 2015, all clearances went through, and the joint venture, named INOVYN, was officially launched. Relations between the new partners, while by no means easy, were at least honest. INEOS had unbending confidence that putting the two businesses together could create a globally competitive player, but the whole deal would have crumbled if it hadn't been for Solvay's Jacques Van Rijckevorsel: 'He was instrumental to the whole process. His vision was critical,' said Tane. There were several moments when the demands on both companies were so tough that people in Solvay wanted out. Tane and Van Rijckevorsel spoke every week and, though they would often argue, both stayed true to their word and saw the process through to its end.

Once the JV kicked off, its projected cost savings quickly grew, and the efficiency of the arrangement became clearly evident. INEOS's early savings estimates of €100 million soon doubled, and the venture has surpassed expectations. Each company benefited from its partner's strengths – while INEOS had proved itself more efficient in managing fixed costs, Solvay's strength lay in variable costs. Improved market conditions also bolstered the strong new company's position, and INOVYN has continued to grow.

The partnership wasn't all plain sailing, something that became evident when Solvay, initially committed to the JV for at least three years, agreed to an early exit after just one. INEOS and Solvay had very different views when it came to steering INOVYN, and different ultimate ambitions for its growth. One of the conditions of the joint venture was a supervisory board with two members from each company. Each had a vote and, if one side didn't agree with the other, nothing happened; there was no tie-breaker. This became increasingly frustrating for Tane: 'I was CEO but couldn't do anything. It wasn't the INEOS way of doing things.' The supervisory process meant it was much more difficult to push anything through, and a lot more time consuming.

The corporate cultural difference between INEOS and Solvay had also started to become a problem, but the friction peaked over financials when EU authorities decided to bring in new regulations that would greatly affect INOVYN's future. Mercury technology, which was the process used in chlorine production, was going to be phased out and eradicated by the end of 2017, on the basis that it was environmentally unfriendly. INOVYN had five mercury plants. Replacing mercury with the newer, cleaner membrane technology was going to cost hundreds of millions of pounds, and Solvay didn't want to make the investment. While INEOS saw INOVYN as a long-term endeavour, Solvay was primarily interested in the short-term gains it could obtain, and was wary of plugging in additional funds. It became clear to INEOS that a 50:50 arrangement wasn't in the interests of the business and, at the beginning of 2016, INEOS approached Solvay to suggest an early exit.

At the start of the unwinding, a dinner took place between the Solvay chairman of INOVYN's supervisory board and their general counsel, and INEOS's Chris Tane, accompanied by legal colleague Jonny Ginns. Gradually, the discussions turned into a formal negotiation, culminating in Solvay's fairly smooth summer 2016 exit. It suited INEOS well, and the owners admit that, while the deal was a strategic stepping stone, they had never wanted a long-term joint venture. 'Jim wouldn't have done it if he didn't think they would exit at some point,' said Tane. Ultimately, Jim was betting on the belief that, after Solvay's CEO had said he didn't see a future being in the industry, the move would happen quicker than anticipated. 'We were always planning on having a conversation before the three years were up,' Tane admitted.

Once again, INEOS's play paid off, but it was likewise a win–win deal for Solvay. 'If Solvay had tried to divest its chlorvinyl assets in 2014 without any synergies and the mercury phase-out issue, they would have struggled,' said Tane. It was also important to Solvay that the business went to long-term, committed owners. Had they tried to sell when the business was struggling, they would probably have attracted the likes of private equity houses. Eventually, Solvay walked away with a €335 million exit cheque on top of the first instalment of €175 million, which they had received in 2015 to redress the 50:50 shareholder split disagreement with INEOS. In total, Solvay made best part of €600 million from the arrangement.

INOVYN is still delivering synergies for INEOS and, by 2018, has a turnover of €3.5 billion. Efficiencies are still being drilled from the business, with the headcount reduced by 500 last year to a current total of 4,000. Like Styrolution, it is now similar in size to the pre-Innovene INEOS. The main challenge remaining is the somewhat disjointed Runcorn Vynova arrangement, described by some of the INEOS executives as a 'dog's breakfast'. This compulsory 'remedy' JV is a more enduring one, which can't be bought out for another ten years. For now, Tane is focusing on running the business effectively and making necessary investments put on hold while the business was waiting for EU clearance, among them construction of new chlorine plants to replace the old mercury technology, due for completion in 2018.

This wing of the company has, it seems, reached its limits of European acquisition – though elsewhere in the INEOS group, new strategic JVs may continue to drive further growth.

CHAPTER 8

GRANGEMOUTH REUNITED

INEOS's suite of successful joint venture deals was by no means its biggest diplomatic challenge. Collaborating or competing among its corporate peers was firmly within its comfort zone since the early days of the business, stemming from Jim's resolute leadership and the owning trio's thorough operating principles. It was negotiations with the company's employees that caused some of the greatest difficulty – specifically, the traditional union culture dominating the Grangemouth refinery site. While the activities of trade unions throughout industrial history have sought to protect workers' rights and privileges, and have ultimately strengthened the hand of both employers and employees, the circumstances surrounding industrial employment have by now changed significantly, especially since membership figures and union power peaked in the post-war years. By the turn of the millennium in wealthy industrialised nations, the strength and culture of union relations had come to vary distinctly among economies. With the INEOS team now running large-scale operations in a number of OECD countries, the British leaders were pointedly aware of the difference in cultural attitude, and collaborative working ethos, of the union–employer relationship across borders. Holding Germany as a prime example of a functional system, where mutual respect and careful negotiation manages to protect both workers' rights and business growth, Jim and the team quickly found that relations at Grangemouth were far more challenging.

When BP included two of its oil refineries with the Innovene deal in 2005, Jim and his partners knew they had quite a challenge on their hands. None of them had any experience running a refinery business, let alone one the size of Grangemouth, and this was ten times bigger, and ten times more expensive to run, than any of the existing petrochemical plants. The learning curve was steeper than they could have imagined. The site, located on the Firth of Forth, the estuary for several Scottish rivers, employed around 1,400 staff between its refinery and petrochemicals complex when Jim bought it, and was a primary employer in the region. Described as the 'heartbeat' of Scotland's manufacturing industry, the Grangemouth site sits at the end of a huge oil and gas pipeline, the Forties Pipeline System, running from the North Sea, and accounts for all the petrol, diesel and heating oil production in Scotland and northern England.

Grangemouth is steeped in energy history dating back to the mid-nineteenth century, after Glasgow scientist James 'Paraffin' Young first discovered how to extract oil from certain forms of coal and shale in 1850. Scotland's oil industry grew solidly from 1851, the year Young established the world's first oil works, in Bathgate, West Lothian, but it was quickly disrupted by further developments in the New World. Once the first oil well was sunk in Pennsylvania in 1859, the development of American oil fields drove down the price of the commodity, suffocating the growing Scottish industry. By 1919, the six surviving oil outfits in Scotland, including Young's Paraffin Light and Mineral Oil Company, came together under the name Scottish Oils – to be acquired in the same year by the Anglo-Persian Oil Company. When this, in turn, evolved into the now well-known organisation British Petroleum, it acquired the crude oil refinery at Grangemouth, built in 1924 and the UK's second oldest refinery.

The Grangemouth works operated under BP until 1939, shut down during the Second World War, and then reopened in 1946 for a new lease of life. In 1947, BP formed a joint venture with the Distillers Company, a Scottish petrochemicals and pharmaceuticals business that wanted to introduce synthetic processes to produce alcohol (ethanol), replacing traditional fermentation. The new venture was called BP Petroleum Chemicals and, in 1951, BP built one of the first petrochemicals plants in Europe, next to the BP oil refinery in Grangemouth, with the refinery's petrochemical feedstock serving as the raw materials. From its opening years, the site was firmly unionised to protect the rights of its workers from the exploitation of big business and, by the time INEOS came to prospect the Grangemouth site in 2005, Unite, Britain's biggest union, enjoyed almost 100 per cent support from the workforce – with unbounded influence. It seemed that, under BP, the union rather than the company ran Grangemouth.

Despite significant investment over the years, the petrochemical wing of Grangemouth proved challenging to manage, and, being tightly integrated into the refinery, BP eventually decided to sell the whole site. Jim and his team could see plenty of opportunities to restructure the business and turn it around, but this confidence was somewhat naïve. They had no idea that they would have to take on the trade unions first – a force unlike any they had faced to date. The concept of owning a business and not being in full control of it was alien to Jim, and it was perhaps unsurprising that he got off to a bad start with the union on site. Tom Crotty, the Grangemouth CEO at the time, recalls the first meeting Jim had with Unite officials. Finding it hard to explain just how difficult it was working with the Unite representatives, Tom had arranged for Jim to come to Grangemouth and meet with Mark Lyon and Stevie Deans, the two full-time union officials who represented the workforce, in an attempt to open dialogue. At first, Tom had trouble persuading Mark Lyon to list any union complaints, defeating the point of Jim's visit. But, as soon as Jim bluntly stated that only at Grangemouth was INEOS experiencing problems, it was as though a switch had flipped in the union leader's mind. 'Mark went berserk, and started ranting,' recalls Tom. 'He said: "Let us tell you who runs this company – we run it."' The meeting ended with both parties walking out of the room in disagreement – portent of a long-term showdown.

There were plenty of factors working against INEOS. Both the union and the workforce were cautious of their new boss from the start because of Jim's background as a venture capitalist. People believed he wouldn't stick around for long and would aggressively cut costs while refusing to invest, before selling the company to someone else. More worryingly, Jim threatened employee comforts from the moment he arrived. The site was promising, but it was clear to the INEOS leaders that there were growing financial issues, one of which was the generous staff salaries and pension scheme. The average operator at Grangemouth earned as much as £55,000, with a company pension contribution of £30,000 on top, well beyond the pay for similarly skilled jobs in the rest of Scotland, where there was an average salary of £26,000. The former BP pension scheme was seen as 'gold-plated' – it was an old-style final salary scheme (increasingly rare back then, and almost unheard of today), which meant that INEOS had to foot the whole pension bill: an average employee leaving Grangemouth on a salary of £55,000 was guaranteed an annual pension of £36,000. Unsurprisingly, the union had safeguarded the pension scheme and warned Jim to keep his hands off it, or they would go on strike. They went as far as calling it their 'birthright'. As a result, pension costs were spiralling out of control, and would soon create a deficit of £200 million.

Another huge financial issue for INEOS was the BP contracts for hydrocarbon supply, particularly ethane feedstock, it had inherited with the purchase of Grangemouth. 'We ended up with a one-sided set of contracts, which basically said we had to take everything BP gave us, even if we got 5,000 tonnes of product one day and nothing the next,' said Jim. It was unworkable. Beyond this, much of the equipment they inherited on site also needed replacing, but even necessary site investment was starting to look challenging. Gordon Milne, Grangemouth operations director, said: 'Even the smallest site improvements that you tried to make had to go through the trade union office to get approval.' Besides, Jim wasn't prepared to make any new investments before significant cost savings were made. The perfect storm was brewing.

Just the threat of a strike was enough to set off serious alarm bells for site management, and Unite played this strategic card often. Because of Grangemouth's strategic location, shutting down the site effectively cuts off the North Sea pipeline, stopping the flow of oil and gas, causing a massive economic impact in a very short space of time. As Tom Crotty explained: 'Within a week there would be no petrol in the stations across the whole of Scotland, the hospitals wouldn't have any heating oil to keep warm, and all the schools would have to close down.' As a result, Unite was on top, and there hadn't been a strike at Grangemouth for thirty years. 'The impact of a strike for BP was so great that it just didn't make sense for them to do anything other than to agree with the unions,' explained Tom. INEOS was bolder in its approach.

Jim decided to offer the union a compromise on the core pension issue and put forward a new proposal that would apply only to new starters, not existing employees. The long-term staff would keep all the benefits they already had, while fresh joiners would receive a less generous pension (although still a good one). Jim and his team were stunned when the union flat out refused the offer – Unite felt that a two-tier pay system would create a divide and that everyone should be paid the same – but they forged ahead anyway, confident the union would back down. Instead, true to its threat, Unite went on strike, taking the whole site offline for two days at the end of April 2008.

The timing was especially unfortunate for Jim – at 3 a.m. on the first day of the strike, his daughter Julia had been born at a hospital in London. Flying up to Scotland straight after the birth, and looking more than a little exhausted, he insisted on showing solidarity with his management team on site. The abuse he received from the unions that day struck more sensitively than usual – 'He just didn't deserve it,' recalls Tom, 'and it made him even more determined to sort out Grangemouth, whatever it took.'

A couple of days later, Tom and Jim held a meeting at a secret London location with the joint general secretaries of Unite, Tony Woodley and Derek Simpson, to try to find a way through the impasse. Jim later pointed out that, although Woodley had said he would help INEOS by making concessions, he had subsequently conceded that the union's currency is its membership, and the leadership could do only those things that encouraged its growth. Jim says: 'It was a real insight into how senior union bosses think. At the end of the day, it was similar to the way that a CEO is principally interested in the bottom line – how much profit, how much cash they've got. The union leaders want to look like heroes by getting more members.' The two groups' ultimate aims were looking impossible to reconcile.

The consequences of this strike for INEOS were huge. Grangemouth runs 365 days of the year without cease, because shutting down and restarting can take weeks, and the safety risks involved are immense. The two-day strike resulted in a loss of €100 million for INEOS, and came at a significant cost to the government, which lost the tax from oil and gas revenues. For Jim and his team, it was a slap in the face – but they had no option other than to back off, reinstating all the original terms and conditions for new employees. It was doubly frustrating to the management team that the union staff could get away with going on strike for just a day or two, which then meant closing the plant for a month or more, and still get paid for the entire period.

The episode was a humiliating blow for Jim. 'The union knew just how powerful they were, and ruthlessly exercised that power,' remembers Tom. 'It wasn't about the wage issue, it was about industrial strength.' More than ever, the battle of wills was getting personal. 'It hit Jim pretty hard. He didn't get over the fact that he tried to make sensible changes and couldn't. This was his company and all he wanted were changes that would ensure its long-term future – and for that he got abused by the union and even in some parts of the press.' Refusing to accept defeat, Jim realised he was going to need to play a longer-term game. He could still see an opportunity to make Grangemouth profitable, but it would be a war with more battles before victory. While awaiting what he knew was an inevitable second confrontation, he went about quietly putting mechanisms in place to reduce the union's power.

First, he made significant structural changes in Grangemouth, splitting the petrochemicals business from the refinery business so that they were more independent, and the ripples of strikes could be better contained. He also split up the European umbrella petrochemical company INEOS Olefins & Polymers Europe into three regions, each with their own separate management boards, to enable them to address their own specific challenges. O&P North, the strongest branch with reliable assets in Norway, Belgium and Germany, was made distinct from O&P South, which includes the refinery and petrochemical complex at Lavéra and a number of smaller, weaker assets whose olefin supply has to arrive indirectly by boat. O&P UK was created to address the unique feedstock and union challenges at Grangemouth, and put under the leadership of the quietly determined and charismatic Scot Calum MacLean, who had worked closely with Jim since the birth of INEOS. The Grangemouth complex continued to flounder, with profitability plummeting, and, by 2012, the site was losing a staggering £10 million per month. On top of existing challenges with high staff overheads and

Artist's impression of the new football stadium planned for Lausanne-Sport, the team bought by INEOS in 2017

INEOS become sponsors of Lausanne Hockey Club following the move to Switzerland in 2010. The team compete in the National League – the top tier of Swiss hockey

Brendan Foster, Seb Coe and Jim at the Queen Elizabeth Olympic Park to celebrate the world's biggest organised children's running initiative, 'INEOS GO Run For Fun', which aims to get children around the world active and off the couch

Jim leaving the INEOS building in Grangemouth, Scotland during the 2008 strike – just twelve hours after his daughter Julia was born

Uncertain times – Grangemouth employees concerned about their future and the future of the plant in 2013

Mark Lyon leading protesters in the second Grangemouth strike, 2013

Protesters line the pavements in Grangemouth during one of the UK's biggest industrial strikes

'Fighting for our Future' – placards lie discarded following the dispute in 2013

Three stages of shale gas production – (1) Drilling to depths of 3,000 metres

(2) Hydraulic stimulation

(3) Completion: the site can produce gas silently for up to twenty years

ABOVE The Breagh field in the southern North Sea acquired by INEOS in 2015

RIGHT A platform on the Siri field acquired in 2017

A dent was found in the Forties Pipeline, south of Aberdeen. Excavation showed this was due to the pipe settling on a granite rock. Repair required shutdown of the pipeline and the Forties sector of the North Sea for nearly a month

Welders work around the clock to repair the Forties Pipeline, which carries 40 per cent of UK North Sea oil production

The launch of the INEOS Dragon Ships in Shanghai, China, 2015

Eight Dragon Ships were built to carry shale gas from the US to Europe – each is 180 metres long, the length of two football pitches

US shale gas arrives in Europe (Rafnes, Norway) for the first time, on board INEOS *Intrepid*, 23 March 2016

US shale gas arrives at Grangemouth on the INEOS *Insight*, 28 September 2016

INEOS's growing reach across the globe

The team behind Projekt Grenadier outside the pub it was named after (from left to right: Tom Crotty, Toby Ecuyer, Jim Ratcliffe, Dirk Heilmann, Chris Tane)

Jim and his beloved Defender; Land Rover discontinued production of the model in 2016. The Defender is believed to be the Queen's favourite car

unbalanced BP contracts, its raw materials from the North Sea were also starting to dwindle, and there was simply not enough ethane gas feedstock to run the petrochemical cracker efficiently. Each year, the situation got worse.

Eventually, Jim realised that the only possible salvation for the site was an unprecedented move, importing cheaper and more abundant stocks of ethane across the Atlantic from the US, in a 'virtual pipeline' of ships. It was an immense and costly gamble, but the situation was grave. Jim was clear about how to proceed: INEOS would draw on its resources to put up some £1.5 billion ($2 billion) for the project, including £200 million in the UK to invest in the terminal infrastructure to receive the new shale gas ships at Grangemouth, and £200 million to float the struggling business there. For this to be viable, however, the employees also needed to make their own contribution. In a move to reduce the pension deficit, Jim put forward a proposal to cut the contribution the company made to individuals' pensions from an uncommonly generous 65 per cent to 11 per cent. The proposal would apply to both existing and new employees, and therefore went much further than his 2008 plan, which the union had brushed aside. Jim and Calum told the workforce that, if they didn't accept the offer, Grangemouth's survival would be threatened.

To support the move, Gordon Grant, Declan Sealy and Ian Fyfe, three senior Grangemouth directors, tried desperately to communicate to the workforce just how drastically the site's financial condition was deteriorating. Management certainly wanted the site to survive – their jobs were on the line, too. They had begun a series of regular liaison meetings with union officials, which, by the summer of 2013, were taking place three times a week, and Calum MacLean, the top boss, was brought in to provide clout. In the background, however, union politics, with a small and a large 'p', were getting increasingly complex – and seeping further into the Grangemouth disarray.

In March 2013, Eric Joyce, the Labour MP for Falkirk West, made national news after he head-butted a Tory MP in a House of Commons bar. His seat was the neighbouring constituency to Grangemouth (which sits in Linlithgow and East Falkirk) and, on being forced to resign from the Labour Party, he announced that he would not stand for the forthcoming 2015 election. As Labour began a process to select his replacement, Grangemouth's Unite senior Stevie Deans was emerging as a local Labour power broker – he had been promoted to chairman of Unite in Scotland, and chair of the Falkirk West Constituency Labour Party. At Grangemouth, Deans and his sidekick, Mark Lyon, saw themselves as invincible. The Unite office at Grangemouth seemed to sum it all up – a huge poster of Che Guevara adorned one wall, with a Cuban flag draped across the other. 'That's how left-wing they had become,' recalls Charles Cameron of law firm Slaughter and May.

Things got further out of balance. Deans, who received from INEOS a full-time salary to represent Grangemouth union members, suddenly found pressing new political duties, and began attending a large number of off-site Labour Party meetings, even during business hours. When the wary management discovered this, tensions with the union began to reach breaking point. Meanwhile, the situation worsened as Deans began to recruit staff from the site as new members of the Falkirk West Labour Party, and allegedly paid their membership fees. Unite wanted their favourite candidate, Karie Murphy, to replace the disgraced Joyce. Some newspapers claimed that INEOS staff were being made members of the Labour Party without their knowledge through forged signatures. Unite leaders were accused of being behind the scam. Then further allegations appeared, suggesting that union backers were paying people to swing the vote in Murphy's favour. When Deans found himself caught up in the scandal, the tension peaked.

The board at Grangemouth carried out an investigation into Deans's conduct, finding emails on the INEOS server that showed he had been managing the affair on INEOS's time, and using the company's resources. With Jim's patience at breaking point, Deans was suspended. 'He was guilty as sin,' said Jim. Unite claimed, nonetheless, that this was 'victimisation' of Deans, and called a strike. INEOS received a call from the head of Unite, Len McCluskey, who threatened to shut the plant down if they didn't reverse Deans's suspension. Unite then held a meeting at Grangemouth, and shortly afterwards announced their strike for 20 and 21 October. The management began, once again, to prepare the site for full closure, starting the process of bringing the plant down to cold where it could safely remain for a while. Then, in a move calculated to wrong-foot the management and cause maximum pain with minimum effort, Unite called off the 48-hour strike planned. They had the site leaders in a knot.

This time, however, Jim called Unite's bluff. INEOS announced that the site would remain closed until Unite confirmed that they would not resort to strike action for the rest of the year. In a bid to reach some sort of deal, urgent meetings were held at the government ACAS (Advisory, Conciliation and Arbitration Service) office in Glasgow. As negotiations progressed, Calum MacLean and Declan Sealy represented the company. 'Declan's a bit of a hard nose, and he was quite happy to trade punches with the unions and not mince his words,' said Calum. The union was used to dishing it out, but seemingly had not yet been on the receiving end of such tough talk. Calum, Declan and their lawyers were put in one room, with a team of Unite officials including Lyon, Deans and Pat Rafferty, Unite's Scottish secretary, in another. Negotiators would then go back and forth between the two, trying to reach an agreement. Alex Salmond, Scotland's First Minister at the time, had been influential in getting the two parties together, and was simultaneously holding meetings with each side, accompanied by Secretary of State for Scotland Alistair Carmichael MP.

It was at the height of this drama that INEOS launched the Grangemouth 'survival plan'. By turning attention away from Deans, and focusing on the main issue at stake – the future of the business – INEOS had a solid footing to make its case. Management proposed their plan by writing to every staff member, with a list of terms and conditions. If employees agreed to the survival plan, INEOS would invest the £400 million required for the new terminal and a new lease of life for the site. INEOS had also applied to the British government for a £237 million loan guarantee, and the Scottish government for a £9 million grant, to help fund the new terminal. The document was not an easy read for many: it included a wage freeze for three years, no bonuses, a money purchase pension scheme and a renegotiation of union convenors on site.

In a concerted bid to gather widespread support for the plan, the board at Grangemouth held meetings around the clock with staff, to reinforce and justify its key elements. Because staff worked on a shift basis, these talks would take place throughout the night, and were often in front of many pairs of hostile ears. Gordon Milne, one of the directors leading the meetings, remembers how intimidating this could be: 'The staff were very angry. There was really bad language in the room. What was amazing was the total denial – many hundreds of workers simply refused to accept that Grangemouth was losing money. I have never been called a liar so many times.' It seemed the team's efforts were futile – Deans and Lyon had the backing of all the blue-collar workers, known on site as the 'collective'. The collective took the view that, even if Grangemouth was losing money, INEOS should just share its profits from other parts of the company to keep it going. They even suggested that Jim should pay for their benefits out of his own pocket. And so it was that, while the board told staff one thing, the union was instructing them the opposite.

In a last-ditch attempt to negotiate some sort of deal, Calum returned to ACAS. The ensuing session was particularly intense, lasting all night and finishing at 6 a.m. the following day. 'After several hours we asked for some food, and the ACAS staff produced just a small plate of stale sandwiches. Presumably the tactic was to force both parties to capitulate due to hunger!' Declan recalls. During the ACAS meeting, Unite demanded an apology from Jim for suspending Stevie Deans. Jim refused. Unite also asked Calum to reinstate Deans, which he refused. It was hopeless. Neither side was prepared to compromise and, in the end, both sides issued a statement blaming the other party for the lack of progress.

In London, INEOS's lawyers at Slaughter and May were anxiously awaiting Calum's call with the outcome of the session. That night, they went into overdrive to write up a 'Settlement Agreement', a proposal to all staff at Grangemouth asking them formally to accept the company's survival plan. It was all hands on deck. Charles Cameron remembers being woken up by a phone call from his senior partner, Robert Stern, at 3 a.m. to read through the document: 'It was very stressful. I almost got a cab in my dressing gown.' They also prepared a defamation claim in response to the union having called Jim 'sinister' – 'We had an interesting discussion about whether "sinister" was in fact libellous,' said Cameron. In the end, the claim was brought forward purely as a tactical diversion, in the hope that the union would back down – play was getting tougher.

In background, tactics went far off-piste – both in legal and in moral terms – as Unite launched its secret 'Leverage' campaign to smear INEOS's leaders. This was a tried-and-tested protest tactic imported from the USA, with the aim to take the dispute away from the workplace to third parties', and even managers', homes. It began with Unite sending groups of protesters to various locations up and down the country to draw attention to their case. They would usually take a giant inflatable rat, and painted banners attacking Jim and the team. At first, they targeted INEOS's lenders, Barclays and Merrill Lynch, its lawyers Slaughter and May, and other suppliers. Barclays was forced to shut one of its branches to customers, which came at a significant cost to the local bank. Then the campaign got personal. One weekend, Jim was warned by a friend not to go into his local high street in Hampshire because Unite were handing out 'Wanted' flyers with his face on them. They were trying to claim that Jim was a criminal. And it wasn't just Jim they were targeting – John Reece, Tom Crotty and Andy Currie also had their faces branded on leaflets in their home towns. Protesters pitched up outside the New Forest hotel owned by Jim and lined the route he would run at weekends. They even disrupted a children's fun-run in a neighbouring village. It was as though Unite had private investigators on the case, hunting down every piece of information they could get to force INEOS to give in. When a threatening gang of Unite activists turned up on the driveway of Declan's home in the middle of the day, where his wife and young children lived, the UK media tuned in, and it became very clear that Unite had overstepped the line.

Jim and his team seized the moment to launch a new attack on Unite. The press had been all over the Stevie Deans story since it leaked, but by now it had gained momentum and journalists were camped out at Grangemouth. Calum agreed to an interview with a local paper about the issue, which then added fuel to the fire. Unite were upset by the coverage and accused INEOS of negotiating through the media instead of directly. It was at this point that Jim and the team finally came up with the solution they thought would end the deadlock. There would be a vote to save the plant. Either the workforce accepted the terms of the survival plan and the plant reopened, or INEOS would shut it down for good.

Every employee was given a voting paper that set out the survival plan, with a 'yes' or 'no' box at the bottom. The voting paper had been drafted at the lawyers' office in London, and Charles Cameron had spent hours working on it. It ended up being two pages long, detailing every eventuality of what it would mean if people accepted the survival plan, and if they didn't. Cameron remembers: 'Jim was obsessed with exactly what the document should look like, even to the point of font size, colour, the width of the boundary around the heading – it became his total focus.' Jim was adamant the paper include a statement that read: 'You must return this form.' The pair fell out over this, after Cameron told Jim there was no legal basis to require people to return a form. 'It was classic me and Jim,' he recalls. In the end, Jim got his way and the statement was added. What was most clever about the voting paper was that it created a divide-and-rule policy – the way the lawyers had worded it meant that, if people accepted the survival plan early on, they would get a higher pension. Stern remembers: 'The company was, in quotes, bribing the people to stay in – because they got a better pension deal.'

Len McCluskey immediately sent the lawyers a letter saying they were in breach of legislation. Unite could certainly have tried suing INEOS for this, but Jim was convinced that they weren't in a strong enough position to do so. The lawyers didn't always share his confidence, though: 'If you had asked me to bet on the outcome, I would have said that INEOS would lose,' said Stern. 'But Jim is the kind of bloke you wouldn't play poker with. He had a very weak hand, but his negotiation skills were fantastic – he out-played them all.'

Jim refused to reopen the plant, and announced that it would remain closed until a decision was reached. It was only then that a sense of real unease began to surface among the workers. The plant had been shut for a number of days already, and the reality of the situation was beginning to sink in. When the results of the vote came in, however, it was devastating for INEOS's management. While the majority of staff on site appeared to have voted 'yes' to the survival plan, none of the collective – which accounted for about half of the total workforce – returned their voting slips to INEOS, instead handing them over to Unite. INEOS never received the papers, and to this day the managing team have no idea of the final result of their vote. Unite's interception had made the exercise null and void.

Jim recalls: 'We were really shocked on the Monday morning when the result came in. It looked like it was an overwhelming "no", and that's because of this intense culture of intimidation and ritual the union had with the membership.' INEOS went on a 24-hour news blackout. Richard Longden and Tom Crotty, who then comprised INEOS's senior press team, were flooded with questions about what was happening, but nothing leaked. On Tuesday 22 October 2013, Jim called an emergency management meeting at Slaughter's office in London, with Gordon Grant, Gordon Milne, Declan Sealy and Ian Fyfe all present. It was during this meeting that INEOS took the decision to shut Grangemouth for good.

Jim remembers delivering the news: 'I said that's it, we're closing it. But I had everything crossed, everything. It was my view that the union would collapse and would come running back. But, if it didn't, then we were going to have to deal with it.' It wasn't an easy call to make – 800 people in the petrochemicals complex would be out of a job immediately, and many thousands more would be affected from the supplier base. Jim and Calum disagreed on tactics. Calum was keen to negotiate further with the unions, but Jim was adamant that this would be futile. 'We would have got to exactly the same place we got to in strike number one because we are dealing with Stevie Deans and Mark Lyon. So that's why we pulled the trigger.' The truth was that closing Grangemouth would have come at a much higher cost to INEOS than most people, even internally, realised. 'It would have come at a very high price,' said Jim. 'But the alternative was to run on, making ever bigger losses, with a union that was totally mismanaged.'

Lawyers Robert Stern and Charles Cameron were aware of

the ramifications and held a meeting at Slaughter and May with Jim, John, Andy, Tom and general counsel Jonny Ginns to go through their options. 'We were never bluffing because we were ready to start the closure process,' said Jim. The group had all bases covered in case their gamble didn't pay off – the same day as the discussions were going on at Slaughter and May, John was in a different room briefing Deloitte to go in as the insolvency practitioner.

When the news was broken to the senior management team in Grangemouth, a deathly silence fell over the room. It was a huge blow to the directors who had fought so hard to keep the site going but, ultimately, 'they were so fed up of being pissed around by these appalling people,' remembers Jim. As the news cascaded through the staff, Milne recalls how traumatic it was: 'The emotion was just horrendous. There were people breaking down.' But there was worse to come. An all-staff meeting followed, held in the works canteen. Calum had the unenviable job of standing in front of the thousand people who had gathered in the room, which was packed to the rafters, and justifying the decision to close. Already the audience knew it wasn't going to be good news but, when it dropped, first silence, then chaos, ensued. Milne remembers: 'There were people screaming. There were people swearing and crying. The vast majority began blaming the union. They had trusted Unite, and now they had lost everything.'

Calum told the gathered crowd about Unite's behaviour: 'I said that Unite had been going to our suppliers and telling them not to give us credit, they had been going to Jim Ratcliffe's home village and abusing him in public, they had gone to Declan Sealy's house and intimidated his wife and family.' The majority of people in the room seemed oblivious to the true battle being waged in the background and were horrified by Unite's actions. There was anger all round, and plenty of it. In what seemed like an instant, the gathered workforce turned against the people they had formerly trusted with their livelihoods. Cries of 'Look what you've done!' were audible above the racket. The union had promised to look after them, but had, in fact, ultimately lost them their jobs. A group of technicians who were part of the collective walked out with their heads down as staff hurled abuse at them. Morale and unity had by now fully broken down.

INEOS didn't come out of the announcement well either, and Calum became the object of immeasurable pent-up frustration. Calum's manner, usually commanding and charismatic, tripped up when a misplaced smile had him branded as callous. 'At one point someone asked me something totally outrageous, and I smiled and said that's a stupid question,' he claimed, but 'it was totally taken out of context. It certainly wasn't a smiling occasion as you can imagine.' As the exiting staff passed swarms of press waiting eagerly outside, a frustrated respondent claimed Calum had looked smug on delivering the verdict – and, sure enough, the next day the CEO was branded a 'smiling assassin'. The seven-day rollercoaster that followed was played out in the eyes of the national and international media.

Ultimately, the media's influence was key to carrying INEOS through the storm that shook Grangemouth. While Jim and his business partners were ensconced in Slaughter and May's offices in London, a media battle raged outside, covering the unprecedented turn of events. At the height of the strike, Jim's public profile grew to the point where his became a recognised household name, and spokesman Tom Crotty became a familiar face on the BBC and other news channels. A false allegation made in Parliament that Jim had left the country mid-strike to holiday on his yacht caused no end of controversy, with plenty of the media keen to paint Jim as a billionaire bully who was out to trample over the unions. The majority, however, made INEOS's case to the public, and helped to forge the path forward. The overarching media view was that the company's loss of £10 million a month wasn't sustainable, and the offer of a reduced but still very decent pension was a fair one. There was also a growing unease that Unite's tactics were going far beyond what was acceptable, and a growing realisation that INEOS was taking on a force that had become an undeniable bully. The privilege the unions had held in decades past appeared to be abused, and was now waning.

Back in Grangemouth, the tension was reaching fever pitch. People were so angry it looked as though a fight could break out any second, and management grew concerned for people's safety. Frustration was soon replaced with fear, however, as the prospect of being unemployed started to sink in. Clusters of worried people began to gather together at various points on site. For many of the employees at Grangemouth, this had been their one and only job, and they had never even considered what would happen if they had to leave. Gordon Milne, operations director, remembers people coming to him for help, asking: 'What do I do now?' Milne told them to go and write a CV. 'They were upset for themselves to a degree, but mainly they were upset about how wrong it all was.'

Fortunately, the turmoil was short-lived. The extraordinary happened just twenty minutes after Calum had delivered the public closure announcement, when Unite called Ian Fyfe to say they wanted to retract their decision. Recognising they had made a colossal mistake, they agreed to accept all of the survival plan's terms and conditions. Grangemouth's directors were clearly stunned. Initially, Ian, Calum and the other directors thought the union's sudden U-turn might be too little too late. They agreed to relay the message back, but the closure story was already leading the *Ten O'clock News*, and was on the front page of every major paper in Britain. For its part, INEOS's board demanded that the union send them a written confirmation of their position, including agreement to all of the new terms and conditions outlined in the survival plan, which was sent on to Jim. The team had to move fast.

Jim, Andy and John were astonished by the turn of events. The three of them sat down and discussed the possibilities of now keeping the site open. Fundamentally, they had never wanted to shut it down – it would have been much easier for everyone to keep Grangemouth going. With the business's fate wholly uncertain, however, the trio would need to be realistic about the measures required to effect a worthwhile turnaround. The requirements notched up as they rolled up their sleeves for the final fight. Jim told Calum that he would now consider reopening the site only if they could get a supportive contribution from BP, which benefited substantially from the Grangemouth site staying open, as well as a contribution from the government. 'It wasn't enough just the union collapsing,' said Jim. 'We had to make sure Grangemouth had a future, otherwise we were going to shut it down. We had loads of other stuff in INEOS to get on with, and this had been a pain in the arse for eight years.'

'We told BP we have to commit to spending £200 million on an import terminal for shale gas,' Jim recalls. 'The only way we were going to go back into this bloody mess called Grangemouth ever again was if they made a contribution, and the government made a contribution.' The following day, Jim received a letter from the government confirming a loan guarantee of £237 million to support Grangemouth's next development, while BP eventually agreed to provide a further significant contribution in the form of a discount worth $150 million on advance sales of BP gas over the next three years. It was quite the radical turnaround, and testament to the critical importance of the site.

A mass email was sent to all staff, inviting them to a meeting the following morning in exactly the same room where they had gathered just days before. No one had a clue what was unfolding, and a U-turn had seemed inconceivable. Calum MacLean was, in the moment, too excited to hold his silence until the scheduled 9 a.m. announcement time, and spilled the news early, feeling 'totally overwhelmed'. Gordon Milne claims he still feels emotional now, thinking back to that day: 'When Calum said that the business was going to carry on, the roars that went up...' Some people were ecstatic. Others were in complete shock and disbelief. It wasn't just relief – the news came as a lifeline for employees concerned about paying their mortgages and providing for their families. In contrast with the real threat of losing everything, the austerity measures imposed on employees now seemed a welcome alternative, and the reactions caught by the media this time around were in complete contrast to the days before.

Exigencies meant, however, that there was no time for euphoria. The plant had been shut for days and money was still spilling away. Resuming site operations as soon as safely possible was critical. Equally important was a workforce emotionally fit to reopen the equipment, a high-risk endeavour even in calm circumstances. The same team that had methodically closed down the plant days before set about cautiously bringing it back to capacity, and, although the ensuing weeks were particularly tough on the whole workforce, a new feeling of commitment to survival started to fill the space left by militant unionist sentiment.

As well as restoring order after the turmoil of the previous few weeks, the management team quickly had to start introducing the new financial measures that would be needed to help the plant survive and secure new investment. Milne recalls how fraught it was: 'Some of the collective decided it was best to leave – they realised that they had nearly destroyed the livelihoods of ten thousand people and weren't exactly popular. What was good was that it allowed a new generation of workers to come on board, breathing new life into the business. It really was the start of something new.' A sense of staff community survived, but union loyalty seemed to wane. The union's popularity in the wider community suffered, too, and Jim recalls a rumour in the weeks after the strike: 'I don't know if it is true, but word got round that Stevie Deans had been knocked out cold in a local pub in Grangemouth by one of the site's contractors, who had nearly lost his business because of him.'

Today, Unite has a much lower profile on the site. 'We negotiated a tough agreement with the union really – it completely neutralised them for three years,' explained Jim. 'So much so that there is not much interest in the union anymore at Grangemouth.' In April 2017, once the three-year agreement with Unite had expired, INEOS announced it was permanently ending its collective bargaining arrangements with the union, after a hair-splitting negotiation over pay rise percentage dragged on.

Though Unite still has a presence on site, INEOS will no longer negotiate with it. It was a tough stance, but allowed management finally to unblock stalled pay rises and bonus negotiations, overwhelmingly supported by the staff.

By 2018, INEOS had managed to deliver on its promise of substantial investment at Grangemouth and secured long-term, good-quality jobs for its 1,400 workers. It had spent hundreds of millions of pounds on the new ethane import terminal, built Europe's biggest ethane storage tank to receive the feedstock, and even erected a brand-new, state-of-the-art headquarters building. The old rusting infrastructure that scarred the site has been cleared away, and areas of the site set aside to promote the development of neighbouring businesses. Perhaps most importantly to its staff, INEOS gave two significant pay rises and a 17 per cent followed by a 27.5 per cent bonus to its workforce. The site has now overcome its biggest demons and is a transformed work environment. To quote John McNally, the current CEO: 'It's moved to the premier league of global petrochemical plants.' For the first time in a generation, Grangemouth is running at full capacity, driven by US shale gas ethane. It was perhaps the battle of Jim's career, but one very much worth winning for nearly everyone involved.

CHAPTER 9

NEW WORLD ENERGY

The saving grace of the Grangemouth site was gas; cheap, abundant ethane gas, brought over from the USA. Formerly drawing its feedstocks from dwindling reserves in the North Sea, the Grangemouth crackers were running at low capacity, losing money all the while, from the day the site was purchased from BP – even reaching a low of 50 per cent in 2013. One of the site's gas crackers was mothballed in 2008, deemed commercially unviable, while at the INEOS site near Rafnes, on the southern coast of Norway, complexities with overpriced inherited feedstock contracts threatened a similar fate for the ethane cracker there. This was not a unique phenomenon – by 2010, other major companies were feeling similar supply pain, and much of the European chemicals industry was facing what looked like a slow and painful decline. Alongside the North Sea's declining production volume, its oil and gas were uncompetitively expensive, while labour costs for extracting them remained some of the highest in the world. With the European chemical industry relying mainly on expensive naphtha or ethane for its manufacturing processes, the resource constraint, combined with wider

European economic stagnation (linked to currency problems and post-recession bruising), meant that very few plants were making healthy profits.

The industry was on the cusp of crisis, and there was no obvious solution. INEOS, which owned two of the four dedicated gas crackers in Europe, required a new plan to keep its plants viable. European gas prices had risen at a much higher rate than those in many other parts of the world, especially the US, which was, by this time, enjoying a natural gas renaissance. 'We needed something major to happen,' recalls John McNally, CEO of INEOS's Olefin and Polymer UK business, the major unit at Grangemouth. At Rafnes, further complexities strangled success, with supply contracts inherited when INEOS first acquired the assets providing insufficient ethane. Having acquired the Rafnes site from competitors Norsk Hydro and Borealis in another strategic joint venture, leading to full buyout over the course of 2006–07, INEOS remained deal-bound to purchase ethane and liquefied petroleum gas (LPG) feedstocks from Statoil in long-running, expensive contracts set to renew in 2015. The team needed to find an alternative to keep the site afloat. After making all possible cutbacks across Europe, INEOS started looking beyond the North Sea, and over to the New World, for potential alternative feedstock supply. 'If we couldn't come up with an answer, we would end up closing down many of our European assets, because they couldn't compete on the world scale,' recalls Jim.

Heading west for feedstock was, at this time, unprecedented, yet an extremely attractive concept. The US was witnessing a remarkable development. The discovery of vast, untouched reserves of shale gas and oil, and the development of a commercially viable way of extracting them, was transforming the country – and breathing new life into US industry. Shale was extremely beneficial to chemicals producers, as it provided not only a cheaper energy supply for manufacturing, but also cheaper feedstocks for an industry that relied on oil or natural gas as raw material. The first large quantities of shale gas were recovered from the Gulf area, where the US chemicals industry was based, and it had begun to experience a remarkable resurgence – INEOS's operations included – with sites very quickly tripling in profitability. Soon, two thirds of the company's overall profits were coming from the US, which comprised just one third of its assets – it was a worrying imbalance, but one with great promise.

When INEOS bought Innovene in 2005, the Grangemouth cracker came in the deal with another, even larger cracker at Chocolate Bayou near Houston, Texas. This was the biggest gas cracker in America. It had by no means been an intended prize in the BP package, merely an obligatory part of the deal – but it ended up transforming INEOS's fortunes in ways far beyond the founding team's imaginations. While oil remained relatively expensive, the shale revolution in America meant that crackers using gas had suddenly become hugely competitive, and the profitability of the Chocolate Bayou site leapt from $300 million per year to $1 billion per year by 2012. It was to change the course of the company's history on other shores, too.

Up until the 2008–09 crisis, Jim claims he had never even heard of shale, and the core team had never discussed it. 'Within just a few years we found shale had transformed one of our businesses. Profitability doesn't increase threefold overnight very often,' he said. It was shale gas, rather than oil, which held primary interest for the company, and they began to investigate its potential further. Its ascendance had been very recent, but its roots in energy extraction history ran deep (the first extraction patent was issued in Britain in 1694), and INEOS soon became part of the story.[4]

As recently as 2006, the US seemed to be on the verge of running out of energy. The country's own resources had been in decline since oil reached peak production in 1970, and oil and gas companies such as Shell, Exxon and Chevron had been forced to go global, drilling offshore in regions such as Africa, Asia and Brazil. Prices soared as the country, a phenomenal energy consumer, became dependent on foreign imports, while indigenous production stagnated. With the housing market collapse in 2007, and the ensuing financial crisis, the US economy was struggling. The shale revolution changed all that, almost overnight.

Technological advances revealed huge untapped reserves of oil and gas in the US, trapped in rock miles beneath the earth's surface, that could be accessed commercially. With that discovery, a booming, though not uncontroversial, industry was born, flourishing quickly across the States. Dubbed 'unconventional' extraction, it was a departure from the energy production norm. Traditional oil and gas fields (such as those in the North Sea) are usually found in 'reservoirs' or pools under impervious layers of rock, formed when their contents migrated from the underlying shale rock towards the earth's surface over millions of years. The reservoirs are drilled into vertically for extraction. The new shale oil reserves were found even deeper in the earth's surface in the base shale layer itself – often more than two miles down. They required more complex drilling to access, involving a horizontal approach along the shale layer, followed by the injection of high-pressure water to create microscopic fractures to release the oil or gas. Geologists had known for decades that there might be substantial energy reserves buried in this shale, trapped in billions of tiny pores and pockets of the dense black 'tombstone' rock, but nobody knew quite how much. The consensus was that it was just too 'tight', making the oil and gas too difficult and expensive to extract.

Since the American oil industry first began with the discovery of petroleum in Titusville, Pennsylvania in 1859, explorers have continuously experimented with new ways of drilling. As Gregory Zuckerman recounts in *The Frackers* (2003), in the 1940s, Standard Oil of Indiana (which later became Amoco) invented a new way to attack reserves inside tightly packed rock. This involved the use of jets of highly pressurised water that, when mixed with detergents and sand, was fired into the rock, separating its layers slightly so the gas and oil within could escape and be collected. The method was called hydraulic fracturing – or 'fracking' for short, and had an inauspicious start. Many of the big energy companies experimented with the method, finding it expensive and disappointing in yield, and quickly abandoned the approach. Nonetheless, a number of maverick energy extraction explorers across the US continued to test the fracking process, determined to access unimagined quantities of oil and gas from deep below US soil. After years of trial and error, these 'wildcats', as they were dubbed by the industry, succeeded, and tipped the balance of the world energy equation in the process.

George Mitchell is often referred to as the 'father of fracking'. He spent decades researching different techniques of extracting gas from shale formations, investing millions of dollars in the process. Often told he was wasting his time and money, he carried on regardless, and his gamble paid off in 1997 when Nick

Steinsberger, one of his engineers, discovered a winning methodology – the so-called 'slick water' frack. This method used a more watery solution with a small addition of chemicals and sand to prise the shale pores open, and produced spectacular results at Mitchell Energy's extensive prospecting fields in Texas. Over the next few years, it gradually became clear that fracking could be scaled up commercially, and other operators began to follow suit. Over the course of the next decade, many existing and new players in the industry began to utilise this form of fracking, paving the way for a spectacular gas boom in North America.

While engineers like Steinsberger were perfecting drilling techniques, geologists were busy re-examining previous estimates of the amount of oil and gas that might be buried in shale. It turned out that even official studies had hugely understated the true scale of reserves. Even George Mitchell's own company had underestimated their reserves in the Barnett shale, until the outspoken geologist Kent Bowker arrived from Chevron and encouraged the company to relook at the numbers. Shale fields such as the Barnett in Texas, the Bakken in North Dakota and, most impressively, the Marcellus in Pennsylvania and West Virginia are now believed to contain billions of barrels of oil and tens of trillions of cubic feet of natural gas. The Marcellus in particular appears extraordinary in scale. As Zuckerman noted, one geologist at Penn State University suggested it holds as much as 50 trillion cubic feet of natural gas, making it one of the largest energy fields in the world, with enough reserve to supply the demands of a country the size of the UK for more than twenty years. By the end of 2010, the shale revolution had produced such a wealth of supply that the price of natural gas in America had tumbled from $12 per thousand cubic feet to $3, producing cheap energy for households and industries across the country. Globally, while oil and gas prices have generally followed each other closely, US production became so abundant that gas prices dislocated from oil for the first time in recent history.

The shale boom provided an historical juncture for Jim and the INEOS founders, too. Their flourishing US plants didn't just keep the company afloat, but provided a potential lifeline for their floundering European operations. It was clear that the future of the Grangemouth and Rafnes chemical plants depended on securing globally competitive feedstock, and the US had it in abundance. Leen Heemskerk, the deft Dutch CFO of INEOS O&P Europe at the time, pushed forward an enterprising suggestion discussed by his team – 'What if we could ship shale gas from the USA to Europe?' It was, of course, unprecedented, and almost inconceivable in the scale of its complexity. Many in the industry dismissed it, saying the company was mad even to consider such a high-risk scheme. But, as a principle, it made sense, and INEOS was ultimately determined to find a way.

In September 2011, the project was given the green light. David Thompson, procurement and supply chain director for the O&P North business, who would become project manager of the multi-billion-dollar endeavour, reflects that 'our [industry] colleagues in the States didn't think for a second that we would ever be able to pull this off'. Andy Bell, an INEOS feedstocks supply manager based in Houston, grasped the project's potential straight away, however, and became a key negotiator working under David. 'It was a challenge, but all I saw was huge potential in the northeast US market. No one had done this before,' he recalls. Fernando Mota, another INEOS feedstocks executive based in Switzerland, was put in charge of European operations, and both men reported to Thompson for the next five years. There were a lot of unknowns, but the team were motivated by the opportunity to disrupt things for the better.

When it came to sourcing their gas, there was one shale field that quickly gripped the company's attention. It was the Marcellus, a 104,000-square-mile formation west of New York and Washington, DC, which stretches across Pennsylvania into West Virginia. By 2012, it had become clear that this was the biggest shale play in America. Operators had been extracting increasingly large volumes of gas there using the new hydraulic fracturing method – and showed no signs of slowing. The natural gas recovered, however, contained high volumes of ethane, unsuitable for selling directly into the US grid as the calorific value would be too high. The developing industry was urgently in need of an outlet for this ethane, and soon INEOS entered into fruitful collaboration with US shale producers, midstream companies (working to separate the gas fractions) and gas transportation services in an attempt to find a mutually beneficial solution. The proposition – to bring US shale ethane to Europe via a 'virtual pipeline' – was to become known as the Mariner East project, an undertaking that would bring together a huge swathe of partners and complex processes, and take the entire industry by surprise. 'It was no secret, but the concept seemed to have been discounted by most others in the industry,' recalls Thompson. 'Maybe to them the whole idea was inconceivable – aligning so many partners. Maybe the idea could have been considered mad. But not to us!'

In 2012, INEOS took the initiative and negotiated a major partnership with Range Resources, the leading Marcellus operator, as well as several smaller producers, for supply of their gas.

The team also struck a deal with Sunoco Logistics, an American oil and gas refining and pipeline firm, to bring the gas from the Marcellus to the port of Marcus Hook in Pennsylvania – a distance of more than 300 miles. The agreements would be valid for fifteen years, and provide the INEOS Olefins and Polymers business with significant supply for the future. At the time of the Sunoco deal in September 2012, Marcus Hook was an almost derelict oil refinery on the banks of the Delaware River on America's east coast. The refining industry in Pennsylvania, as in many other regions of America, was in peril, and the site was about to be shut down after 100 years. INEOS's deal reversed its fortunes and would breathe new life back into the moribund site and its surrounding community. The deal aimed at transporting approximately 70,000 barrels per day of ethane and propane, via a huge new pipeline, from a shale gas processing centre in Pennsylvania to the Marcus Hook terminal. At Marcus Hook, the ethane would be cooled in huge tanks down to liquid state at -90°C, ready to be transported to Europe.

The next issue, then, was shipment. Ethane gas had never been shipped on this intended scale before, and INEOS would need to build a new fleet of boats to extend the virtual pipeline across the Atlantic and provision its European plants. 'People said it couldn't be done,' recalls Jim. But the fact that ships large enough and specialised enough to make such a journey did not exist simply meant that INEOS would have to build them. When the time came to progress this element of the project, Thompson was made head of a newly created division, INEOS Trading and Shipping, which was ultimately to oversee the whole supply chain for ethane, naphtha and LPG to the company's European crackers. His first task: to commission these boats. With a chemistry background, he knew little about shipping, but INEOS knew plenty of people who did. For years, the company had been using ships to transport ethylene, the highly volatile product produced by cracking ethane, to and between its manufacturing sites. Thompson began the process of approaching prospective shipping companies to collaborate on the project. Most declined, but one, a Danish company called Evergas, spotted an opportunity. 'They shared a similar innovative mentality to us,' said Thompson.

With a shipbuilder on board, INEOS now had to work out the most efficient route to deliver the gas to Europe. The ethane ships would dock directly at Rafnes, which was both geographically and strategically simpler to organise than delivery to Grangemouth. The latter site required both a longer route by sea and a few more months to resolve its pension and asset strategy issues, in the wake of the earlier strikes. After considering the possibility to land the liquefied gas at the Finnart oil terminal on the west coast of Scotland and pipe it on to Grangemouth, the company decided that the giant ships should ideally sail directly to the plant, approaching from the North Sea in the east, avoiding further earthworks. On landing at both sites, the new influx of feedstock supply would require construction of brand-new ethane storage tanks, too, and engineering company TGE was recruited to undertake these mammoth building projects, first at Rafnes then at Grangemouth.

The entire endeavour, including the pipeline and the 10–15-year gas supply contracts, would end up costing the company upwards of $13 billion – making it an investment on a scale to rival the Innovene deal. The only way INEOS could justify an investment of this size was the guarantee of a significant cost saving, 'futureproofed' against market fluctuations. At the time, ethane was trading at about 80 to 90 US cents a gallon – historically a very high price (this would later fall to about 25 cents a gallon). Most in the industry were sceptical that INEOS could buy the ethane, ship it to Europe, and still make a profit. The team had sensed, however, that if INEOS could somehow open up the US market, this could bring down the cost of European gas, too. Ultimately, pricing innovation was key to the deal's success and, to allay their partners' concerns about future price volatility, INEOS changed its pricing policy to exempt the contract from the Mont Belvieu Index, which sets the standards for many gas commodities. INEOS also sought to make best use of its new infrastructure by expanding US exports from ethane into propane and butane using the virtual pipeline, maximising the asset's potential.

A deal of such complexity, with so many different partners, was bound to be challenging to realise, and threw up an inevitable rollercoaster of stresses. Along the way, one potential partner, Williams, a leading US gas producer, withdrew from the supply agreement, but a replacement deal struck with Pennsylvania-based Consol Energy ended up providing an even better partner. There were additional, more predictable problems, such as delays in upgrading the Marcus Hook terminal, and major equipment needing to be replaced as the project unfurled. INEOS's own operations slowed proceedings too; a rather late technical problem occurred with the new Rafnes storage tank at the very end of the pipeline, when the country's harsh temperatures caused unanticipated damage requiring urgent repair. According to the INEOS team, however, the ultimate key to the deal's success was the formation of especially strong relationships with the companies in the supply chain: 'Our approach was to create long-term deals,' recalls Andy Currie.

There were other, albeit cosmetic, problems which arose around the launch of the ships, too. Initially, Evergas required the vessels to be painted green, the company's brand colour, with its logo on the funnels. It also wanted to include the letters 'JS' on the bows, which stood for Jaccar Shipping, the Evergas parent company. INEOS, of course, wanted its virtual pipeline to bear its own company colours, and dogged negotiation ensued. The Danish firm conceded the INEOS blue and logo, but insisted on keeping its own mark on the chimney and 'JS' alongside the ships' names. When the stubborn 'JS' was making relations fraught, INEOS decided that JS would simply have to stand for 'Jim's Ship', and proceedings once again edged forward. Success, as they say, is a matter of perspective.

The ships were built in yards at Qidong, near Shanghai, and Danyang, further upstream on the Yangtze, and were painted with symbolic dragons to reflect their Chinese heritage. The whiskers of each dragon outlined the numbers 5 and 2, representing '52', the year of Jim's birth and the Chinese year of the dragon, and the vessels were dubbed the 'Dragon Ships'. The eight ships' names were, appropriately, decided by Jim. Every moniker had the prefix 'in' and represented a core INEOS value: *Intrepid*, *Insight*, *Ingenuity*, *Inspiration*, *Innovation*, *Intuition*, *Invention* and *Independence*. It took some time with the dictionary, though, to mine the English language for positive 'in's, and, as Thompson recalls, added plenty of humour to proceedings.

While construction of the land-based infrastructure for the mammoth project rolled on somewhat modestly, the launching and landing of the Dragon Ships were highly celebrated and symbol-laden occasions. The first two ethane carriers were unveiled at Qidong in July 2015 amidst an elaborate party on the water's edge, attended by media, film crews and politicians. Maritime superstitions were duly observed – champagne bottles were broken against the boats and the vessels were christened by godmothers (Jim's partner Alessia and Andy's wife Dawn), who cut the tape and entered into lifelong obligations to send the crew Christmas cards. Thompson remembers it being an ecstatic day, if an uncomfortable one: 'It was sweltering hot, the film crew was mopping our brows between takes, and the boats' last-minute paintwork was still drying!'

The first ethane landings, however, held the greatest weight for the INEOS leaders, their project partners and the company's wider European operations. The INEOS *Intrepid* picked up its first load of transatlantic shale gas from Marcus Hook on 9 March 2016, and brought the virtual pipeline to life over a thirteen-day ocean crossing. It landed at Rafnes on the 22nd, greeted the following day by a huge crowd of project partners, local politicians and the many Norwegian engineers who had tirelessly collaborated with the project's US suppliers and partners to bring the gamble to life. The stakeholders on the site had committed to a significant start-up risk to make the virtual pipeline a reality, and were eventually rewarded significantly. Principally, the site was able to secure cheaper US ethane to displace its original overpriced contracts when these came up for renegotiation, maximising site capacity, which had been suppressed by higher pricing of the alternative LPG. Beyond this, the plant gained the negotiating power to purchase future alternative ethane and LPG supply at more competitive prices, and ultimately overhauled its capacity and profitability. David Thompson notes: 'If we had not had US ethane, we would have had to continue to pay a much higher price for Norwegian feedstock, and we would not have the optionality and financial benefit we now have today.'

Months later, when the ethane ships finally docked at Grangemouth, the wider industry and media saw the significance of the hard-won project. A Scottish reception event had been organised, and the INEOS *Insight* had been moored off Orkney for several days to await its grand entrance into Grangemouth. Carrying 27,500 cubic metres (970,000 cubic feet) of liquefied shale gas, the giant ship – covering the length of two football pitches – dominated the water as it passed under the iconic Forth bridges in the early morning of 28 September ahead of a crowd of waiting journalists. On board, a lone piper played the bagpipes, and the TV pictures were broadcast around the world. For the expectant media, however, this moment was the peak of the day: an emergency diversion due to winds reaching 100 kilometres per hour made the final docking unsafe until the following morning. This didn't dampen festivities at the Grangemouth site, though.

A wind-battered marquee stood on the dockside edge, filled with over 300 guests – including Grangemouth employees, the businesses' suppliers, local luminaries, Secretary of State for Scotland David Mundell, the shipping project partners and, of course, INEOS's founders. A band played, speeches and toasts were made, and a new era of Grangemouth prosperity was celebrated. After six years, the impossible had been made possible, and INEOS's virtual ethane pipeline was remaking the company's fortunes in Europe. The system gave INEOS's businesses new flexibility and control over their raw material supply, and almost overnight turned Grangemouth from a loss-making to a profitable plant, with its mothballed cracker coming back online and its new equipment ready to yield new production levels.

The benefits weren't only limited to INEOS; as Thompson notes: 'We've enabled a new era of feedstocks to gas plants in Europe, so when Shell and Exxon come knocking on our door asking for raw materials for their Scottish plants, we can supply them from our tank in Grangemouth.' Very soon, other competitors began to follow INEOS's lead, and new and more technically developed ethane ships continue to be commissioned. For Jim, it was a great feeling to have led the world and delivered such a huge project on time and within budget. 'I think INEOS is one of very few companies that could have done that,' he says proudly.

CHAPTER 10

BREAKING GROUND

The first Dragon Ship's momentous landing at Grangemouth in 2016 was a highly publicised and well-attended event – but some significant invitees were conspicuously absent. Nicola Sturgeon, the governing Scottish National Party leader, as well as her ministers, declined to attend the celebration, prompting a *Scottish Mail on Sunday* story headlined: 'Churlish Nicola and a petty game of power poker.' Controversy was, quite clearly, raging behind the scenes. The rebuke was not, perhaps, a mark of disapproval at INEOS's pioneering shipment of ethane gas to revive the Grangemouth site, which was the biggest industrial investment Scotland had seen for a decade, nor even a remonstration that this particular gas was the product of fracking. Rather, it was, more likely, a protest against INEOS's broader plans brewing in the background – plans to establish an indigenous shale industry in the UK. This project was potently political.

INEOS had brought fracked US shale gas to the UK to address the need not only for competitively priced feedstock for its plants, but perhaps more importantly, for competitively priced energy for its operations. By now proven leaders in the

UK manufacturing sector, the INEOS team's hard-won experience of turning chemical businesses around in a competitive global market gave them sharp awareness that the cost of energy in the UK, and in many nations in Europe, is too expensive – and a significant deterrent to manufacturing investment. For this traditionally fundamental sector to continue supporting the economy in so-called 'developed' nations, the cost of energy – a major expense for manufacturers – needs to be managed. For Jim, the answer was simple: to begin investing in domestic energy resources.

In the past twenty years, the UK has gone from being a net energy exporter to a substantial net importer. Reliance on imported energy is around 50 per cent, a circumstance not experienced since the 1970s, and a number significantly above import levels of neighbouring EU nations, such as Germany, Spain, France and Italy, which have worked harder to maintain domestic supplies. External reliance at this magnitude not only subjects the UK to international political uncertainties, but also drives up the cost of supply, with huge impact on both ordinary consumers and businesses. In the past ten years, according to one analysis, the real price of electricity for ordinary UK customers has risen 63 per cent, while real gas prices have soared by 115 per cent.[5] For UK industry users, the price of electricity is the highest in the top fifteen EU countries, and rose 40 per cent between 2010 and 2016 alone. Industry electricity costs on average 63 per cent more in the UK than in other EU nations, due in large part to new green taxes. Meanwhile, average gas prices for households across the EU are 2.5 times higher than in the US and Canada. Not surprisingly, this is an issue at the forefront of political debate.

There is little doubt that coal has become too 'dirty' to meet modern environmental standards, and coal-fired power stations are seeing out their final years. Nuclear power, of course, is carbon-free and will continue to be a significant energy source in the near and medium term, but the UK's own fleet of nuclear power stations is ageing and needs to be replaced. The government is encouraging, via guaranteed pricing, the investment of billions of pounds into renewables, such as wind and solar energy, though these sources are weather-dependent and cannot yet provide reliable energy. Moreover, they are years, perhaps decades, away from being able to meet a large nation's energy needs (UK electricity consumption from these sources has risen from 1 per cent to 9 per cent in the past twenty years, with research and investment continuing). The widespread international goal to bring renewables to dominance in the energy supply mix looks to be a way off and, while gas and nuclear provide 60 per cent of the UK's needs (excluding transport fuel such as petrol and diesel), many believe natural gas is the obvious bridge to a new energy economy.

INEOS backs this view, with Jim emphasising that, 'as a country, we are totally dependent today on gas and nuclear. There are no viable alternatives on any sensible time horizon.' He argues that, for international independence and domestic cost, developing a domestic gas supply should be a national priority. If we can stimulate the UK's economy by producing cheaper energy in the form of relatively clean natural gas, this would spark a renaissance in manufacturing. The gas in question, a gas the UK potentially has in abundance, is of course shale gas – the resource responsible for the current US energy boom. If shale gas can be extracted safely and with no damage to the environment or people's health, it will be a game changer. It is, at the moment, a game playing out under more public scrutiny than any other manufacturing sector activity, and a truly historic debate.

In the past decade, the issue of shale gas extraction has become polemical. Worldwide, though conventional oil and gas is becoming more difficult to extract on a commercial basis, an apparent abundance of shale gas lies largely untapped. A recent US Energy Information Administration report shows that potential shale gas resources across forty-six of the world's countries could total a staggering 7,576 trillion cubic feet (tcf) – while the UK consumes, comparatively, some 3 tcf of gas per year. Only four countries were, at the time of reporting, producing any gas from their reserves on a commercial scale – China (reported to have 1,115 tcf of shale gas), Argentina (801 tcf), the USA (622 tcf) and Canada (573 tcf). The US was far ahead of the rest of the world, accounting for 90 per cent of all shale oil and gas production.[6] In Europe, differences in public acceptability, population density, laws on mineral ownership rights and even geology meant that shale gas extraction was only at the exploration stage. Any bid to kickstart a UK shale revolution, even by a seasoned deal broker like Jim Ratcliffe, was bound to be challenging. Shale was not, however, a wholly new phenomenon.

Unknown to many, the history of shale exploration in the UK runs deep. In 1875, the first well to encounter shale gas was drilled by the Subwealden Exploration Company, a group of Victorian academics funded by private gentlemen and supplemented by the Royal Society, the Geological Society of London and the British Association for the Advancement of Science. The group drilled two wells into the crest of a small hill at Netherfield, in East Sussex, in a scientific bid to investigate the depth of the Palaeozoic rocks beneath the Weald; although the first well failed for mechanical reasons, the second reached 1,905 feet. Strange oscillations in the water level in the borehole were reported and, when a naked light was lowered into its depths, an explosion occurred, ending all further exploration. The team had struck gas. As Richard Selley, the historian of UK shale, noted, this was effectively the first discovery of shale gas by drilling in the UK. Subsequent drilling for water several years later found commercial quantities of gas in Heathfield, twelve kilometres to the west.[7] The significance of these accidental finds went unnoticed for more than a century, however, as attention focused on abundant conventional gas reserves offshore, or those more easily accessible on land.

It wasn't until the mid-1980s that academics at London's Imperial College began exploring the economic potential of gas from shale in the UK. Research published was at first ignored by scientific journals and the government. The British Geological Survey followed shortly afterward, delivering a report in the 1990s noting the potential for UK shale gas production, similarly falling on deaf ears.[8] Shale's first political breakthrough didn't come until 2003, when the Labour government under then Prime Minister Tony Blair repealed the Petroleum Revenue Act, exempting shale gas from the petroleum revenue tax. This gave explorers the green light, and early commercial investigation began.

Unbeknownst to the majority of the public, fracking has already taken place at numerous sites around the UK, and has been doing so for decades. More than 2,000 wells have been drilled onshore in the country during the past thirty years, and about 10 per cent of these have been hydraulically fractured to enhance recovery. As a 2012 report by the Royal Society and the Royal

Academy of Engineering observed, a combination of fracking and horizontal drilling allowed the development of Wytch Farm field in Dorset in 1979.[9] This field, discovered by British Gas in the 1970s, was later bought by BP and subsequently Perenco, and is Europe's largest onshore oil field, responsible for the majority of UK onshore production. Sited on the scenic Dorset coast in the midst of a number of environmentally sensitive areas, the field has 200 wells, extending horizontally out to sea beneath the Sandbanks estate off Bournemouth, one of the UK's most popular resorts. One of its wells held the world record at the time for horizontal drilling, reaching a lateral distance of 10.1 kilometres.[10] Similarly, in 1996, British Gas hydraulically fractured a well in the Elswick gas field in Lancashire, very close to Cuadrilla's now infamous Preese Hall well, and gas has been produced there ever since. These developments, of course, have been focused on conventional oil and gas rather than on shale reserves. But the potential to apply the methodology to shale layers remains.

With shale gas extraction taking off in America in the first years of this century, the UK government began to look more seriously into the resource's potential, while geologists began pointing to the tantalising possibility that the huge Marcellus shale field running north-east across Pennsylvania and West Virginia might actually extend out under the Atlantic, all the way to the Bowland Shale area across large swathes of northern England. In 2006, the government announced a round of new UK licences for onshore shale exploration, named the '13th Onshore Round', with several companies expressing an interest in applying for shale gas acreage, especially in the Bowland area and in the Sussex Weald. When the results of the round were allocated in 2008, a total of ninety-seven petroleum exploration and development licences (PEDLs) were awarded to companies looking to explore for oil and gas in the UK, including shale gas. Subsequently, the 14th Onshore Round licensed more land for exploration – and exploration is, at this early stage, the focus. While these blocks of land have been identified by geologists as sitting on potential reserves of gas, commercially profitable extraction at scale is still in question.

Since its first investigations into importing US shale led to a deeper awareness of the industry, INEOS has invested in several of the most promising British PEDLs and purchased others from fellow shale pioneers. A new INEOS Upstream business was established in 2014, with Grangemouth senior Gary Haywood at the helm, and, by 2017, the company held thirty-six licences to explore shale deposits, covering more than 1.2 million acres of land. 'Jim's an entrepreneurial character,' said Gary, 'and he could see that the UK's licensing regime meant that if you could prove you were technically and commercially capable, you would be granted licences for little or no upfront cost.' The cost is, of course, incurred in the exploration and production development of these licences. At present, the company is, by acreage, the largest, and certainly one of the most publicised, shale explorers in the UK.

Despite the company's lack of experience in the field, its sheer size and resources gave it a real advantage over the smaller UK onshore companies that were less financially able, though INEOS was quick to acknowledge the need to bring in technical expertise. Drilling and geology experts were hired, and the desire to draw on the experience of industry veterans from the US, where fracking had taken place successfully, was prioritised.

The Upstream team explored the concept of a strategic partnership with a US shale company but, after several failed attempts, it became clear that the credible US partners were just too busy. 'There's such a lot of opportunity in the US, and the general view was that they would be giving up a guaranteed win there for a potential benefit here, so they weren't convinced it was worth the risk,' explained Gary. Instead, the Upstream business decided to hire in independent consultants, and the industry's best.

It was relatively easy to identify who INEOS wanted to work with – Dan Steward, Nick Stensinberger and Kent Bowker. Dan, Nick and Kent were three of the key members of the Mitchell Energy team, whose story was told in Gregory Zuckerman's book *The Frackers*, a popular history of the shale industry in the US. Dan was the team leader, was trusted by George Mitchell, and had accepted the challenge from Mitchell to develop the vast Barnett field in Texas. Kent Bowker was an outspoken and highly rated geologist from Chevron, who had done significant technical work on shale geology, and believed that the shale resource in the Barnett was significantly underestimated. Nick Steinsberger was the veteran petroleum engineer who had developed the original commercial 'slick water' hydraulic fracturing method at Mitchell Energy. Together, these three had been the driving force behind the unlocking of the Barnett shale, the first such demonstration of the commercial potential of shale gas. They were true legends in the shale business.

Getting hold of them proved somewhat more problematic. The INEOS shale operations director, Tom Pickering, would not give up, though. He managed to get the mobile phone number of Nick Steinsberger (by means that would make the CIA proud) and commenced a relentless effort to contact Nick. After many voicemails, perseverance won the day, and eventually Nick agreed to meet with the INEOS team. Nick and his cohort are approached regularly for consulting services and have declined many opportunities – but the INEOS project sounded different. His interest piqued, he agreed to meet the team in Houston.

The INEOS team's initial US visit proved to be the beginning of a strong collaborative partnership. The first meeting took place in a rather edgy Houston café, because the team's budget hotel didn't serve breakfast. 'We were a bit concerned that we might blow it,' recalls Gary. However, the quirky café proved to be a perfect venue for this first meeting. Nick was impressed by the INEOS team's honest and down-to-earth approach, and left with a positive view of the opportunity. Next, Gary and Tom met with Dan Steward, Kent Bowker and Dan's wife, Gilda. Over a nice bottle of Malbec in Houston's Pappadeaux restaurant, the relationship was cemented. The fracking pioneers were quickly dubbed 'The Legends', and were formally contracted into the UK project team to advise on exploration and extraction. The Legends were unconventional operators, succeeding because they had gone against the industry grain, and were drawn by INEOS's innovative approach and its desire to break new ground in a frontier shale resource in the UK. 'If we had been a traditional oil company type, I don't think they would have taken to us,' said Haywood. 'But I think they quite liked that we were a bit different, and very keen.'

Early trips to the US showed Jim and the Upstream team how a successful shale industry could come to look. Sites in the Appalachian area in Pennsylvania, parts of Oklahoma and the Fort Worth sites in Texas demonstrated shale operations successfully embedded in local communities and existing productively alongside everyday life. This was the result of many years of teething issues and, accordingly, Jim spelled out the ground rules for INEOS's UK shale project. If the company was going to invest hundreds of millions of pounds in shale gas, he did not want to be repeating any of the errors already experienced in America. Jim was also adamant that they use the best available technology, and at US costs: 'Everything in Britain costs more than in America. I wouldn't approve anything until they could prove all the work – the seismic, drilling, etc. – would be at the same cost.'

The US experts were quickly becoming aware, however, of how different the shale development project would be in the UK – the regulatory and licensing framework as the first hurdle was many degrees more complex. The UK system for acquiring mineral rights like shale is vastly different from that in the US, because UK mineral rights are owned by the state (the Crown) rather than by individual landowners, as is the case in the US. The right to explore and drill shale in the UK is granted every few years in government licensing 'rounds', which offer rights to prospective blocks of land, each 100 square kilometres in size. In contrast, individual leases in the US are agreed directly between landowners and the oil and gas company. Hence, the US system is far more flexible and nimble than the UK system. On the other hand, the UK system provides a route to gaining large areas of prospective licences at very low cost, which is perhaps a more suitable route to encourage the exploration of a frontier resource.

The hurdles to gaining approval for exploration and production activity on these leases were also vastly different in scale and complexity between the US and the UK. The US has a longer and more concentrated history of successful onshore development of unconventional oil and gas resources alongside communities and landowners, and the approval processes have been tried, tested and streamlined. Regulation in the US does vary among the states, and is not as stringent as UK legislation in some regions, but more similar in others. Even in the states with more stringent regulation, the drilling application and permit awarding process is usually complete within a few months, and can, in simple cases, happen in just a week.

The UK proved to be far more problematic in terms of gaining approvals for drilling wells. The INEOS team quickly found that their primary barriers were the views of local landowners and communities, with local authorities regularly refusing planning permission for applications to test or drill for shale gas. The UK context was vastly different – the industry was unfamiliar, and there had been some bad publicity (and a subsequent moratorium on hydraulic fracturing) from the tremors arising from the Preece Hall well (more on that later). The environmental lobby also created a successful scare campaign – which took some genuine but manageable concerns, and used exaggeration, untruths and out-of-context arguments to create a climate of fear in local communities. Fear led to resistance to any activity, regardless of the measures taken to ensure acceptable community impact. This resulted in delays and legal standoffs, including between local and national government. Despite literally years of INEOS sharing public education campaigns and building trust with local communities in town hall consultations, the social licence to operate has been very slow to win.

The exploration acreage now licensed to INEOS in the UK covers a total of five different geological basins, though it is unlikely that all these areas will prove commercial. Based on data so far collected, the company's best guess is that just one in four will turn out to be commercially viable. The process of getting to the starting line for production is expensive and complex, and INEOS have so far committed to investing £400 million for exploration alone. The scoping process is a long one – with seismic data and test drilling taking months even in the most favourable political conditions – and requiring an INEOS investment of an additional £20 million in related equipment. Once seismic data has created a picture of the size and continuity of a shale layer, exploratory drilling takes core samples to test the quality of the rock, and, if deemed appropriate, a suitable well is hydraulically fractured (or 'fracked') to test the gas flow. While it can cost millions of pounds to sink and fracture a full-scale shale well, the rock may not even yield enough gas, though wins are big when they come. With a successful shale field, a single development of a few hundred wells could produce hundreds of millions of pounds' worth of gas. A successful shale gas development in the UK could provide a significant proportion of the nation's gas demand, which is a very attractive opportunity given that the UK has a huge gas deficit and relies upon European gas to balance demand – while Europe relies upon gas from countries such as Russia.

Getting to the point of production has thus proved an impossible task for INEOS so far. As a political issue, the UK's energy future is divided along party lines. The topic of shale extraction is contentious, discouraged by green groups demanding faster moves towards renewables, and protested by many individuals fearing both the process itself and the impact on house pricing if such an industry grew in their vicinity. The tangle of information and misinformation available about the extraction process, interwoven with local and national politics, has led the

Green, Labour, Liberal Democrat and Scottish National parties to oppose the technology in the UK, swayed by voter opinion. Only the Conservatives have largely backed the process in the name of energy security, independence and business growth, and debate rages on.

It was against an initial fertile backdrop of support from the Conservative government that INEOS began to commit significant investment into shale, and a new energy industry appeared to beckon on the horizon. In January 2014, former Prime Minister David Cameron declared that his government was 'going all out for shale', launching a series of financial incentives for local communities with the intention of pushing the agenda rapidly forward. The political rationale behind this support had been the desire to boost economic growth, especially in the former industrial heartlands where whole communities have been left behind. It was declared that local councils would be allowed to keep all of the business taxes raised from fracking sites, generating potentially millions of pounds of localised funds, while onshore prospecting firms were told that their tax charges on early profits would be halved to encourage investment in domestic oil and gas, including shale. In 2015, the then Chancellor of the Exchequer, George Osborne, set out plans for a Shale Wealth Fund, seeded with up to 10 per cent of tax revenues from shale gas production in England, to ensure that the communities hosting shale sites directly felt the benefit of the industry's development. With those revenues ostensibly providing up to £1 billion in total funding over twenty-five years, individual communities were promised as much as £10 million depending on local shale productivity, with individual households also receiving up to £10,000 each. Industry body UK Onshore Oil and Gas proposed an even more generous package, promising £100,000 in community benefits at the exploration stage per well site, with a further 1 per cent of revenues to be paid out once wells are flowing.

Despite these proposals, INEOS was keen to learn from the US model, where landowners are paid a direct royalty from shale gas production based upon the well production revenue, and not only a profit component. This paradigm created a much more aligned partnership between the community and the gas producer. It seemed to INEOS that sharing the value of the resource was fair to the UK as owner, and ensured host communities also directly benefited. Not all the UK players were initially keen on this proposal, but INEOS was confident it was the right approach, and promised to set aside 6 per cent of future shale gas revenues for local communities hosting development (with 3–4 per cent going to landowners hosting the wells, and another 2–3 per cent being shared with the local community). In due course, an industry-common structure was agreed with the other UK operators that accommodated this form of community benefit.

Despite such commitments, the concept of fracking in the UK has been met with popular resistance. As alluded to earlier, the reasons for this are several, complex and interwoven. Some are grounded in fact, others grounded in political leanings, others grounded in fear that flies in the face of scientific findings. It is undeniably an emotive issue and, though by now exploration licences are widely distributed among prospectors poised to begin drilling, the social licence required to progress the shale agenda seems still a long way from being secured. To that end, the major British oil companies such as BP and Royal Dutch Shell have so far stayed away from tapping into UK shale reserves. They likely fear that the environmental controversy stirred by anti-fracking groups is not worth the trouble, at least until shale gas extraction is shown to be commercially attractive. Smaller UK firms, such as Cuadrilla Resources and IGas Energy, along with the French utility giant GDF Suez, have been securing licences alongside INEOS, though the company has largely felt it is leading the charge alone.

The question of the likely economic benefits of shale is ultimately uncertain, and needs to be verified by exploration. The most credible reports have suggested fracking could create 64,000 new jobs, and claim the supply chain for the new industry alone is estimated to bring in $33 billion (£24.3 billion) in investment in England over the next twenty years, though it all ultimately depends on how much gas lies beneath large parts of the countryside, and how much of this can be commercially extracted. Scientists from the British Geological Survey have estimated the total volume of gas in the Bowland-Hodder shale in northern England, the largest known basin, at some 1,300 trillion cubic feet – more than 400 years' worth of gas at current consumption rates. If just 10 per cent could be recovered, the UK would be energy-independent for fifty years. Without investigation, however, this remarkable potential remains an unknown.

Some of the widespread public fear around fracking is logical. In the early days of shale exploration in the United States, industry regulation was often poor, experimentation by maverick prospectors became common, and mistakes such as gas leaks and drilling into water tables created widespread concern in local communities. Scare stories and extremist messaging pushed forth by activists has, by now, been far outweighed by a growing volume of scientific evidence for a safe and reliable method of extracting shale oil and gas, though the former still has the dominant share of voice. This rhetoric-laden climate of fear has attached itself to the very term 'fracking', itself an unfortunate and aggressive-sounding word, and has not been easy to assuage. Despite stricter regulation bringing extraction to account in the States, and reassurance from the UK government that the tightest regulatory standards would frame the practice here, the young industry perhaps requires the weight of years of more positive experience to turn the tide of public opinion.

So far in the UK, the development of indigenous shale has been blighted by successive unfortunate trip-ups. The first of these was a true blunder: a drilling-induced earth tremor caused by early pioneer Cuadrilla Resources, which had embarked on a three-well exploration programme in 2010. In April 2011, it hydraulically fractured its Preese Hall-1 vertical well near Blackpool, but misinterpreted geological data and caused a series of minor earth tremors to the magnitude of 2.3 on the Richter scale. Despite being the smallest quake possible to sense above ground, this understandably raised alarm and, following renewed fracturing of the same well the next month, when further, smaller earthquakes occurred to the magnitude of 1.5 on the scale, the UK government announced an immediate shutdown of all exploratory fracking for the next eighteen months. Ministers ordered an independent report to determine what caused the earthquakes, and to develop appropriate regulations to mitigate the chances of any further incidents. While the effect of the tremors was not significant enough to cause damage to humans or to any buildings nearby, public anxiety was stoked and damage to the nascent industry was significant.

Further research continued, and the government's chief scientific adviser, Sir John Beddington, commissioned an independent

Review of Hydraulic Fracking from the Royal Society and the Royal Academy of Engineering, published in June 2012.[11] This found no meaningful evidence that environmental or health damage would be caused by the fracking process if carried out sensitively and within a tightly managed framework. In response, ministers lifted the shale fracking moratorium that December, and began to reiterate that they 'actively' supported the launch of a shale industry in the UK. The following March, the Office of Unconventional Gas and Oil was established within the Department of Energy and Climate Change to promote the 'safe, responsible and environmentally sound' recovery of unconventional energy sources, such as shale gas and coal bed methane. Michael Fallon, then energy minister, told the UK shale 'Making it Happen' conference in July that year that the government was being 'extremely active creating the right framework to accelerate shale gas development in a responsible way'. Prime Minister David Cameron stated that shale had 'a huge potential' for keeping energy bills down, and George Osborne introduced the new tax regime, which he described as 'the most generous for shale in the world'.

Such talk didn't translate into tangible progress, however, and locally and in the devolved regions, this enthusiasm was not widely felt. Although it had been identified as a prime shale area, Scotland was particularly reluctant to allow the industry to develop within its borders, and the issue became central to regional politics as the Scottish National and Scottish Labour parties adopted staunch anti-fracking stances to attract voters. Despite energy independence being critical to the SNP's *raison d'être* – Scottish national independence – the ruling party has taken a hard line on the matter, first imposing a moratorium on shale exploration back in 2015 and, by October 2017, extending this to an indefinite ban, which Paul Wheelhouse, minister for business and energy, claims was based on 'a cautious, evidence-led approach'.

His announcement came as a shock to the industry, and stirred further controversy. The Scottish government's respect for independent research was fundamentally questioned, because the weight of formal scientific reporting had by now fallen largely in favour of the potential to create a robust and safe fracking industry, discrediting many scaremongering reports of health or environmental risks. Ultimately, the Scottish decision seems to have come down to political pressure – the need to appease a majority of voters who had declared themselves against fracking and in favour of renewable energy as the primary means of reducing greenhouse gas emissions. Despite the lack of ready renewable technology to realise this agenda in the near future, the debate has now seemingly settled on this axis – the ideological versus the evidence-based and pragmatic.

INEOS is not, however, the only party looking to draw attention to the contradictions surrounding fuel provision in the UK, and to bring public awareness to the wider nuances of the issue. Responding to the Scottish ban on fracking, the GMB union, which represents over 630,000 industry employees and is one of the Labour Party's three largest affiliates, stated that the SNP's fracking ban decision was 'dishonest and hypocritical'. Gary Smith, GMB Scotland secretary, pointed out that the SNP was still happy to allow shale gas to be imported by INEOS: 'Scotland is importing a huge amount of shale gas from [President] Trump's America. If the government wants to be consistent, it will now ban shale gas imports, threatening a huge number of job losses. The government has failed to explain where the two million households in Scotland using gas to heat their homes will get gas in the future.' Ken Cronin, chief executive of UK Onshore Oil and Gas, called attention to the fact that, in the past twenty years, thirty wells had been drilled to produce gas within Scotland's Central Belt area, without any impact on the natural environment or public health, while a continual dependence on imports will create environmental issues of its own. INEOS Upstream also pointed out, when trying to discuss the matter with senior Labour Party politicians in Scotland, that the current Scottish Labour Party holds double standards with regard to the North Sea: 'We cannot understand why Scottish Labour are actively encouraging investment in the North Sea when their reason for banning fracking is that fossil fuels should stay in the ground. If that's the case, they should be against the North Sea, too.'

Despite these setbacks, INEOS has continued navigating the complex political climate in England in a bid to develop a shale success story. By early 2018, it began seismic testing in a handful of its licence areas, but is still facing a wall of polarised public opinion and protest, significantly hampering its efforts. Fuelled by media attention, the anti-shale protesters are still winning the war of public sentiment and, in the world of energy generation, emotion dominates fact. Even our existing national dependence on gas is not truly examined with scrutiny, because our imports from other nations and our extraction from offshore areas keep the realities of energy generation out of sight. A deep-rooted public view that oil and gas companies are innately malevolent is one major barrier to success and, as Upstream's Gary Haywood has noted, the balance of trust between the charitable and commercial interests here is often far from even: 'People think that the Greenpeaces of this world don't have an axe to grind, that they are just trying to do the right thing by the climate. Whereas we are portrayed as being interested in money and that's it.' INEOS unquestionably has a commercial motivation for its position, but also firmly believes in the importance of shale for the UK's political and economic future. 'We believe shale gas could revolutionise UK manufacturing,' explains Jim, and the INEOS team have made known their hope to see indigenous UK shale gas one day powering the refinery and gas crackers at Grangemouth, and the INEOS chlorine plant in Runcorn. 'Establishing a properly supervised UK shale gas business makes economic and environmental sense for the country,' insists Haywood.

Though it was anti-shale activists whom INEOS initially expected to be the major stumbling block to success, in practice the planning process itself has threatened the death knell for the project. Offering 6 per cent of its shale revenues as financial incentive to communities local to proposed wells, INEOS became the industry leader in attempting to collaborate with everyday stakeholders, with Jim arguing that 'it's what they do in the USA and we think it is right to do it here. It democratises the shale gas revolution.' Such empowerment has not been locally embraced, however, with most planning departments recommending approval for shale development efforts, only to have planning committees turn applications down. The overextended timescales and extended fights to win permission for exploratory science look to stifle the industry in its tracks, as processes taking less than five weeks in the US are being stretched to as much as five years in the UK. With government support failing at the local level, the voices of communities craving investment still mute, and an abundance of uncertainty and misinformation still resounding, INEOS knows well when to walk away. For the core team, the shale project is a matter of pragmatism and, ultimately, one of principle – driving forward the values of entrepreneurial thinking, scientific rigour, economic sense and community empowerment towards a tangible energy future. After twenty years of industrious growth, however, Jim, John and Andy are shrewd in their talent for weighing opportunity cost.

CHAPTER 11

AGAINST THE CURRENT

The senior INEOS team, while overseeing an ever-growing and shifting business portfolio, have not been best suited to slow and singular focus. Since the earliest days of INEOS's founding, the enterprising trio have been constantly analysing, deal-brokering and seeking opportunities to broaden their company's scope and profitability, often with several options in play at one time. After recovering from the fallout of the global recession, opportunity-scoping resumed in earnest, and the company's US shale gas successes weren't the only fast foray into the energy production sector. Besides the intention to invest in a potential UK shale industry, INEOS was looking to wade into more established upstream channels – the waters of the North Sea. In an era when the North Sea oil and gas industry had been pronounced in terminal decline, severe job losses battered the economy, and the major prospectors were looking to decommission or divest, INEOS sought to step in and do what it had come to do best – take ageing and unloved assets from the hands of larger players, vigorously reduce their costs, maximise their capacity and create great leaps in profitability. A better-known industry than the chemicals sector, North Sea energy production and its future was looked upon with scepticism by most commentators. The move seemed more than mysterious to many.

The North Sea, Britain's own slice of the Atlantic Ocean, covers thousands of square miles bordering the UK's eastern edge, extending to the west coast of Europe from Norway down past Germany, the Netherlands, Belgium and France. For centuries, the North Sea had given the country one of its most famous resources, providing livelihoods for thousands of fishermen at ports up and down Britain's east coast. But, by the early 1960s, the prospect of a brand-new mineral source much further beneath the water came to reshape Britain's future. For more than a century, Britain had boasted a small onshore oil and gas industry, but its output supplied just a fraction of the country's total energy needs. Two world wars had underscored the importance of sourcing politically reliable and abundant energy and, by the middle of the twentieth century, as mapping technology developed at pace, so did the earnest search for indigenous energy sources.

Geologists had long suspected that there might be large oil and gas reserves hidden deep below the vast North Sea and, in the 1960s, legislation was introduced to encourage companies to explore the area. In 1964, the UK Continental Shelf Act formally identified a huge tract of the North Sea as an area to which Britain now claimed exclusive mineral rights, and early explorations looked promising. In 1965, BP made the first commercial gas discovery in Britain's sector of the North Sea, the West Sole gas field off the coast of Easington in Yorkshire. In 1969, Norwegians discovered the Ekofisk field, the first commercial discovery of North Sea oil. Soon after, the US oil and gas giant Amoco revealed the discovery of the Montrose oil fields, 135 miles east of Aberdeen on Britain's continental shelf. Aberdeen would quickly become the UK's own 'Houston', hosting tens of thousands of new jobs in direct and indirect support services for companies extracting fuel resources.

Each major find was followed by another. In 1970, BP discovered the giant Forties oil field, 110 miles off the coast of Aberdeen. It became the largest oil field in the North Sea, covering 50 square miles with a depth of at least 7,000 feet. Then, a year later, Shell announced the discovery of the giant Brent field to the north-east of the Shetland Islands, one of the most significant oil and gas finds ever made (which went on to give its name to a major crude trading classification, now setting a price benchmark for oil sales worldwide). A wave of oil explorers from around the world descended on the continental shelf, creating tens of thousands of jobs and yielding a multi-billion-pound tax trove in their wake. Energy firms poured tens of billions of pounds into gigantic offshore rigs, hundreds of miles of subsea pipelines, storage facilities, refineries and other infrastructure. North Sea investment was further fuelled by the geopolitical 1973 OPEC (Organisation of Petroleum Exporting Countries) oil embargo, linked to the Israeli Yom Kippur War, which led to global shortages of crude oil and a quadrupling of oil prices. Offshore production became a compelling opportunity for many prospectors and, within just a couple of years, the network of offshore rigs in the North Sea began to yield a profusion of black gold.

Over the next fifteen years, the dramatic rise in North Sea oil and gas output transformed Britain from a net importer to a net exporter of energy. In 1999, annual production peaked at 398 million barrels. The Forties field alone was producing 500,000 barrels a day by 1979, and the North Sea boom was the economic high-water mark of Prime Minister Margaret Thatcher's administration in the 1980s. This new fuel rush had made Britain self-sufficient in energy, and tax revenues from the North Sea were upgrading the economy and improving living standards across the country. The boom was, however, short-lived. Global dynamics shifted yet again and, after the year 2000, North Sea oil and gas production declined rapidly, with Britain resuming its status as a net energy importer by 2004. It seemed the fields that held so much promise thirty years earlier were starting to run low, and oil majors such as Royal Dutch Shell and BP began to divert resources where supply was more abundant, where production and labour costs were lower and margins still robust. Areas such as the Gulf of Mexico, Kazakhstan and the African coast became the new hotspots.

This decline in North Sea oil and gas production, combined with a dramatic drop in the price of oil in the second half of 2014, quickly made many of the North Sea oil fields unprofitable for the extracting companies. As workers were steadily laid off, dozens of the gigantic offshore rigs were shut down, and eventually towed into ports for decommissioning. 'The assets appeared to be dying quickly in the hands of the oil majors,' recalls INEOS's Bill Reid, who would soon come to play a major role in the company's unpredicted upstream venture. Meanwhile, the US shale revolution and global drop in oil pricing had injected new life into the chemicals industry, with majors such as Dow and BASF as well as other global players making significant margins. Global demand for plastics was once again on the up, rising at a rate higher than GDP, and the share prices of many of the big chemicals companies were surging, making acquisition opportunities tougher. The cheaper cast-off chemical plants INEOS formerly sought out were now elusive, and it was no longer a buyer's market in that sector.

INEOS was also enjoying the boom, but was struggling for a suitable next move. Deeming most expansion opportunities within chemicals now to be overpriced, Jim and the INEOS team looked instead to take a strategic step sideways, and scope out the residual profitability of the apparently floundering North Sea. Having grown so close to the upstream sector in both geography and supply chain, it made business sense. After all, oil rigs were basically chemical plants on stilts in the sea, and Jim and the team knew that INEOS had the inbuilt capability to run such assets, whether onshore or not. The machinery and equipment required is almost the same in both sectors – pumps, pipes, valves and steelwork. The same disciplines are required to run the operations efficiently and safely. The same financial and management toolkit can improve reliability and costs and, moreover, there was plenty of scope to trim these key ingredients. In the heady days of the 1970s and '80s, as oil and gas gushed in huge quantities and profits were sky-high, the majors running the rigs weren't exactly focused on their fixed costs. In the oil price crash of 2014, however, the many large asset owners did not have the ready agility to reassess these costs, and ageing fields were starting to be put up for sale.

It seemed an ideal matrix of opportunity, following the tried-and-tested INEOS process of acquisition and turnaround, though this time at the top of the supply chain. When Jim assembled a team of trusted senior colleagues to work on the new upstream project in a Swiss coffee shop meeting in November 2014, it was no secret that the team was inexperienced in the sector. Bill Reid, who was by then heading up INEOS's lean mergers and acquisitions department, admits: 'I knew nothing about oil and gas. We unashamedly called ourselves enthusiastic amateurs.' By 2015, North Sea oil and gas was being added to the shale portfolio managed within the recently formed INEOS Upstream company. INEOS's bank backers needed convincing, of course, and John Reece and the team again had to work hard to persuade their financiers that the firm was capable of mastering this new domain and running the assets profitably. With an oil refinery at Grangemouth on the western side of the North Sea, and the Rafnes petrochemicals facility in Norway, to the east of the energy basin, the business had perfectly placed infrastructure to capture the best of the resource, and, 'eventually, they understood that we are good operators capable of reducing costs and breathing new life into such unloved assets,' said Reid.

With financial backing to proceed, serious scoping soon began, and the company instigated talks with major players BP and Shell. The first opportunity that really caught Jim's eye, however, was linked to the lesser-known German oil and gas producer DEA (Deutsche Erdoel AG). The Hamburg-based operator was looking to sell all of its UK assets, comprising twelve North Sea oil and gas fields, along with their platforms, infrastructure and highly skilled teams, and had been recently acquired by LetterOne, an investment firm owned by Russian billionaire Mikhail Fridman. Among the twelve fields were two heavyweights: the Breagh field located in the southern North Sea, 65 kilometres off the coast of Middlesbrough, and the Clipper South even further south and 100 kilometres off Lincolnshire. Between them, they provided enough gas to warm one in ten British homes – and it seemed the Russian Fridman's acquisition of this promising package was in debate.

Due to the geopolitical disputes of the time, as Western powers threatened economic sanctions on Russian interests in response to the 2014 invasion of Ukraine, Fridman's move was obstructed. Though the LetterOne deal went through in March that year, before the UK government could intervene, the company was within months instructed to dispose of its new UK acquisition in order to avoid a conflict of economic interest. It was an uncanny window of opportunity for a UK company to make a bid, especially since Lord Browne, the former BP chief who had approved INEOS's Innovene deal, was by now on the board of LetterOne Group. INEOS's general counsel Jonny Ginns contacted Browne and kicked off negotiations towards a sale. Jim and Lord Browne did the deal directly this time and, by October 2015, INEOS had acquired DEA's UK assets for a still-undisclosed sum. The deal comprised 70 per cent of the Breagh field and a 50 per cent interest in Clipper South, with INEOS also inheriting 110 staff in the German organisation's UK subsidiary and fifty operations contractors. The new company was based in London, trading under the name of INEOS Breagh, and came to sit alongside INEOS Shale under the umbrella of the Upstream business branch. INEOS was now a key new player in oil and gas.

Norwegian senior manager Geir Tuft, an INEOS employee since 2008, had been working in Grangemouth as a business director, and was asked to head up INEOS Breagh as CEO. 'The beauty of the DEA acquisition was that it came with a complete organisation which we inherited,' he said. It was a steep learning curve, however, as Tuft and his transferring INEOS team were all new to the sector, while fluctuating gas prices including a sudden gas price drop on completion of the deal quickly challenged the new business's profitability. The first priority here, as with all past acquisitions, was a forensic focus on fixed-cost reduction, stripping the business back to run as lean and efficiently as possible. 'We created value by driving down our own costs,' said Tuft. As with many of INEOS's acquisitions, there was a clash of corporate cultures which became immediately apparent when the turnaround toolkit was deployed, and DEA's hierarchical and bureaucratic approach to business was completely at odds with INEOS's more agile and accountable style. Once Tuft took over, he embarked on a series of major changes, starting with internal spending – 'These guys were allowed to spend a lot of money without even asking,' he recalls. Tuft took away senior management's corporate credit cards and enforced new rules whereby only directors could spend money, and even then no more than €10,000 at once. Every purchase above that figure required Tuft's personal approval. Not surprisingly, this caused some early disquiet.

Tuft explained the attitude clash: 'If you stay in chemicals for ten or fifteen years, you are always going to feel poor at some point, because it's cyclical and your margins slim down. In contrast, people who work in oil and gas tend to have grown up in an environment where the sky's the limit, and it creates a bit of a culture where cost doesn't matter.' At INEOS, the ethos governing spending was universally encouraged to be: 'Would I spend this money if it were my own?', with personal expenses largely needing to be shouldered by employees and reclaimed retrospectively. It certainly worked. After a year of applying this tightening to Breagh, the business's costs had fallen by a third. Despite widespread reports of North Sea decline in the media, the business was already thriving, and making a significant €100-million-a-year contribution to the INEOS Group's profits.

Two years on, in 2017, the company was already working on its second major North Sea acquisition. Jim and the team had always been interested in acquiring the Forties Pipeline System (FPS), the UK's largest oil and gas pipeline network, which fed into the Grangemouth site. The 235-mile underground complex connects eighty-five North Sea oil and gas sites to the UK mainland, and provides 80 per cent of Scotland's fuel and 40 per cent of the UK's oil – more than 450,000 oil barrels and 3,500 tonnes of raw gas a day. FPS as an asset package included the offshore gathering system from the Unity Platform, the pipeline both at sea and onshore, and the BP Kinneil terminal at Grangemouth. Kinneil stabilises the crude and separates the associated gas into feedstock for industrial use, major quantities of which are delivered to the Grangemouth cracker to make chemicals, or exported via tankers to be sold in the open market. The stabilised crude is either exported (via the Dalmeny terminal on the Firth of Forth) or fed into the Grangemouth refinery, which in turn delivers petrol and diesel to service stations across Scotland and the north of England. As a strategic asset, this was in the premier league of upstream acquisitions.

BP first built the pipeline network after its historic discovery of the Forties field in 1970, and had connected it to its Grangemouth crude oil refinery, later sold to INEOS in the Innovene deal. When negotiating in 2005, Jim wanted the FPS to be included in the package because together, the two parts form a vital strategic asset, but BP had resisted then and continued to for more than a decade. 'Unfortunately, we didn't see eye to eye with BP on what were the key value drivers of FPS,' said Tuft. BP insisted that the infrastructure was more valuable than INEOS's own evaluations. As the FPS business's major customer, however, with 20 per cent of the oil passing through the system going to feed the INEOS refinery, and the Grangemouth cracker taking all the gases that could not be exported from the site, 'the business relied heavily on us', said Tuft. This put INEOS in negotiating lead when sale became strategically necessary. After fifty years of ownership, as BP rationalised production and restructured some of its operations, the decision was eventually made to sell the FPS business – and INEOS was ready to bid.

In April 2017, the deal was finally struck. INEOS would pay up to $250 million for the whole business, including the pipeline network, the Kinneil terminal and plant, the nearby storage farm at Dalmeny and the unmanned Forties Unity platform. The price was $125 million in cash, combined with an earn-out agreement over seven years that would make up the remaining half. Some 300 people would transfer from BP to INEOS Upstream. When the deal was announced, Jim emphasised the benefit of this unified ownership, indicating that INEOS is now the only UK company with refinery and petrochemical assets directly integrated into the North Sea. 'We will now be able to produce greater efficiencies and help secure a competitive, long-term future for this important piece of UK oil and gas infrastructure,' he explained. Tuft is confident the purchase will improve the network's profitability: 'I think it will greatly benefit from the kind of focus that we can give it'; while Reid emphasised that 'we can make it more efficient just by focusing on reliability and costs. It's what INEOS does.'

The first months of integrating the pipeline, however, provided as much challenge as opportunity for the new INEOS FPS business. In early December 2017, just five weeks after the formalisation of the purchase, the pipeline had to be shut down. An

Actor Steve McQueen and model Kate Moss wearing iconic Belstaff jackets. INEOS bought the motorcycle fashion brand in 2017

Jim shaking hands with Professor Sir Andrew Likierman, Dean of the London Business School, after donating £25 million

Jim cutting the ribbon on the newly named Ratcliffe Building, a Grade II listed wing in the heart of the London Business School campus

INEOS teams up with Sir Ben Ainslie and the Royal Yacht Squadron to challenge for the 2021 America's Cup. INEOS is committed to spending £110 million – the biggest ever British America's Cup investment – to bring the cup back to the Britain for the first time since the competition was established in 1851

Jim backs Pride of Britain Award winner Elaine Wyllie and her Daily Mile campaign, which aims to get every primary school child running or jogging for fifteen minutes every day

Jim riding through the surf on the Atlantic coast, Namibia

In collaboration with the Strengur Angling Club, which provides the best quality fly-fishing in the world, Jim has initiated a series of investments to help protect the land, rivers and salmon in north-east Iceland

Observing rhino darting as part of a conservation project, Africa, 2017

RIGHT In 2012, Jim celebrated his sixtieth birthday by travelling 10,000km around Africa on a BMW F800 motorbike. After breaking his foot, he used a ski boot for the remainder of the adventure. Here Jim is joking with an 88-year-old bushman, known as The Doctor

BELOW Taking a well-earned rest from mountain biking and running 600km across the Namibian desert in 2016

INEOS's petrochemical and refinery site at Grangemouth, Scotland

internal inspection had previously shown a dent in the underground pipeline south of Aberdeen. Excavation of the site indicated the pipe had settled over the years and was resting on a granite rock. While removing the rock, a hairline crack appeared in the dent area, requiring immediate attention. The team fast learned that repairing a 36-inch-diameter pipe operating at 35 atmospheres pressure is not a simple task, requiring a pipeline shutdown and production suspension involving more than eighty oil and gas platforms. The interruption caused the wholesale gas price for same-day UK delivery to surge by nearly 30 per cent and, though an expert team managed to devise a repair plan to bring the pipe safely back into full service within twenty-one days, it was an unwelcome and very public learning curve for the new owners. Misfortune aside, however, the new FPS business sees as much opportunity as challenge in the maintenance and development of the asset, with Reid suggesting: 'We think we can link the FPS beyond its current footprint.' Though it would require major new investment, one option is to expand the pipeline to the west or east of Shetland, on to Norway, and beyond.

With the company's growing success in the North Sea, Jim and the Upstream team continued to scout further opportunities, and, alongside the BP Forties Pipeline deal, the company began brokering what was to be its largest acquisition since Innovene in 2005. In May 2017, INEOS purchased the entire exploration and production business of DONG Energy (Danish Oil and Natural Gas) in a $1.05 billion deal. This suddenly positioned it as the biggest privately held company operating in the North Sea, and one of the top ten oil and gas producers in the North Sea basin. It was a turning point that redefined INEOS as a chemicals and energy giant in equal measure, and epitomised its strategy of tacking against the business current to maximise pragmatic opportunities. The DONG E&P business was sold as the result of a bold move to divest from fossil fuels and focus on operations and investment in wind energy. It owned shares in some of the largest offshore oil and gas fields in the UK, Denmark and Norway, with potential resources estimated at 570 million barrels of oil equivalent. In 2016, it was producing on average 100,000 barrels of oil a day, and still represented a very promising opportunity for a savvy and efficient operator.

DONG CEO Henrik Poulsen had spent nearly three years trying to sell the business but, in a climate of North Sea pessimism, had not yet found a suitable buyer. Meeting Jim, however, the two energy bosses immediately saw eye to eye and, as Reid described: 'Jim's entrepreneurial spirit made the deal happen very quickly. He is a very personal deal maker.' When the deal went through in May 2017, INEOS acquired a mix of long-life operated and non-operated assets, with inherited expertise running the platforms. One of DONG's gas fields included part of the Ormen Lange, the second largest field in Norway and third biggest in Europe, and while DONG's share was bought by INEOS in the deal, it continues to be operated by Shell. Similarly, the Laggan-Tormore, a new project west of the Shetland Islands, remains operated by Total, the French oil giant. The deal also saw INEOS take control of oil production in the Siri field and a significant share of one of the largest oil and gas fields in Danish waters, Syd Arne, operated by Hess. Some 440 staff transferred from DONG to INEOS, taking the entire INEOS Upstream business headcount to over 1,000 employees. 'It increased the size of our Upstream business threefold,' said Tuft, 'and was a major step up for INEOS.'

For the future, the company sees 'attractive exploration potential' in the west-of-Shetlands area, as well as 'significant near-field exploration and appraisal opportunities' close to its newly acquired core fields in both Norway and Denmark. In total, the company now owns all or part of twenty-eight North Sea fields, and has a deepened and broadened understanding of the oil and gas sector far beyond its early forays two years ago. Against widespread gloom predicting the North Sea's impending demise, INEOS has not only stepped in as a major stakeholder, but made known its desire for continued growth. It has been to a great extent encouraged in this venture by government support, with changes in the tax regime (including a reduction in the petroleum revenue tax from 50 to 35 per cent announced by the Conservative-led coalition government in 2015), and is now recognised as a key force in reviving the North Sea's fortunes for the near future.

Since 2015, the company has spent over $2 billion expanding its Upstream business, and continues to scour the horizon for opportunities. Rumours circulate that it is now in discussions over a fourth energy acquisition, which could be even larger than the first three, while there is further speculation that the company is aiming to become the largest petrochemicals firm in the world, overtaking competitors BASF and DowDuPont, the newly merged mega chemical company. Reid is excited: 'Back in 1998, we certainly didn't expect to have grown to this scale in twenty years, so maybe global energy company is where we are headed. Those aren't Jim's words, but you can see it in his eyes.' Jim is more coy, however, admitting that he isn't primarily driven to be number one. 'We look at opportunities and invest as they come along,' he says. 'I can't tell you where oil and gas will be in five years' time, or shale. I just think at the moment the investments look sensible and we'll carry on. I have no reason to change strategy.'

What the new Upstream venture does mean, however, is that INEOS by now has a stable and predominant foothold in two major fields of industry. At twenty years old, with business breadth and profitability at an all-time high, the team's drive towards growth has brought the organisation to secure adulthood with plentiful profit to play with, and the leading team's appetite for pioneering risk still shows no sign of abating. Rather than seeking to retire, the driven owning trio appear to have resolved to usher in another new era of INEOS, bringing their now-heavyweight resources and proven acumen to areas of business which combine professional and personal passions. The chemicals and energy giant is branching out of the industrial shadows into even braver new worlds, it seems; worlds that capture broader public and media attention. INEOS's next steps are starting to look unpredictably intriguing.

CHAPTER 12

DRIVING FORWARD

Jim Ratcliffe has been fascinated by cars since childhood. On the day he passed his driving test, he took his father's Ford Corsair 2000 company car to Hull's Anlaby bypass with his brother Bob in the passenger seat. The two trialled his top speed and 0–60mph acceleration with his grandfather's stopwatch. Both brothers soon came to own identical first cars – white models of the venerable Volkswagen Beetle, with consecutive registrations WWH 315K and WWH 316K – which had been retired from their father's company's fleet. It was this which took Jim from Bolton to Worthing twice, to interview for his first pharmaceuticals job at Beecham. Later working at Courtaulds, he drove an unexciting but reliable Vauxhall Cavalier. His big break at Advent International was marked by a significant upgrade, to a BMW 5 Series.

After twenty years of INEOS success, Jim now owns a collection of practical, sentimental, classic and working vehicles, including a 1933 Alfa Romeo 8C, an unrestored 1955 Series I Land Rover, a 1966 red Ferrari 275GTB, and a 2015 limited edition Porsche 911R. He still drives for leisure – be it around racing tracks or across the African bush. Certainly, cars have always meant more to Jim than functionality or status; above all, they represent adventure. This became increasingly significant as he got older. In his early thirties he flirted with racing in a Caterham 7, the iconic amateur racing car of the 1970s, but as he raised his family and travelled more widely, his passion gravitated towards off-roading, often spending long stretches in Africa on expeditions and safaris in the Land Rover Defender.

The budding industrialist's passion for driving was increasingly accompanied by a keen interest in the car business, a market that had seen a complete overhaul since the 1970s when he first began to drive. From the end of the 1960s, the post-war economic boom stagnated and the following decade ushered in a long-running period of economic strife, beset by high inflation, rising levels of unemployment and frequent strikes. Manufacturing was hardest hit, and car factories became daily battlegrounds as workers turned against their bosses in bitter disputes. The British Leyland conglomerate, which incorporated much of the British-owned motor industry, was partly nationalised at crisis point in 1975 amidst an extended shuffle of mergers and divestments that tried to consolidate marques in decline. Despite this, by 1982, UK car production had fallen to a low of 888,000 vehicles and when British Leyland's later guise MG Rover Group went into administration in 2005, mass production by British-owned car manufacturers had officially ended.

Trade union relations clearly played a significant role in this fall, driving the UK's manufacturing fortunes along a very different trajectory to major rival Germany. Quality had reduced as bosses seemingly fought to control workers' attitudes and behaviour, and constant anti-management battles seemed to wage around issues of pay, pensions, tea breaks and holidays. In comparison, Germany had eventually managed to forge an industrial revolution following the Second World War, rebranding itself as a forward-thinking, hard-working nation, and was enjoying manufacturing success. Union relations were starkly different to those in the UK, with management and unions working collaboratively and putting 'works councils' in place to get through tougher times. Constructive bodies fought for increased investments and long-term security for workers, and negotiated effectively. In 1978, for every day that German manufacturers lost to industrial action, the UK lost ten. Jim believes to this day that one of the most significant distinguishers of the fortunes of the UK and German manufacturing sectors is this union relations barometer, convinced that, while German unions tend to focus on tomorrow, the British have been comparatively short-sighted. The success of the automotive sector had become the ultimate symbol of Germany's industrial revival, just as 'Red Robbo' and the British Leyland saga signalled the collapse of Britain's manufacturing industry. Today, Germany's total manufacturing sector is more than twice the size of Britain's, accounting for 23 per cent of GDP, compared with 9 per cent in the UK (figures from the World Bank).[12]

During the second half of the 1980s, the British automotive industry was boosted once more by the Conservative Thatcher government, when foreign car manufacturers, incentivised by improving industrial relations and government support, started to open production plants in the UK. In 1986, Nissan became the first Japanese car maker to set up a production facility in Sunderland. In the same year, Peugeot acquired Chrysler's European operations in the Midlands and, by 1994, Toyota had a site in Derby. It seemed, however, that the British marques had had their day, with drivers increasingly favouring German brands such as Mercedes, BMW and Audi. In the mid-'90s, Rover Group, the last volume British-owned car producer, was sold to German giant BMW; the symbolic end of an era. In 2000, the group was split up, with the Land Rover and Jaguar divisions sold to Ford. In 2008, the two brands were sold again, to Indian conglomerate Tata Motors, who merged them into one, now named Jaguar Land Rover.

Under Tata's ownership, Jaguar Land Rover has enjoyed great sales success, particularly with the Range Rover and Jaguar marques, well placed as it has been to take advantage of the growth of the 'sports utility vehicle' market. Alongside the Evoques, Range Rovers and F-Types, one model carried on unruffled – the much-loved Land Rover Defender – until Jaguar Land Rover announced in 2013 that it was discontinuing production to make space at its Solihull factory for another new model. The Defender is seen by many, including Jim, as the archetypal off-roader. It is a car with as much sentimental as practical appeal and, despite long-recognised challenges with reliability, it was held as an authentic lifestyle vehicle, and one of the greatest cars ever made. Jim himself is a true believer: 'If I am in Africa on safari where roads hardly exist, I want to be in a Defender, not a Toyota Land Cruiser' – even if he did need to keep a picnic basket in the back for when it inevitably broke down. Jaguar Land Rover blamed the move on new European laws regarding fuel emissions and safety, which the Defender would not be able to meet. It also acknowledged that a change in market direction, with the growing popularity of SUVs, meant producing Defenders was no longer sufficiently profitable.

The Defender model is steeped in history. The first of its kind, the Land Rover Series I was revealed in 1948 to a design by Maurice Wilks. Maurice was chief engineer for manufacturer Rover, and based his concept on the original American wartime Willys Jeep. Seeking to replace the working Jeep he used on his Warwickshire farm, the legend goes that he sketched an image of this new vehicle in the sand at Red Wharf Bay on Anglesey, while staying at his holiday cottage. He worked up the idea more formally and took it to Rover, which shortly after began producing the vehicle at its Solihull site, outside of Birmingham. Post-war shortages were a major driver of the manufacturing concept – the unavailability of steel necessitated the use of surplus aluminium, and the original Land Rover green paint was contributed by the aircraft industry. The Land Rover was built with a tough, box-section chassis and low gears, intended to be a practical, functional workhorse. It soon became the vehicle of choice for British farmers, and both its look and its usage have lingered to this day. It proved an instant hit with the general British public, too, with Rover selling 8,000 vehicles in the first year of production. Through the '50s and '60s, improvements were made to the car including wider wheels, enhanced petrol and diesel engines, and a twelve-seater version, with production volume peaking at 55,000 units in 1970.

Since its birth, the Series Land Rover (which didn't become the Defender until 1990) has grown to become a quintessential symbol of Britain and British values. Her Majesty the Queen received her first Land Rover after coming to the throne in 1952, and has been a devotee ever since. Legendary Prime Minister Sir Winston Churchill was given one as an eightieth birthday present. The Defender has also featured in several James Bond films (most recently in *Skyfall*), and, in military guise, has been a mainstay of British Forces for many years and millions of miles. What is so unusual about the vehicle is that it hasn't changed much since it was first designed in 1948. There have been several editions made, but the basic concept hasn't altered. The Defender was, and still is, hailed as an enduring piece of Britishness, in both its design and its engineering. Since its launch, two million have been manufactured, and, remarkably, the majority are still in use today. It has enjoyed international popularity, too, and been overwhelmingly coopted by a mass of urban drivers who, despite buying into the off-roading dream of the vehicle's capability, ultimately choose it for its style and timelessness as much as its workhorse credentials.

Following the 2013 announcement that Jaguar Land Rover was ceasing production of the Defender, demand went up by 20 per cent, with the firm's Solihull plant building 122 Heritage models a day in 2015. Jim was one of a small number to snap up one of the last models ever made – a special edition bright orange Land Rover Adventure, which would accompany his well-worn (but still functioning) original 1955 Series I Land Rover as a demonstration of the car's long lifespan and collectability. When the final Defender rolled off the assembly line at the Solihull site in January 2016, after sixty-seven years of production, generations of families that had worked on the car turned out alongside the national media for an emotional send-off. Jim didn't attend, but was watching from a distance with great interest. Meanwhile, he had been making plans of his own.

It was a casual Wednesday evening in the Grenadier pub near INEOS's London HQ in Knightsbridge when the concept of creating a follow-up to the deceased Defender first took root. Jim and a group of friends were lamenting the announcement of the car's demise when an innocent suggestion was raised. Jim was, by now, a very experienced and sufficiently wealthy manufacturer – could he not approach Jaguar Land Rover and discuss the possibility of reviving the Defender in some way? Failing that, could he create a spiritual successor to the vehicle under a new British marque? It was a conversation fuelled by a few casual pints, but quickly grew into a powerful preoccupation for Jim – and soon for John Reece and Andy Currie, too, who came to back the venture as an INEOS project.

The Grenadier pub itself, unbeknownst to the car-dreaming drinkers, was a very fitting place for such a conversation. Tucked away down Wilton Row near Old Barrack Yard, it had an esteemed (and supposedly haunted) heritage, originally serving as an officer's mess for the First Royal Regiment of Foot Guards from its original launch in 1720. It was supposedly frequented by King George IV, and when the First Royal Regiment defeated the French Grenadiers at the Battle of Waterloo in Belgium in 1815, they were renamed by Royal Proclamation as the 'First Grenadier Regiment of Foot Guards' – the only regiment in the British Army to be named for one of its battle honours, who lent the pub its name. The Grenadier became a licensed premises for public drinking in 1818, and has hosted many British legends, including, notably, the first ever long-distance expedition in a Land Rover. In 1955, the pub was the starting point for the historic 'Oxford and Cambridge Far Eastern Expedition', now known as the 'First Overland' expedition, which saw six Oxford and Cambridge university students drive from London to Singapore in two Land Rover Series I Station Wagons. The expedition was filmed and broadcast on the BBC, and backed by a young David Attenborough. Land Rover donated the vehicles as a road-test, as well as a publicity opportunity, and it was the very first time such a journey, which took six months and six days to complete, was made in any car. Setting off on 1 September 1955, the team arrived in Singapore on 6 March 1956, covering a gruelling total of 18,000 miles by their return and paving the way for decades of overland adventuring.

There was, then, no better place to begin planning a future descendant of these pioneering cars. As the conversation in the pub developed, the team became convinced there was now an emerging gap in the market for a newer and better 'classic' 4x4 off-roader to fill the space vacated by the outgoing model. The esteemed departing vehicle could certainly be improved, since Jim along with many others recognised its one major flaw: its reliability. A well-repeated saying in the off-roading community follows the line 'If you want to go into the outback, take a Land Rover. If you want to come back, take a [Toyota] Land Cruiser.' Jim and the team soon decided that if they could combine the classic British style and off-roading ethos of the original Land Rover with the world-renowned reliability of German-engineered vehicles, they would create something truly worthwhile. The potential to build on the formula of, and improve, a much-loved vehicle wasn't the sole appeal for Jim and the INEOS leaders, either. If they were able to build a new car in the UK, this could also help boost the country's flagging manufacturing sector.

The pace of productivity is undeniably fast at INEOS, and this pub scheming soon became an official company project. Initial talks with Jaguar Land Rover regarding collaboration on a next generation of the vehicle did not work out, and so in 2016, unperturbed, a new INEOS Automotive business was formed, combining a team of experts and off-road enthusiasts from around the world. A young senior manager, Dirk Heilmann, was put in charge of the new division as CEO. An experienced and long-term engineering and project manager, he had risen by 2015 to head up engineering and technology for one of INEOS's largest businesses in Cologne. Dirk had international work experience in the UK and the US, a first-hand knowledge of the German way of working and, critically, a passion for Defenders and off-roading. Chris Tane, the influential CEO leading the turnaround of INOVYN, was put on the board as chairman, bringing some hard-edged and driving-dispassionate business nous to the team. Tom Crotty, INEOS's director of corporate affairs, was elected to lead the early public communications on the project, by now dubbed 'Projekt Grenadier' to reflect its Anglo-Germanic DNA.

This dual nationality was central to the conception of the new vehicle and the team built around it. Design and heritage was to be proudly British, while the engineering was to draw on stereotypical – and proven – German reliability. By early 2018, the growing business had come to partner with MBtech, a former subsidiary of Mercedes-Benz, to manage the vehicle's engineering, and recruited some 200 engineers to be located near Stuttgart in Germany. Design was decidedly closer to home, however, with Jim going off-piste to elect friend and talented boat designer Toby Ecuyer to draw up the initial vehicle sketches. A protracted process of many months of design proposal, engineering alignment and design reiteration kicked off from the earliest days of the new business, with Jim having first-hand involvement in each fine detail of the vehicle's styling. Conventional contemporary vehicle designers, with their relentless bent towards curved-edged, homogeneous, SUV-type vehicles, did not make the cut, despite several rounds of consultations.

The ultimate vision for the vehicle, espoused by Jim and adopted by the team, was to bring to life a highly functioning triangle of characteristics: off-road ability, good looks and reliability. It is, however, a deceptively simple formula, and one which the original Land Rover couldn't solve – the Defender was a very good-looking, very capable off-roader that often broke down. When it came to design, Jim felt strongly that the new 4x4 should not be a 'posh, poncy, city car', but should remain at heart a rugged 'farmer's vehicle', appealing to urbanites only as a by-product of its performance credentials. It should be classless, and equipped to drive cross-country, pull a plough, lead a safari, clear a minefield, cross a motorway and drive up to Buckingham Palace. 'It should also be pretty much unbreakable, but easy to maintain in the field,' says Jim. 'We're looking at the engineering to give it what the Land Rover was missing.'

There are a broad number of improvements, intended to overcome some of the more obvious engineering flaws in the original Defender, that INEOS has committed to make. For example, its vulnerability to corrosion and ergonomics more suited to the slighter frames of the Second World War generation who were Land Rover's first customers. 'There's nowhere to put your elbows and not much leg room,' explains Jim, who at 6 feet 4 inches tall struggles to fit inside. 'It's a real testament to the Defender's character and the fact it's fantastic off-road that it thrived for sixty-seven years.' It has been a car widely forgiven for its faults by a passionate following of drivers.

The design process so far, following early talks with Jaguar Land Rover (JLR), has not been straightforward, with the company rightly proud of its heritage vehicle and fiercely protective of their commercial interests. It is a complex case, with

JLR openly admitting they are not ever going to reproduce the original design, but being nonetheless guarded about other companies attempting to follow in its tyre tracks. JLR announced their intention to launch an all-new vehicle under the Defender name in 2019, with a very modern look far removed from the original, though, after Jim's automotive project announcement, the company was quick to try to trademark certain features of the discontinued version.

With INEOS's design not due to be revealed until 2019, further details about its intended offering are also somewhat limited, as the team work to an extremely ambitious project deadline – planning to roll the first vehicle off the production line by 2021. What has been announced, however, is the intention to enter several different sales markets – certainly Europe and the US, where the Defender has not been sold since 1996 due to regulatory compliance issues. INEOS will also look to make a splash in the fast-growing Asian and Australian markets. This will require a high degree of adaptability to international regulations discrepancies, a factor needing to be built into the vehicle's engineering from the earliest project stages. Beyond this, perhaps the biggest question the young endeavour faces from the worldwide media is the growing issue of emissions reduction, with several mainstream manufacturers committing to cease production of diesel engines in the very near future to reduce environmental impact. A number of major car brands have already committed to produce predominantly hybrid vehicles to meet changing legislation targets, while others are investing heavily in all-electric technology with a view to imitating the likes of disruptors such as Tesla. INEOS is not clamouring to join their ranks yet.

For launch, INEOS Automotive plans to release a range of powertrains for the vehicle – petrol, diesel and hybrid – to suit different markets and uses. The team are typically pragmatic in approach, sharing that they will seek to adopt all-electric technology only when this is proven fit for off-roading in their various target regions worldwide – the vehicle must be reliable. While the net lifecycle resources consumed by electric vehicles are still higher than simple 4x4 combustion engines, and generation of electric power still sometimes relies on coal, INEOS will focus on building a responsible and enduring vehicle, with a lifespan longer than an average seven-year battery life. This should ultimately carry a reduced carbon footprint. It will also draw on INEOS's own materials expertise, to source and develop technical solutions to enhance fuel efficiency and performance. This project defines itself, as with other INEOS ventures, as a realistic bridge to future technologies.

Beyond design and engineering, arguably the greatest challenge for the new car company will be making a success of the manufacturing process – one completely different from INEOS's experience managing chemical plants, and equally complex. The initial intention to build 25,000 vehicles a year, at an affordable purchase price, is a bold one for a new player; such an output represents more than double that of long-standing British brands such as Aston Martin, McLaren, Bentley and Rolls-Royce. This will require heavy cost commitments upfront, and INEOS have announced the intention to invest £600 million in the project to kick off, with no patience to entertain losses on a 'vanity project'. The potential demand for such a vehicle is there, with JLR producing over 25,000 Defenders in the model's swansong year, though the newcomer's success will depend on its ability to build a desirable brand to fill this gap in the market left by the departing heavyweight.

To find or build a production facility capable of turning around this quantity of vehicles in such a short lead time is no simple task, and INEOS Automotive has spent its early months considering a range of manufacturing solutions. The team have not been shy about their desire to build the vehicle in the UK, nor about their admission that they would need some financial support from the government to make this a financially viable option. There are currently over 800,000 people employed in the UK car industry, and INEOS estimates that Projekt Grenadier could generate up to 10,000 additional jobs, with 1,000 in the production facility itself, and the rest in the supply chain. Potentially a very lucrative move for the government, Jim suggests that, with an investment of some £200–300 million, 'you would end up with 10,000 really good-quality, long-term manufacturing and support service jobs.' For Jim, John and Andy it comes down to the national attitude towards the manufacturing sector, which they see as clearly lagging behind others: 'It is what a government would do in every other country in Europe where they value manufacturing,' adds Jim.

To build in the UK would require negotiating more complex trade union relations than elsewhere, which INEOS is naturally wary of after years of struggle at Grangemouth. Beyond this, a UK workforce would also require a heavy upfront investment in skills, given, as Jim perceives it, the vast discrepancy in training between INEOS's facilities in the UK and elsewhere, largely due to a decline in quality apprenticeships in recent decades. 'The plumbers, the welders and the electricians are all better trained in Germany than they are in the UK, their attitude is more disciplined and there are more of them,' he notes. To turn this around will inevitably take time, and some well-coordinated government and industrial effort.

Apart from human resourcing, the creation of suitable production facilities on British soil, in areas with sufficient broader infrastructure and port access for materials and export, will likely mean building sites from scratch, increasing the cost, risk and timescale of the project. Early options being considered were green and brownfield sites on the UK's east coast, around Hull and Teesside, where there is easy port access to mainland Europe, and also south Wales, where existing car production infrastructure and proximity to the port of Bristol offer advantages. Ultimately, however, while Jim admits there is an element of romance to building the vehicle on British soil, he does not believe it has to be fully built here for the project to be a success. Many well-known brands nowadays split their production processes to improve viability in a competitive global market. At the end of the day, Jim concludes, this should be a discerning business venture: 'In an ideal world I would love to build it in the UK, but I have to believe that it is economically viable and that I can make it at the right quality.'

INEOS Automotive's alternative option is to take over an existing car-making facility in Europe, perhaps even with a ready-trained staff. After making the project announcement, the team were inundated with interest from European sites keen to produce the new 4x4, the two most appealing alternatives to the UK being Germany, with its well-established automotive infrastructure and workforce, and Scandinavia, with a couple of options offering existing capacity and workforce capability. Of course, every step away from a brand-new bespoke build limits the company's manufacturing options further, and the final potential route for INEOS, to begin production with an existing established automotive supplier, would carry both the least risk but also the least flexibility. At the time of writing, the INEOS Automotive team remain open to all options, because, as Jim has made clear, the numbers ultimately need to stack up: 'We wouldn't be doing it if we didn't think we could make money out of it.'

Both UK and European manufacturing options do, of course, raise the very public question of Brexit, and the impact the UK's impending departure from the European Union will have on the automotive industry on both sides of the new fence. In 2016, around 1.7 million cars rolled off production lines in the UK, marking a seventeen-year high. Brexit uncertainty may be secondary to concerns about diesel in the market decline since then, but it is a real concern for the industry. Many UK-based motor manufacturers and commentators fear the industry's resurgence could be put at risk by Britain's departure from the European Union. Automotive industry investment by the end of 2017 stood at £1.1 billion, down from £1.7 billion in 2016 and £2.5 billion in 2015. In a pre-Brexit referendum survey, some 80 per cent of the Society of Manufacturers and Traders (SMMT), whose membership ranges from giants such as JLR, Nissan and Toyota to smaller supply chain companies, declared their desire for the UK to stay in the EU. Jim, however, who has been open about his pro-Brexit stance, remains optimistic that there are advantages to be gained by leaving the EU, largely around increased legislative and bureaucratic freedoms, and he has faith that 'there will be a common-sense outcome to Brexit'. Indeed, the markets are likely to remain closely entwined, as 'big commercial organisations in countries such as Germany are not going to be cut off from such a big market – they will not allow politicians to get overly emotional about it'.

Regardless of design and manufacturing specifics, the unfolding project as a whole has been received with both great interest and great scrutiny from the automotive industry itself. Some analysts, warning of stiff competition within the already rather saturated 4x4 market, have questioned the wisdom of the move. 'People probably think we're crazy because we're not in the car industry,' admits Tom Crotty. David Bailey, professor of industry at Aston University, has suggested that 'there may be a small niche market for certain uses and for fans of extreme off-road driving, but there is already quite a lot of competition. It is not clear to me if the business case stacks up.' Others have questioned INEOS's ability to succeed in an industry where they have no experience, with sceptics warning that, just because INEOS has the financial power to try this, doesn't mean it is easy, and many other UK upstarts have failed in the past. Indeed, if INEOS manages to pull it off it will be a seriously bold feat. 'We're not doing this on some nostalgic dalliance,' says Jim. 'It is a manufacturing project, a business proposition, and a very interesting challenge.' Crotty argues that the project has been thoroughly assessed from a business perspective, as with any other INEOS venture. 'There's risk in everything you do, but we can manage that risk. We are manufacturers at heart, we have confidence in what we're doing, and we know we need to bring on board the highest quality people in the industry.' The ambition to create a spiritual successor to one of the UK's most famous cars is not necessarily the end of the line, either. According to Projekt Grenadier's chairman, Chris Tane: 'When we make this successful, we will take it further. There are no limits.'

When Projekt Grenadier was publicly launched to a media audience in the Grenadier in September 2017, Jim honoured one of the haunted pub's traditions by paying off the gambling debts of Cedric, the resident soldier ghost. He did so by tacking a new UK £5 note, made with INEOS-supplied polymer, onto the establishment's ceiling, watched by John, Andy, the entire new Automotive team and the gathered journalists. It was a comical moment, but also a more symbolic one – imbuing good luck to a game-changing new venture that, in that instant, united two decades of petrochemical success, a concern for British manufacturing, an appetite for risky opportunity and a lifelong personal passion. Jim and the INEOS team are heading off-road, and the expedition is now being followed closely by many.

CHAPTER 13

HORIZON

It is twenty years since Jim Ratcliffe sat down with his two sons at the family's New Forest home to pore over dictionaries and dream up the name INEOS. From a single site in Antwerp bought for £84 million and employing just 400 people, the company has grown exponentially since it was formed in May 1998. It is now a multinational giant, with 20,000 employees at over 100 sites in twenty-two countries across Europe, Asia and North America. The scale and speed of its expansion have been surprising. By 2018, the company comprised thirty-two separate business units (including joint ventures), eighteen of which had an annual turnover of €1 billion or more – substantial enterprises in their own right. The rise in INEOS's profitability has been similarly exceptional. Today profits are just shy of $7 billion. Whether or not its trend towards doubling EBITDA every few years can continue, the pattern and pace of the company's upwards growth is impressive. Indeed, INEOS's rise is unprecedented in British corporate history. While the likes of well-known giants Royal Dutch Shell, BP, HSBC, GlaxoSmithKline and Barclays can trace their origins back beyond one hundred years, no other

British company of this size has been grown from scratch during this century.

The fact that the company has been owned, grown and so tightly controlled by a trio of leaders for the duration of its existence is also unusual. The relentless growth and change within INEOS is perplexing to keep track of, though Jim and his partners John and Andy maintain a constant and burgeoning portfolio of expansion opportunities which they manage with real focus. The three northern grammar-school boys have a low public profile, but a large circle of family and friends, and have attracted direct, diligent and rounded employees to their team. The company culture they have created has managed to maintain a small-scale, tight-knit, 'start-up' feel despite the organisation's size, and it is the high level of personal responsibility, emphasis on sport and baseline of good humour which staff comment on most commonly. Jim in particular has been outspoken about the importance of challenge in working life, and it seems the trio have built an environment of empowerment for all employees.

Jim, John and Andy are self-professed friends as well as partners – perhaps both a saving grace and a necessity in light of the tumultuous journey INEOS has taken over the past two decades. It certainly hasn't been an easy ride. Many of the trio's biggest decisions, including several refinancing deals, the near-loss of the company and the near-closure of Grangemouth, required unwavering adherence to the team's shared principles and a very bold attitude to risk. None of the leaders claim to have held particular plans or ambitions to grow INEOS to its current scale, though their collective appetite for pushing the limits of the possible and committing to action is evident – exemplified by Jim's extra-curricular endurance and adventure quests. Grit has been defined by Jim in particular as a central INEOS value, and this has been manifest, especially in the darkest nights of the company. Several existential threats in the past years have been weathered with a solid dose of northern common sense, an unshakable faith in instinctive judgement and a clear eye on the next move.

After twenty years of building success in the core petrochemical domain, then expanding to become a major player in oil and gas supply, Jim and his partners reached retirement age with no interest in slowing things down. Indeed, the drive that put the INEOS owners at the forefront of British industry is not the kind that is easily assuaged by the slow life, and it was perhaps inevitable that a change would be better than a rest. The announcement of the Automotive project in 2016, underway to produce its first car by 2021, was followed in October 2017 by the unexpected announcement that the INEOS team had bought iconic British fashion brand Belstaff, with a view to reviving its fortunes. Established in 1924, the brand is best known for its waxed motorcycle jackets, worn by Lawrence of Arabia as well as Steve McQueen in *The Great Escape*, and its early aviator jackets adopted by the 1930s plane pioneers Amelia Earhart and Amy Johnson. David Beckham, legendary former star of Jim's favourite football team Manchester United, has even promoted the brand. Many commentators saw the move into fashion as 'off-centre' and unconventional, but others discerned a certain logic, interpreting this as being part of a strategy to expand INEOS's motoring operations. The company has not yet elaborated.

Alongside core business interests, the trio support and run a number of not-for-profit projects in line with their interests, with a particular focus on sport. In April 2018, they announced their backing of Olympic sailing legend Sir Ben Ainslie, providing £110 million to create INEOS Team UK in a bid to bring the America's Cup home to Britain for the first time in its 167-year history. INEOS also funds two successful charities, based in the UK but with international reach, to help young children grow up fitter and more active. Supported by John and Andy, Jim passionately believes in the importance for public health of getting young people moving, in the shadow of a growing obesity crisis – as well as advocating sport's wider power to transform quality of life. Jim and the team have for the past two years proudly funded the Daily Mile campaign, bringing it to international attention. Initially introduced in Scotland by primary school head Elaine Wyllie, the disarmingly simple concept of allowing teachers to take children outside to run around for fifteen minutes each day in all weathers, covering on average a mile, has had transformative outcomes for children and schools – enhancing mood, behaviour, academic performance and all-round wellbeing, as well as lifting children's base fitness. The public health promise of allowing children to be active for a guaranteed slice of every school day has been widely noticed, and as academic studies proving its positive impact are shared, local authorities, local governments and even national governments have come on board to promote the habit as educational policy. Already, over 3,000 primary schools around the world have adopted the Daily Mile.

With the same motivation, the GO Run For Fun Foundation, initially established with the assistance of Newcastle's well-known Great Run Company event team (founded by Brendan Foster), has for four years travelled between primary schools delivering free two-kilometre fun runs and fitness education. As well as touring annually throughout the UK, the concept has now been brought to schools within INEOS's neighbouring communities across the US and Europe. With almost 250,000 young participants to date, a plethora of sports star supporters and further growth planned, the team are committed to nudging children out of sedentary lifestyles through proving that fitness is fun and worthwhile. Meanwhile, in a very different context, Jim is also exploring plans to establish football academies in Africa, starting in Botswana and Namibia, to nurture local sporting talent and provide quality education.

Jim's love of the African continent, which he has explored by motorbike, on several athletic endurance trips and on countless safari visits, merges his passion for sport and for unspoiled wilderness – and recently a long-held interest in conservation has led to sustainable investment in Tanzania and Mozambique. The Selous and Ruaha national parks are two huge and under-recognised protected areas where wildlife numbers have fallen dramatically in recent years, caused by human encroachment and poaching. Jim is beginning to build camps and lodges to attract tourists to the regions, providing hundreds of jobs alongside. With an emphasis on engaging communities, the resorts seek to empower locals to protect the elephants, rhinos and lions being hunted out of existence, in both an ecologically and a financially sustainable way, bringing business success to broader benefit. Other sporting and conservation passions have combined for Jim in Iceland, where his more sedate interest in salmon-fishing led to him buying wild land to protect it from invasive development. In December 2016, he became one of Iceland's larger landowners when he bought a 300-square-kilometre estate in the salmon breeding grounds in the north-east of the island, committing to improve the prospects for the Atlantic salmon that breed in the six major rivers of the region. It is this pragmatic and measured approach to sustainability which informs the spectrum of INEOS projects, and has led to robust results for the business, too.

The company's current health is well celebrated, but stands against a backdrop of continued concern for the UK's manufacturing sector – a cause rallied by Jim and his partners as the company comes of age. A long-term decline in manufacturing, concerns around high energy prices and the uncertainties created by Britain's pending exit from the EU have combined to generate fear for the health of the industrial sector, one that Jim firmly believes is fundamental to the stability of any national economy the size of Britain. Like the very production of petrochemicals, oil and gas, such a preoccupation may be unfashionable, with industry often sitting on both the physical fringes of our communities and the fringes of our consciousness – but it is undeniably fundamental. As well as enabling us to better manage the production and consumption of our material goods, a healthy national manufacturing sector provides secure, high-quality jobs and investment to communities across the country, particularly in the north, which have suffered long-lasting decline.

In 1981 some 5,713,000 people worked in manufacturing in Britain, amounting to 22 per cent of the workforce. By 2017 that figure had fallen to 2,685,000 – just 8 per cent.[13] Manufacturing was once the backbone of the UK economy, but it has suffered a huge decline, even in INEOS's short lifespan. Today, while Germany's manufacturing has retained its 23 per cent share of that country's economy, UK manufacturing has collapsed. The reasons for this are multiple, such as uncompetitive energy costs, lack of technical skills, frequent confrontational rather than collaborative union relationships, and general government indifference to the sector compared with other countries. The results manifest themselves most prominently in parts of northern England, Wales and Scotland, exacerbating an economic north–south divide. The human effects of this shift have been marked, and the hollowing out of Britain's industrial heart has been correlated with job losses, incapacity benefits and social security needs. On the world stage, it looks inevitable that the UK will be punished for undervaluing its industrial base, with multinationals able to pick and choose where they want to invest their billions in an era of unprecedented globalisation. INEOS is proof that manufacturing, if done well, can create immense value, growth and plentiful high-quality jobs. At present, INEOS and British manufacturing are heading in opposite directions.

* * *

INEOS today celebrates its twentieth birthday, having enjoyed tremendous growth and change through its adolescence. It is intriguing to consider where these industrial 'alchemists' will take it over the next two decades, and indeed how the world might look by that time. In our globalised world of ever-quickening technological change, predicting the future is as impossible as ever, but there is perhaps one certainty in business: the organisations that are leaner, faster-moving and most flexible are likely to be fit to face it. INEOS looks set to remain dynamic, and now, having stepped into oil and gas, automotive and onto the fringes of fashion, invites us to question how the company will come to reshape itself in its adult years. Alongside their core interest in the health of British manufacturing, the INEOS leadership's concerns for childhood obesity and wildlife under threat are issues which will reshape the world over the next two decades, as the company matures. However, this eclectic organisation's energy holds promise for forging positive shifts in the causes it commits to, through its defining spirit of pragmatism and grit. Three northern grammar-school boys have certainly played their part in reshaping the petrochemicals industry already.

REFERENCES

1 Snow, C. P. 'The Two Cultures and the Scientific Revolution'. Rede Lecture, Senate House, University of Cambridge. 7 May 1959.

2 Wilson, Harold. 'White Heat' speech. Labour Party conference, Scarborough. 1 October 1963. In 'Labour's Plan for Science', reproduced by Nottspolitics.org. http://nottspolitics.org/wp-content/uploads/2013/06/Labours-Plan-for-science.pdf (accessed 15 April 2018).

3 Atkins, Peter. 'Where Would We Be without Chemistry?' *Chemistry International*. Vol. 3, No. 2 (2011). At www.iupac.org. https://www.iupac.org/publications/ci/2011/3302/1_atkins.html (accessed 15 April 2018).

4 Moody, Richard (20 April 2007). 'UK Oil and Gas Shales – Definitions and Distribution in Time and Space, History of On-Shore Hydrocarbon Use in the UK'. Weymouth: Geological Society of London.

5 OVO Energy Guides. 'Average electricity prices around the world: $/kWh'. OVO Energy. https://www.ovoenergy.com/guides/energy-guides/average-electricity-prices-kwh.html (accessed 15 April 2018).

6 US Energy Information Administration. 'World Shale Resource Assessments'. EIA.gov. https://www.eia.gov/analysis/studies/worldshalegas/ (accessed 15 April 2018).

7 Selley, Dick. 'Shale Gas – Blessing or Curse?' www.geolsoc.org.uk. https://www.geolsoc.org.uk/Geoscientist/Archive/May-2011/Shale-Gas-blessing-or-curse (accessed 15 April 2018).

8 Shelley, R. C. 'UK Shale Gas: The Story So Far'. *Marine and Petroleum Geology*. Vol. 31 (2012), p. 103. (Shelley cites Smith, N. J. P. 'Unconventional Hydrocarbons: Changing Exploration Strategies'. Earthwise 7, pp. 14–15.)

9 The Royal Society & The Royal Academy of Engineering. 'Shale Gas Extraction in the UK: A Review of Hydraulic Fracturing' (June 2012). royalsociety.org. https://royalsociety.org/~/media/policy/projects/shale-gas-extraction/2012-06-28-shale-gas.pdf (accessed 15 April 2018).

10 Knott, David. 'BP Completes Record Extended-reach Well'. *Oil and Gas Journal*. Vol. 96, Issue 3 (1997). www.ogj.com. https://www.ogj.com/articles/print/volume-96/issue-3/in-this-issue/drilling/bp-completes-record-extended-reach-well.html (accessed 15 April 2018).

11 The Royal Society & The Royal Academy of Engineering. 'Shale Gas Extraction in the UK: A Review of Hydraulic Fracturing', op. cit.

12 World Bank. 'Manufacturing, value added (% of GDP)'. Data.worldbank.org. https://data.worldbank.org/indicator/NV.IND.MANF.ZS (accessed 15 April 2018).

13 House of Commons Library. 'Manufacturing: Statistics and Policy'. Briefing Paper 01942, 2 January 2018. www.parliament.uk. http://researchbriefings.parliament.uk/ResearchBriefing/Summary/SN01942 (accessed 15 April 2018).

APPENDIX 1

THE BUSINESS STRUCTURE OF INEOS

INEOS

PETROCHEMICALS

- Olefins & Polymers Europe:
  - North
  - South
  - UK
  - Trading & Shipping
- Olefins & Polymers USA
- Oxide
- Oligomers
- Phenol
- Nitriles
- Enterprises
- Styrolution
- INOVYN

OIL & GAS

- O&G UK
- O&G Denmark
- O&G Norway
- Forties Pipeline System
- Shale

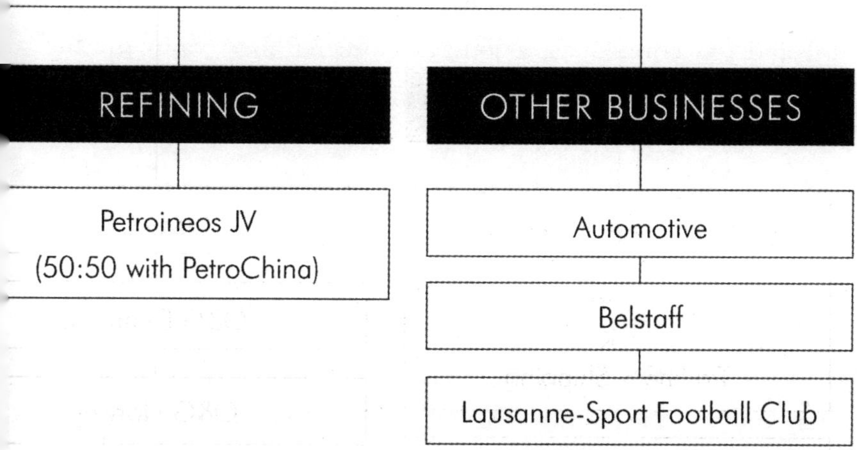
REFINING
Petroineos JV
(50:50 with PetroChina)
OTHER BUSINESSES
Automotive
Belstaff
Lausanne-Sport Football Club

Figure 1

When INEOS was formed in 1998, there was one major site near Antwerp, Belgium with sales of $200 million a year. It became the Oxide business. Twenty years later INEOS sales were $60 billion in 2017, with twelve petrochemicals companies, five oil and gas companies, a joint venture refining company (with PetroChina) and three other businesses.

INEOS has found the best way to manage such a large and wide-ranging portfolio is to break down activities into manageable chunks. The overall organisational structure by businesses is shown in Fig. 1. Each business has a chairman, a chief executive and a board, typically comprising a chief financial officer and directors for operations, business and procurement. A chairman is either Andy Currie from INEOS Capital or one of the senior directors who has already substantial experience as a chief executive. A board is responsible for all aspects of its business including activities, such as IT, that in many companies would be handled centrally. The INEOS central office numbers only around forty, compared with hundreds in many companies of comparable size. It gives supporting advice at a high level, e.g. finance, tax, insurance, legal, human resources, manufacturing operations, technology, mergers and acquisitions, and communications – but only in very small departments! Businesses participate in a half-day meeting every month or so with INEOS Capital to cover recent performance, safety as well as financial, together with budgets and investments.

Olefins & Polymers Europe, spanning a variety of countries, benefits from segmentation into four separate businesses. Besides Olefins & Polymers USA, the other petrochemicals businesses are global in scope. The oil and gas portfolio expanded substantially in 2017 with the acquisition of DONG (Danish Oil and

Natural Gas) and the Forties Pipeline System. Once more, manageable units have been formed.

Enterprises is a mini-INEOS with nine smaller diverse business units, each independently managed, and ranging from solvents to salt, and sulphur chemicals to chlorotoluenes.

Styrolution started life as a styrenics 50:50 joint venture with BASF in 2011 and became the world's largest player. INEOS acquired BASF's share in 2014. INOVYN also began as a 50:50 joint venture, this time with Solvay in 2014, when INEOS ChlorVinyls combined its chlorine, caustic soda and PVC (polyvinyl chloride) with Solvay's equivalent activities. Solvay sold its share to INEOS in 2016.

The Petroineos joint venture was set up in 2011 covering the two oil refineries at Grangemouth, Scotland and Lavéra, France. It combines INEOS's strength in safe operation of the refineries with PetroChina's capability in purchasing crude oil and trading petrol (gasoline) and diesel.

Automotive and the recent acquisitions, Belstaff fashion brand and Lausanne Football Club, all of which are consumer focused, complete the pack (at the time of writing).

APPENDIX 2

THE PETROCHEMICALS WORLD AND INEOS

FLOW CHART FOR INEOS PETROCHEMICALS MANUFACTURE

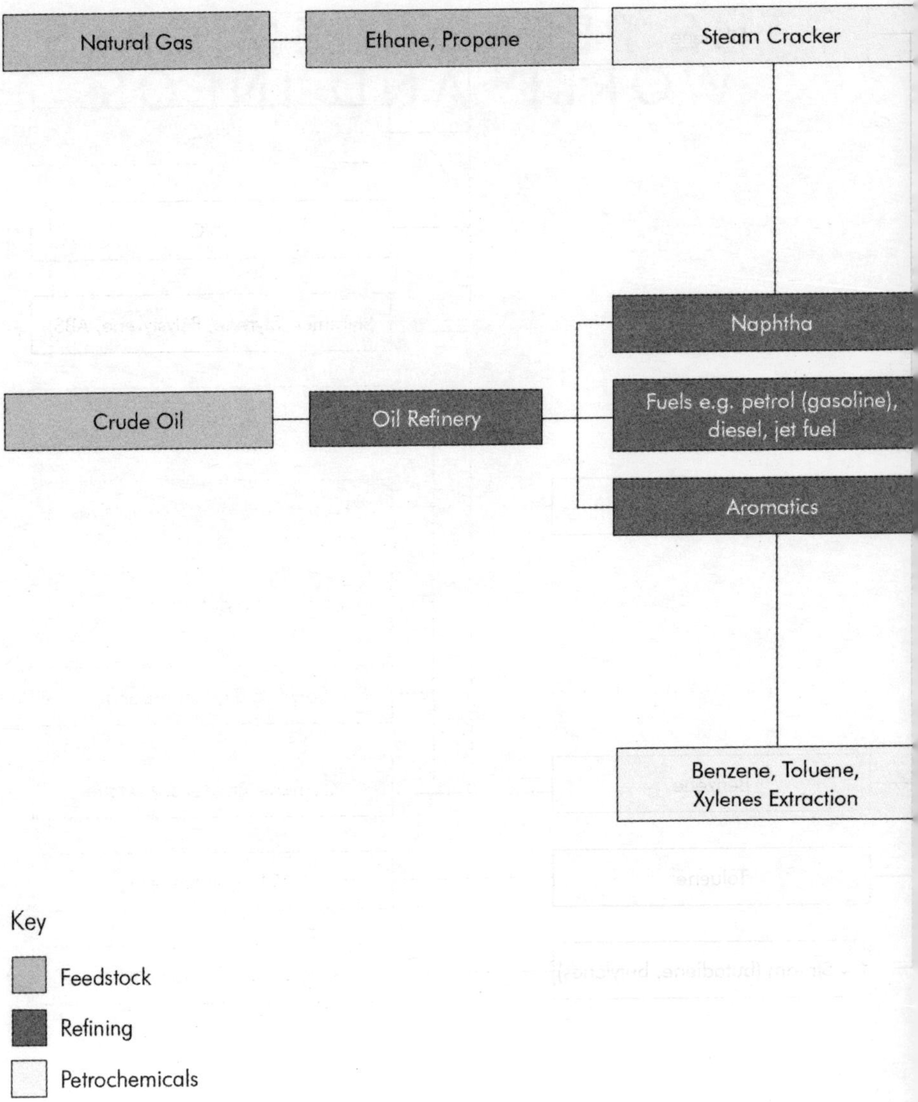

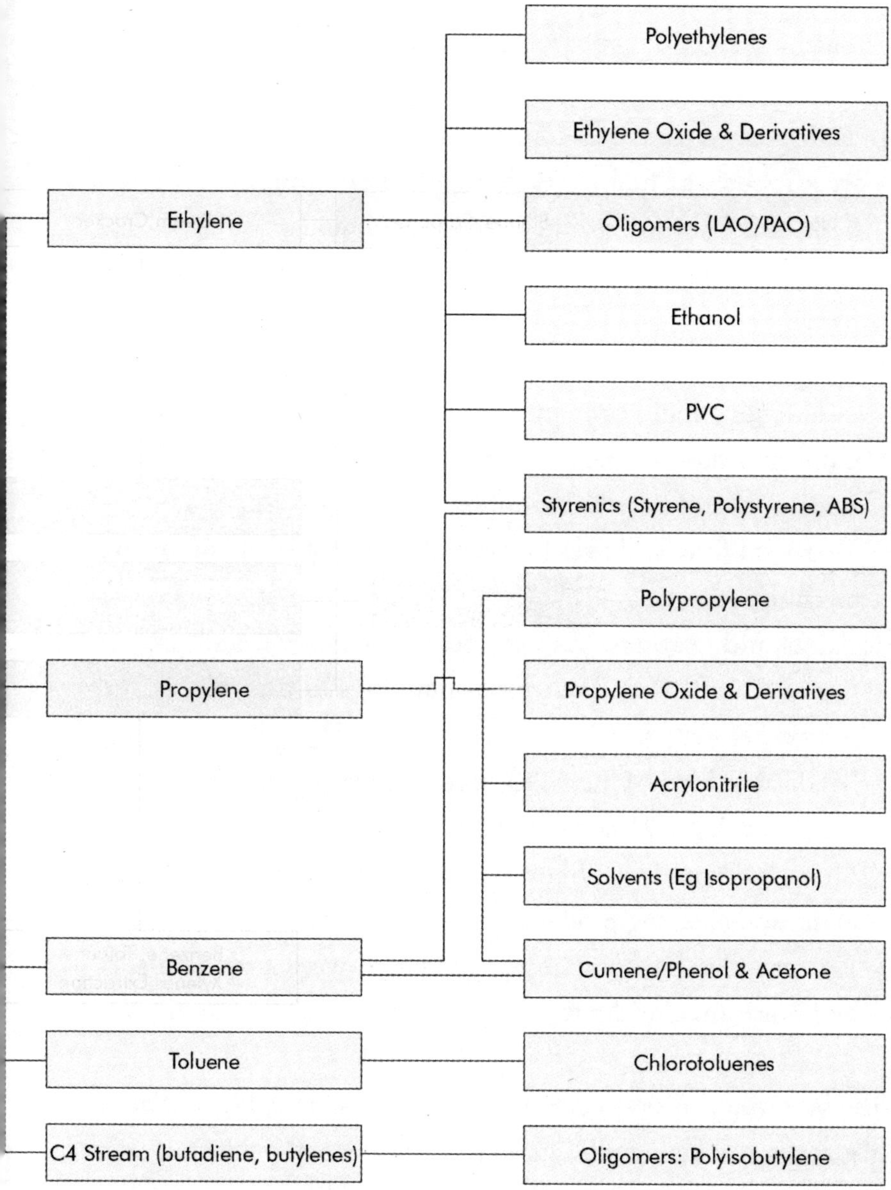
Polyethylenes
Ethylene Oxide & Derivatives
Ethylene
Oligomers (LAO/PAO)
Ethanol
PVC
Styrenics (Styrene, Polystyrene, ABS)
Polypropylene
Propylene
Propylene Oxide & Derivatives
Acrylonitrile
Solvents (Eg Isopropanol)
Benzene
Cumene/Phenol & Acetone
Toluene
Chlorotoluenes
C4 Stream (butadiene, butylenes)
Oligomers: Polyisobutylene

Figure 2

Products from the petrochemical industry are found everywhere and are essential to modern life. They are used in an astonishing array of applications, examples being:

- Transport: Structural components to protect and lighten weight such as fuel tanks, bumpers, headlamp lenses; tyres; brake fluid, antifreeze and screen wash liquids;
- Construction: Insulation; window frames; piping; protective paint;
- Packaging: Materials to keep food fresh and safe from contamination; liquid containers;
- Communications and electronics: Smartphone casings and screens; circuit boards; headphones;
- Textiles: Fibres and dyes for warm, comfortable and protective clothing; carpeting;
- Paints and coatings: Paints used for decoration and protection, both inside and out, from buildings to cars, planes and infrastructure;
- Medical industry: Chemicals used in making pharmaceuticals; eye drops; hip replacement cement;
- Household products: Shower and bath soaps and gels; detergents and cleaning products;
- Energy: Gas transport pipes; biodiesel; wind turbine blades and lubricants for the turbines.

The versatility of petrochemical products is clear to see. Some, like soaps and detergents, are sold to the general public but over 80 per cent of petrochemicals are purchased by other businesses to convert by chemical reaction or moulding into products consumed by the general public. Thus a milk container is moulded from high-density polyethylene (HDPE), and acrylonitrile is the precursor of acrylic clothing and tough computer housings.

What are these various petrochemicals made from? There are several basic chemicals that are building blocks in their manufacture. These are ethylene, propylene, butadiene and the so-called aromatics benzene, toluene and xylenes. These basic chemicals are themselves derived from the constituents of crude oil and natural gas (Fig. 2).

Crude oil contains a mixture of hydrocarbons (molecules containing hydrogen and carbon) of various size and boiling point. When crude oil is heated, various constituents boil off and can be recovered. Propane and butane appear first, followed by naphtha, similar to petrol (gasoline). At higher boiling points emerge kerosene/jet fuel, diesel, fuel oil (used to power large ships) and bitumen, the tarry stuff used for road surfaces. These activities take place in an oil refinery.

In a steam cracker (also called an ethylene cracker), naphtha is indeed mixed with steam and heated up in furnaces to around 850°C for a very short period of time, typically fractions of a second, and then immediately cooled to prevent further reactions. This treatment breaks down the naphtha molecules – called cracking – into smaller ones such as ethylene (two carbon atoms), propylene (three carbon atoms), butadiene (four carbon atoms) and benzene (six carbon atoms in a ring). The steam helps reduce coke formation in the furnaces.

Gas is also a source of raw material for steam crackers. Natural gas is mainly methane, used for domestic heating and electricity production in power stations. Methane is also consumed to make methanol, another basic building block chemical. Slightly heavier molecules, such as ethane and propane, are present as a few per cent in natural gas. These can be separated and cracked in a steam cracker to produce ethylene and also propylene.

Besides steam cracking of naphtha and ethane/propane contained in natural gas, some building blocks are produced in oil refineries during processes to improve the quality of petrol. Examples are propylene from catalytic cracking and benzene, toluene and xylenes from catalytic reformers, a process used to increase the octane rating of petrol.

Many hundreds of different petrochemicals can be manufactured from basic chemical building blocks. Ethylene and propylene can be linked together in chains of any length, known as polymers. Items made from polyethylene and polypropylene are familiar, as are those from polystyrene and PVC (polyvinyl chloride). Many polymers soften when heated and can be moulded into many shapes and in some cases drawn into fibres. These are called thermoplastics, or plastics for short.

Polyethylenes in various forms are the main consumers of ethylene. Another big use is the production of ethylene oxide, much of which finds its way into ethylene glycol for engine coolant and polyester fibres.

It is also possible to link ethylene into shorter chains to form linear alpha olefins (LAO) with between six and twenty carbon atoms. They can be used to make detergents and lubricant additives. A derivative product called PAO (poly alpha olefin) is the main component of high-end synthetic motor oils.

After polypropylene, an important consumer of propylene is acrylonitrile, a precursor of rigid, tough ABS for consumer goods and transport, acrylic fibre in textiles, and carbon fibres used in sports equipment and transport.

Of the aromatic hydrocarbons, benzene is the most important

building block. Combined with ethylene it leads to styrene, the basis of polystyrenes and also expanded polystyrene (EPS) with good insulation properties. Benzene is also used to make phenol, a product with a wide range of applications including polycarbonate, a tough, transparent polymer found in spectacle lenses and car headlight housings.

The chemicals industry is an important contributor to the wealth of a country or region. Thus in Europe it amounts to over 1 per cent of total GDP and to 7 per cent of GDP generated by all manufacturing industries. Food and motor vehicles have a bigger turnover but chemicals is considerably larger than electrical and electronics equipment.

In recent decades, manufacturing as a percentage of GDP has fallen in most developed countries to the 10–15 per cent range, a notable exception being Germany, where it remains at around 23 per cent, mainly owing to its world-class automotive, machine tools and indeed petrochemical industries. This change has been partly due to the rise in services such as retail sales, finance and healthcare but substantially related to the movement of industries, such as textiles and consumer goods production, to cheaper areas in south-east Asia, particularly China.

In this changing global environment it is remarkable that INEOS has been so successful. After twenty years of growth, INEOS has annual sales of $60 billion, the majority of which is from petrochemicals. This places the company comfortably among the top five global chemicals manufacturers along with BASF, Sinopec (China) and Dow Chemical.

This growth has not been to the detriment of fundamentals such as personal safety of employees. The general standard is to express injury rates per 200,000 hours, equivalent to 100 people working for a year. For all manufacturing and construction industries in developed countries, the injury rate is over 3. For petrochemicals manufacturers and oil refiners, the average rate is in the 0.35–0.4 range; INEOS managed a world-class 0.23 in 2017.

The company has 18,600 employees at over 180 manufacturing sites including joint ventures. Its petrochemicals capacity is 54 million tonnes, and 20 million tonnes of oil refinery products, mainly petrol (gasoline), diesel and jet fuel, are sold each year, equivalent to 400,000 barrels/day. INEOS is now a top-10 producer of oil and gas from the North Sea with a daily production of 100,000 boe (barrels of oil equivalent) per day, backed up by 570 million boe of reserves.

Many of INEOS's manufacturing plants are in the USA, Germany, Belgium, the UK and France. Their original locations, often coastal, reflected the need for a steady supply of raw materials – oil, gas, ethylene – as well as proximity to markets for the resultant petrochemical products. Future investment decisions will depend on other factors as well. The availability of a skilled workforce to operate large, capital-intensive plants is crucial and often depends on the quality of and respect for a technical education, notable in countries such as Germany.

Competitive energy costs are also essential. The USA has really benefited from shale gas production in recent years and this has been one of the key drivers to growth in new petrochemical plants. Gas prices are two to three times more expensive in Europe than in the USA. Around $180 billion of new investments have been announced since 2010 and amazingly the petrochemicals industry accounts for around half of all investment in American manufacturing. There is understandable concern about more expensive energy prices in Europe and the impact on future investments.

Finally, a number of other important elements are key in investment decisions, including corporate tax rates, constructive labour relations, and government attitudes to the importance of manufacturing in a mixed economy.

APPENDIX 3

TWENTY YEARS OF INEOS: MILESTONES

TWENTY YEARS OF INEOS: MILESTONES

1998

INEOS ACQUIRES ANTWERP SITE FROM INSPEC (FORMER BP SITE)
The birth of INEOS. Becomes the Oxide business

1999

INEOS BUYS THE ACRYLICS (PERSPEX AND LUCITE) BUSINESS FROM ICI, IN PARTNERSHIP WITH CHARTERHOUSE DEVELOPMENT BANK
INEOS operates the manufacturing sites in Europe, N America and East Asia

2001

INEOS PURCHASES CHLOR CHEMICALS, FLUOR AND SILICAS BUSINESSES FROM ICI
Substantial investment in NW England, also Louisiana (Fluor)

ACQUIRES MAJORITY OF EVC (REMAINDER PURCHASED IN 2005)
Expansion into vinyls, films, and compounds

BUYS PHENOL BUSINESS FROM DEGUSSA
New business area. 3 phenol plants – Germany, Belgium and USA (Mobile, Alabama)

PURCHASES ETHANOLAMINES AND GAS TREATMENT (GASPEC) FROM DOW
Expands Oxide business into USA

2002

OXIDE, FLUOR, SIL AND PHENOL COM TO FORM INEOS G AND REFINANC
First major levera finance transact (€900m) for INE

2013

AT THE END OF OCTOBER, GRANGEMOUTH PETROCHEMICALS AND REFINERY RESTART AFTER A STRIKE
New terms and conditions, necessary for Grangemouth survival, are agreed by Unite the Union

2014

BUYS SOLVENTS BUSINESS FROM SASOL GERMANY
Expands range of solvents

INEOS PURCHASES BASF'S 50% SHARE IN STYROLUTION
Styrolution fully owned by INEOS

2015

INEOS AND SOLVAY COMBINE THEIR EUROPEAN CHLORVINYLS BUSINESSES IN A JV CALLED INOVYN
World scale business formed

INEOS PURCHASES UK NORTH SEA ASSETS FROM DEA GROUP AND FAIRFIELD ENERGY
First strategic investment in the North Sea

INEOS IS AWARDED 21 NEW SHALE GAS LICENCES AS PART OF THE UK 14TH LICENSING ROUND
With access to 1 million acres of potential gas reserves, INEOS becomes UK's leading shale gas company

2016

INEOS INTREPID LEAVES MARCUS HOOK, NEAR PHILADELPHIA, BOUND FOR RAFNES, NORWAY, WITH 27,500 M³ OF SHALE GAS ETHANE FROM THE MARCELLUS FIELD
First shipment of shale gas from USA to Europe in world's largest ethane carrier. One of a fleet of 8 Dragon class ships which will creat a virtual pipeline across the Atlantic of feedstock for ethylene cracker replacing declining North Sea production

INEOS PURCHASES SOLVAY'S 50% SHARE IN INOVYN
INOVYN fully owned by INEOS

INEOS INSIGHT DOCKS AT GRANGEMOUTH WITH 27,500 M³ OF ETHA
A game changer for Grangemouth and British manufactu
First time US shale gas ethane is shipped to the UK. Culmination of $2 b investment by INEOS

NEW UK HEADQUARTERS OPENS IN KNIGHTSBRIDGE, LONDON
Move reflects INEOS growth in the UK, both petrochemicals and oil & g

2005

BUYS POLYSTYRENE BUSINESS IN N. AMERICA FROM BASF
New business area. Manufacturing facility at Joliet, Illinois

INEOS PURCHASES INNOVENE FROM BP FOR $9 BILLION
Transformational. Includes olefin cracker complexes at Grangemouth, Cologne, Lavéra (France), and hocolate Bayou (Texas) plus many derivatives. Gained 19 sites in Europe and N America. 2 refineries (Grangemouth, Lavéra)

2007

INEOS AND NOVA COMBINE THEIR EUROPEAN JV WITH THEIR RESPECTIVE STYRENICS ACTIVITIES IN N. AMERICA
Larger styrenics JV with simpler structure, called INEOS NOVA

BUYS 51% OF ABS ENGINEERING PLASTICS BUSINESS OF LANXESS
Participation in a new global business

ACQUIRES BOREALIS POLYOLEFINS BUSINESS IN NORWAY (INCLUDING 50% OF NORETYL ETHYLENE CRACKER)
Norwegian production facilities

2008

PURCHASES CHLORVINYLS BUSINESS FROM HYDRO POLYMERS, AND REMAINING 50% OF NORETYL ETHYLENE CRACKER
Expanded activities in Norway and Sweden

INEOS COMBINES SILICAS BUSINESS WITH PQ CORPORATION
Global speciality inorganic chemicals

PURCHASES VINYL ACETATE MONOMER (VAM) AND ETHYL ACETATE BUSINESS FROM BP
Portfolio expanded with ethylene consuming businesses at Hull (UK)

BUYS SEAL SANDS (UK) SITE FROM BASF
Expands Nitriles portfolio

2009

INEOS BUYS REMAINING 49% ABS FROM LANXESS
Fully owned INEOS ABS business

INEOS AGREES WITH ITS BANK LENDERS TO RESET COVENANTS AND INCREASE INTEREST PAYMENTS
Refinancing settles the future of INEOS following the 2008/09 financial crisis, but increases finance costs by €800m over the next 4 years

2010

INEOS CAPITAL MOVES HQ AND TAX RESIDENCE FROM UK TO SWITZERLAND
To remain internationally competitive

2011

:OS BUYS NOVA'S 50% SHARE IN THE INEOS NOVA JOINT TURE, AND THEN COMBINES STYRENICS ACTIVITIES WITH BASF TO FORM A NEW 50:50 JV, STYROLUTION
Global leadership in styrenics

ORMS JV WITH PETROCHINA IN OIL REFINING AND TRADING
mpany called Petroineos. Combines INEOS's strengths in safe ry operations with PetroChina's oil and oil products trading. $1 billion cash proceeds used to reduce Group debt

2017

INEOS ANNOUNCES PROJEKT GRENADIER
exciting venture to build a world class, uncompromising 4x4 off-road vehicle

INEOS PURCHASES OIL AND GAS BUSINESS FROM DONG ENERGY
Production of 100,000 boe/day plus 570 million boe reserves. Assets in Danish, Norwegian and UK sectors. INEOS now a top 10 company in the North Sea

BUYS NORTH SEA FORTIES PIPELINE SYSTEM AND KINNEIL TERMINAL FROM BP
Reunites North Sea and Grangemouth assets under INEOS ownership

BUYS BELSTAFF GROUP FROM JAB LUXURY
Iconic British clothing brand with 100 years of heritage

ACQUIRES LAUSANNE-SPORT FOOTBALL CLUB
Continues INEOS investment in youth and sports in the Lausanne, Switzerland area

2018

INEOS TEAM UK FORMED TO CHALLENGE FOR THE 2021 AMERICA'S CUP. HAS PARTNERED WITH SIR BEN AINSLIE, AND WILL REPRESENT THE ROYAL YACHT SQUADRON'S AFFILIATED CLUB, ROYAL YACHT SQUADRON RACING
Sir Ben Ainslie, world's most successful Olympic sailor, will lead the design and build programme and skipper the racing yacht. INEOS will spend £110 million, biggest ever British investment, in an effort to bring the trophy back to Britain for first time since competition established in 1851

INDEX